Charlecote and the Lucys

Alice, Lady Fairfax-Lucy is the daughter of John Buchan. She married Brian Fairfax-Lucy in the late 1930s and they were the last private owners to live in Charlecote. Her son now lives in the house, of which he is life-tenant under the National Trust.

Introduced to the reading of history by her father, Alice Fairfax-Lucy is the author of several books: *A Stuart Portrait* (1934); *Joan of Arc and the Recovery of France* (1948); *Charlecote and the Lucys* (1958, Gollancz Paperback edition 1990); and *Scrap Screen* (1980), an account of her mother's family, the Ebury Grosvenors. She also edited the memoirs of Mary Elizabeth Lucy (1803–1889), published under the title *Mistress of Charlecote* (1983). Alice Fairfax-Lucy lives in Burford, Oxfordshire.

Charlecote and the Lucys

The Chronicle of an English Family

ALICE FAIRFAX-LUCY

'By truth and diligence'

LONDON
VICTOR GOLLANCZ LTD
1990

Original edition first published 1958
by Oxford University Press

This revised edition first published 1990
as a Gollancz Paperback
by Victor Gollancz Ltd
14 Henrietta Street, London WC2E 8QJ

British Library Cataloguing in Publication Data
Fairfax-Lucy, Alice
Charlecote and the Lucys : the chronicle of
an English family.—Rev. ed.
1. Warwickshire. Social life, history
I. Title
942.48

ISBN 0-575-04824-7

Typeset in Great Britain by CentraCet, Cambridge
Printed in Finland by Werner Söderström Oy

Contents

Illustrations

The young Shakespeare, accused of poaching deer, is brought before Justice Thomas Lucy in the Great Hall at Charlecote (*courtesy the Mansell Collection*)

Bust of the first Sir Thomas Lucy (*courtesy Jarrold Publishing*)

The Great Hall as it is today (*courtesy the National Trust Photographic Library*)

The Lucy coat of arms

Richard Lucy (*courtesy Jarrold Publishing*)

The west prospect of Charlecote, c. 1695 (*courtesy Jarrold Publishing*)

Captain Thomas Lucy (*courtesy the National Trust Photographic Library*)

Colonel George Lucy, Mary Bohun and Jane Bohun (*courtesy Jarrold Publishing*)

George Lucy (*courtesy Jarrold Publishing*)

Charlecote prior to its nineteenth-century restoration

Busts of George Hammond Lucy and his wife Mary Elizabeth (*courtesy the National Trust Photographic Library*)

Alice Fairfax-Lucy (*courtesy Jarrold Publishing*)

Foreword

In the first edition of this book I gave thanks to all the people who helped me on the long uphill road. I knew it would be a long road and I dreaded that it might be dull in patches. Dr George Trevelyan had warned me that anyone who attempts to write the history of a long-descended family is writing a history of England. Dr G. M. Young in his own words lit a taper to put my feet on the right path. I set out with such confidence, loving the place and the Shakespeare connection, but I knew very little about the craft of writing a family history.

In the 40th year of her age my husband's great-grand-mother Mary Elizabeth Lucy, with no qualms about it, sat down to write the history of the Lucy family. By then a widow in early middle age, she embarked on her self-imposed task with the fervour that the house evokes to this day, starting with an introduction addressed to her eldest son:

'That you, my dearest son, may know something of your ancestors I have compiled from worn out parchments and old books this brief account of the Possessors of Charlecote. May God through you prolong the line of Lucys till Time itself shall End.' (It was not to be. He outlived her by six months and had no son.)

She had wished to be buried in the little churchyard of the church she had built in the Park, '. . . to lie beside the loved Dead below the soft green grass and know that my children would water my resting place with their tears'. That too was not to be. Custom and tradition both demanded that as Mistress of Charlecote she should be buried in the family vault.

By the time she died in her eighties she had wept her eyes

dry over the deaths of husband and children. Among the
coffins in the family vault, many of them so pathetically
small, one must contain the baby who had died when they
were making the crossing of the Mont Cenis pass; she sat for
eleven hours in the coach with the moonlight pouring in at
the carriage window cradling him in her arms.

'How closely mingled the strands of joy and woe had been
in my life,' she wrote on the last page of her journals. 'The
grave buries every error, covers every defect, extinguishes
every resentment. From its peaceful bosom spring none but
fond regrets and tender recollections.'

BAGINTON : *Bromley*

BELDESERT : *De Montfort*

CHARLECOTE

CHERRINGTON : *a Lucy manor until the end of the 17th century*

CLAVERDON : *Spencer*

CLOPTON : *Clopton*

COMPTON VERNEY : *Verney*

COUGHTON : *Throckmorton*

FINHAM : *Bohun*

FULBROKE : *acquired by the Lucys in about 1615*

HAMPTON LUCY

HASLEY : *Throckmorton*

HUNSCOTE : *part of the manor of Charlecote after 1492*

IDLICOTE : *Underhill*

NORTHBROKE : *Grant*

SHERBORNE : *Lucy property until 1685*

SHREWLEY : *Lucy property in the Middle Ages*

SNITTERFIELD : *Shakespeare*

STONELEIGH : *Leigh*

THELESFORD : *added to Charlecote at the Dissolution*

UMBERSLADE : *Archer*

WARWICKSHIRE

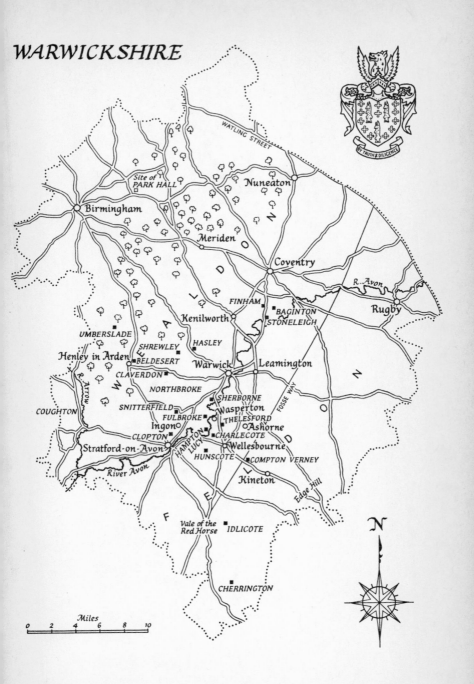

WATLING STREET

Site of
PARK HALL

Nuneaton

Birmingham

Meriden

Coventry

R. Avon

FINHAM

BAGINTON

STONELEIGH

Rugby

Kenilworth

UMBERSLADE

HASLEY

SHREWLEY

Warwick

Leamington

Henley in Arden

BELDESERT

CLAVERDON

NORTHBROKE

SHERBORNE

SNITTERFIELD

WASPERTON

FULBROKE

THELESFORD

COUGHTON

Ingon

Ashorne

CLOPTON

CHARLECOTE

Stratford-on-Avon

HAMPTON LUCY

Wellesbourne

River Avon

HUNSCOTE

COMPTON VERNEY

Kineton

Edge Hill

Vale of the
Red Horse

IDLICOTE

FOSSE WAY

CHERRINGTON

N

Miles

0   2   4   6   8   10

CHAPTER I

Charlecote Today and Yesterday

'Gentlemen and Friends, the longest summer's day hath his evening, Ulysses arriveth at last, and rough winds in time bring the ship to Safe Road.'

John Lyly: *Euphues*.

Charlecote stands on the banks of the Warwickshire Avon in the rich plain of the Felden. Four miles downstream lies Stratford; four miles upstream is Warwick, the county town. The broad, slow river washes the terrace steps of Charlecote on the west side; on the east the first sunlight catches the gilt weathervanes on the gatehouse roof. On the north side the garden rides like the prow of a ship, breasting the green wash of the park which Capability Brown planned; to the south an avenue of great limes planted by an Elizabethan Lucy winds to join the Stratford road.

The pattern of the house is one that is happily yet to be found all over England, an Elizabethan half-H of red brick groined with stone, with turrets at its four corners, its arms enclosing a gravelled court. Before it lies a gatehouse under whose arch the casual visitor now passes.

Towards the close of an autumn day mallard and teal flight in great numbers along the river's bank, printing a lonely pattern against the sunset. As the day wanes the aeroplanes go back to their base; a thrush flutes briefly, a robin whistles. A widower swan, who lives solitary in the rushes below the terrace steps, swims very slowly up the darkening river and makes ghostly pause above its own reflection. The gatehouse clock strikes, but seems to have no relation to time as it is understood by those who hurry blindly from one point to another.

In summer the cedars on the lawn shade only picnickers.

In winter the avenues are padlocked, and no lights wink at the upper windows where the household servants had their dormitories. Yet there is no sense of diminution of personality. Some singularity in the conformation of its building makes the house reverberate imperiously: footsteps along a stone passage, voices at a distance, set up a clamour of echoes; a clock striking hits the ear with the impact of a shot. Charlecote has no ghosts, but holds the past as a shell holds the sound of the sea.

The true sightseer, filled with an insatiable curiosity for getting inside other people's lives and minds, derives particular enjoyment from the sense of invading prohibited ground—of seeing what he was never intended to see. All these windows, keeping a sightless vigil, remind him that the house not so long ago brimmed with an intense life and could do so again.

It is not the England of Elizabeth I that is felt at Charlecote as it is felt at Hatfield or Hardwick or Kirby, but the robust, comprehensible England of a century and a quarter ago, the England of William IV and his niece, Victoria, that was still in everything but name the England of the eighteenth century.

The marriage in 1822 of George Lucy and Mary Elizabeth Williams, great-grandparents of the present generation of Lucys, lifted Charlecote out of shabby, crumbling obscurity, and brought it into line with the taste of their day. Lady Louisa Stuart, the friend and correspondent of Sir Walter Scott, wrote with approval: 'He [Mr Lucy of Charlecote] has had the sense to re-edify his curious house without destroying its character or pulling it down and building a Cockney cit's box in its stead.'

People of discrimination liked to preserve the appearance of antiquity. Edward Fitzgerald wrote: 'I have been to see two show places lately, but these kind of places have not much character in them; an old Squire's gable-ended house is much more English and aristocratic to my mind.'

Sir Walter Scott himself visited Charlecote, his curiosity kindled by Washington Irving's description of the venerable hall where the young Shakespeare had been brought to justice. He found quite delightful the associations of the armorial glass and the deer's antlers lining the walls.

At the end of the century, a compatriot of Washington Irving's took up his pen to describe it: '. . . in Shakespeare's day, no doubt the coat of nature was far from being so prettily trimmed as it is now; but there is one place, nevertheless, which as he passes it in the summer twilight, the traveller does his best to believe unaltered. I allude, of course, to Charlecote park, whose venerable verdure seems a survival from an earlier England, and whose innumerable acres stretching away in the early evening to vaguely seen Tudor walls, lie there like the backward years receding to the age of Elizabeth.'* The equipage hired to drive him about the haunts of Shakepeare's youth paused before the park gates. Great elms and limes (owing more to Dutch King William's taste for trees planted with parade-ground precision than to the age of Elizabeth) led to the gatehouse of untouched Tudor workmanship, and beyond to turrets with cupolas and gilt weather-vanes catching the sun that was sinking out of sight across the river. He had put an unerring finger on it; here was something Shakespeare could have known. Not, of course, still looking exactly as it had done in the poet's day, but in substance the same.

The Lucys had been formerly a little shy of the Shakespeare cult and had not encouraged random sightseers; such public attention they found faintly distasteful. After all, there was no actual proof. The dreaming trees, the calm vistas of the park did not suggest a poaching brawl. Polite but distant, the family withdrew, leaving the place to defend itself. Meanwhile, Shakespearian scholars were outdoing themselves in their efforts to place the poaching legend on a basis of probability which should absolve England's greatest poet from any taint of vagrancy or dissoluteness. This mental gymnastic once accomplished, it was agreed that Charlecote was hallowed ground and that the legend, though lacking the accident of documentary evidence, was established beyond question.

* Henry James, *English Hours*, 1905.

By the early nineteenth century the English public had taken Charlecote to its heart and has never relinquished it. Every schoolchild learnt that the youthful Shakespeare had been caught in the act of poaching Sir Thomas Lucy's deer, and been hauled before the Justice in his Great Hall. The subject was popular with lithographers, and the corridors of most country inns harboured a large steel engraving, rosewood-framed, of the Poet in the Hall of the Justice.

A few soberer critics hinted that there might have been other reasons for the poet's sudden departure from Stratford, but public opinion, which still held the landed classes in awe, preferred to believe that Sir Thomas Lucy had made Warwickshire too hot to hold anyone of the name of Shakespeare.

The deer-stealing legend has by now a hold on popular affection that no argument can weaken. If it were ever authoritatively disproved, children of the future would be deprived of something that for centuries has made the poet live for them. The portraits of Shakespeare are few and of debatable authenticity. In the shadowy throng of the Great he cuts an uninspiring figure. But set him against the background of Charlecote warren or Fulbroke park some night near dawn, with moonlight whitening the turf, and there you have reality. Theft, capture, punishment, flight— these are all within the compass of ordinary experience.

When questioned, in after-years, the village people of Charlecote found they could recall too many such incidents. Stratford boys were always out at Charlecote after game; the danger of a beating from a warrener never frightened them off, though the keepers would often seize and hang their dogs as a deterrent. Memories of this sort, hoarded by generations who had no cheap travel, newspapers, or easy entertainment to dull their sense of wonder, struck deep roots.

In Charlecote brake there were rabbits and hares and foxes, wood-pigeons and magpies and rooks, but few deer. Boys from the neighbouring villages, in spite of the warrener's vigilance, trapped moles for their skins, baked hedgehogs in hot clay, and netted sparrows, but for real sport went further afield to Fulbroke across the river, and risked being seen on its open slopes.

Fulbroke had once been a royal park. It was granted by Queen Mary to a Catholic gentleman, Sir Francis Englefield, but as the castle was a ruin and all the fences were broken, it was declared disparked. A few harts and does of the fallow deer survived, and these *ferae naturae* were looked on as fair game by the neighbourhood. Englefield left the country on Elizabeth's accession, and Fulbroke became again a kind of no-man's-land. In 1584 Parliament declared Englefield a recusant and traitor, and granted Sir Thomas Lucy the advantage of his property. It is often said that the unsuccessful Bill introduced by Sir Thomas into the Parliament of that year to ensure the better preservation of grain and game by making poaching a felony was an indication of his strong proprietary instincts. Perhaps it was. Elizabethan landowners all shared that foible, as do most landowners even in these days.

The circumstantial evidence of Shakespeare's connexion with the Lucys, so painstakingly built up throughout the seventeenth and eighteenth centuries, blurred where before all had been plain. The poet's early marriage, the failure of his father's business, the wife and children to be provided for were reason enough for his leaving Stratford, where the wool and leather trades, in which the Shakespeare family fortunes were sunk, had begun to decline. A father must support his young when starvation stares them in the face, and a deer's carcass roughly divided in a ditch as morning began to dapple the drowsy east was provision fairly taken. '*Change places and handy dandy, which is the Justice, which is the thief?*' Thomas Lucy had not been backward over appropriating his Catholic neighbours' land.

A Mr John Jordan, a wheelwright of Stratford with literary leanings (1746–1809), claimed to have discovered in a piece of furniture in a cottage in Shottery the complete version of the doubtful ballad alleged by Rowe (1674–1718) to have been hung on Charlecote's park gates; 'He had, by a misfortune common enough to young fellows, fallen into ill company; and amongst them, some that made a frequent practice of deer-stealing engag'd him with them more than once in robbing a Park, that belonged to Sir Thomas Lucy of Charlecot, near Stratford. For this he was prosecuted by that gentleman, as he thought somewhat too severely; and in order to revenge that ill-usage, he made a ballad upon him.'

Rowe's information about Shakespeare's life was provided by an actor called Betterton, who went enquiring round Stratford in about 1708 for details about the poet's life. There were still people living who could remember Shakespeare's daughters, among them William Shakespeare Hart whose aunts they were, and Betterton's rather meagre findings could have been had from this source. But Oldys ventured to doubt whether Betterton had ever been near Stratford. Malone, a much more serious critic, writing in 1821, thought this doubt unworthy, and so the game of discrediting each other's findings and giving an individual twist to meagre scraps of information has persisted among Shakespearean critics down to our own day.

Sir Walter Scott, when he visited Charlecote in 1823, was solemnly told the same story, that Thomas Lucy, in order to clean up Fulbroke, resided for a time in the lodge there. The theory neatly fitted Shallow's accusation of Falstaff: 'Knight, you have beaten my men, killed my deer, and broken open my lodge,' and was found most acceptable by nineteenth-century critics. (But Sir Walter did not altogether believe it.)

The keeper's lodge at Fulbroke has long ago gone, though some nineteenth-century cottages near the site of its barn still go by the name of Deer Barn Cottages, but the truth of the deer-stealing episode does not need such dubious support. Shakespeare himself voices it over and over again.

When all the arguments for the Lucy-Shallow contention have been fingered threadbare, we are left with only a few small shreds of certainty: the references in *The Merry Wives of Windsor* (written fourteen years later) to the white luces 'that do become an old coat well'; Shallow's threat of making a Star Chamber case of a poaching incident; and the gentle fun poked at Justices of the Peace, and all foolish, elderly men in authority (Shallow, Polonius, Verges, and a score of others)—little enough to build a legend on.

Suspected recusants, not poachers, were Sir Thomas's quarry, and industriously he tracked them down, tearing up floor-boards for hidden mass books, smoking priests out of their hideouts in chimneys and haystacks. This was not Shallow, the forked radish with his homely talk, or the ineffectual Justice of *The Merry Wives*. Sir Thomas lies stiffly on his tomb in Charlecote Church, a small, spare man, with his wife beside him; even in their effigies they seem to be strenuously keeping up appearances. The threat of making a Star Chamber matter of the killing of a deer on land not emparked would have been much beneath the dignity of an agent of Her Majesty's Privy Council. No, we must look elsewhere for Justice Shallow's prototype, perhaps among the Coombes or Quynys of Stratford.

As a Justice of the Queen's peace Sir Thomas had continually to deal with thefts, of which poaching was the most common. To be caught literally red-handed—ensanguined with the blood of a newly-killed buck—was punishable either by imprisonment or a fine. With these went generally a stinging rebuke from the local JP before whom the wrongdoer was hauled ('*See how yond justice rails upon yon simple thief*').

Charlecote was the first Elizabethan mansion to be built in Warwickshire—one of the earliest to be built at all. Lying low by the river, it was invisible on two sides from the dense growth of the warren; only by taking a boat upstream from Alvescot before the barriers halted you, could you get a glimpse of its red brick turrets quoined with stone and its many gables. It had cost a fortune (Sir Thomas's wife's fortune)—and the Queen had stayed there, sleeping two nights in a goose-feather bed. This, joined to Sir Thomas's reputation as a Commissioner for Recusancy, caused the place to be looked on with awe.

Shakespeare's father had moved into Stratford, hoping to make his fortune there as a trader in corn, wool, and hides. The family connexion with Snitterfield, however, continued during the lifetime of an old Shakespeare uncle. The boy

must have many a time taken the ancient bridleway from
Snitterfield that skirted Hampton Great Wood to follow the
windings of Avon back to Stratford. By Fulbroke with its
ruined castle, past the Great Wood where the deer's slot
could be seen, by spongy meadows, breeding-places for
duck and heron, the path led over the Great Meadow over
the river from Charlecote. With its gilt weather-vanes glinting in the sun, it rose above the trees, the local Great House,
about which gossip fermented; where it was said that the
women wore the breeches, where it took forty wax tapers to
light one room alone, where there was sewed work on the
chairs, and on the walls pictures of stag-killing, as lively
painted as the deed was done. *''Fore God, Master Shallow, you
have here a goodly dwelling and a rich.'* The reality, which was
mutable and has perished, is preserved in the boy's dream,
which is immortal as long as words last. Whatever he saw,
mazed from rough handling, plastered with the mud of a
night's vigil in a wet ditch, it was enough.

Charlecote does not depend on the alleged caricature in
The Merry Wives for its immortality. It is to be found in the
plays; in the lord's hunting lodge to which Christopher Sly
is conveyed, where painted hangings tell the story of Diana
and Actaeon, in Petruchio's rustic grange where the house
servants fall over each other in their anxiety to please, in
Portia's Belmont, in Illyria, at the Court of Navarre.

Thomas Lucy was a type common to all ages, the man
who hunts with the pack. But because of a routine episode
that took place early one morning, between being shaved by
his man and helped on to his ambling gelding by his groom,
he lies in Charlecote church, secure of immortality. His
regard for posterity's opinion can be seen in the epitaph that
he placed above the table tomb to which his wife preceded
him:

Here entombed lieth the Lady Joyce Lucy, wife of Sir Thomas
Lucy of Charlecote, in the County of Warwick, Knight, daughter
and heir of Thomas Acton, of Sutton, in the County of Worcester,
Esquire, who departed out of this wretched world to her heavenly
kingdom, the tenth day of February in the year of our Lord God,
1595, of her age 60 and 3. All the time of her life a true and faithful

servant of her good God, never detected of any crime or vice, in religion most sound, in love to her husband most faithful and true; in friendship most constant; to what was in trust committed to her most secret; in wisdom excelling, in governing of her house and bringing up of youth in the fear of God, that did converse with her, most rare and singular. A great maintainer of hospitality; greatly esteemed of her betters; misliked by none unless of the envious. When all is spoken that can be said, a woman so furnished and garnished with virtue as not to be bettered and hardly to be equalled by any. Set down by him that best did know what hath been written to be true—Thomas Lucy.

It is a singular document, and reveals more than Sir Thomas perhaps meant the world to know, by refuting imputations that otherwise would never have been made. It is on *aperçus* like this that this chronicle is based, since, as will be seen, almost no direct evidence has survived of Lucy personalities.

Dr G. M. Trevelyan has said in his *An Autobiography and other Essays*: 'Anyone who undertakes to write a history of England down the ages must needs be out of his depth in one part or another of the course, and must make good as best he may by lusty swimming.' Striking for the shore after nearly submerging in rough water, we approach our own age with the relief of finding our feet at last touching the bottom.

Everything that happened to Charlecote after the eighteen-seventies, when the shadow of taxation was creeping over it, seems like a reflex, a mechanical process growing slower all the time, and creaking as the wheels run down. The true refulgence had died, and in the large, comfortless rooms austerity was tamed by basket chairs, by fans of fluted paper in the fireplaces, by Japanese screens, by palms with sterile-looking, blade-sharp leaves, and economical arrangements of bulrushes standing in painted drainpipes. Taste no longer knew its own mind; the calm certainties of the Age of Elegance died with George Hammond Lucy and Mary Elizabeth Williams.

After their marriage in 1822, Charlecote had entered its

last phase of prosperity. Swept away were the rattling panes, the old worn floors, the furniture blurred by the touch of countless fingers. All that was tarnished and time-worn was replaced. Once the old windows were refurnished with sheets of plate glass the rooms looked smaller, and the imported Florentine marbles and mosaics less imposing, while the family pictures, unused to such exposure, appeared to shrink. Looking-glasses were placed to duplicate the multitudes of small tables and cabinets crowded with glittering objects. Everything had a shine to it, from the wallpapers of red and blue flock on gold, down to the glacially-white tablecloths damasked with the family crest.

The court was planted out with box-edged beds, and urns, wherever room could be found for them, spilled over with richly-scented heliotrope, verbenas, and geraniums. The carriage horses had coats like varnish; in the coach-house the crested carriages, painted in black and red, and upholstered with corded silk woven with the Lucy pike, were glassy with polish; in the harness-room harness shone like mahogany.

In the safe there was a service of gold plate, gold wine-coasters and candelabra and *epergnes* by Paul Storr and Paul Lamerie; on the walls hung a collection of pictures bought on Buchanan's advice by George Lucy, who had some natural flair and a good deal of luck, at about the same time that the National Gallery collection was being formed. The pearl of the collection was Raphael's *Marquis of Mantua*, which Vertue in his catalogue of Charles I's pictures described as 'A young man's head without a beard, in a red cap whereon a medal . . .' The Prince Consort begged Mr Lucy to be allowed to have a copy made. (George Lucy bought it from Buchanan in 1830 for £1,150, and his son sold it to Baron Lionel de Rothschild for £3,000 in 1883.) Of the interior by Pieter de Hoogh of sun-checkered marble and bright satins, Emmerson, the art dealer, wrote to George Lucy in 1827, 'You will be pleased to know that it is a Picture which is not known in the Market and has never been hacknied about.' With Teniers' *Wedding Feast*, and Hobbema's *View in a Wood near Haarlem*, it, too, was bought by Rothschild. In the year 1875 alone Spencer Lucy received

£16,000 from the sale of half a dozen pictures from his father's collection. Wertheimer bought the two small and lovely Holbeins of an unidentified man and woman, the Clouet of *Henry II of France* and *The Travelling Musicians* by Karel du Jardin.

The Canaletto of the Grand Canal at Venice, decorated for a gala, and the immense canvas by Van Dyck of St Jerome with a lion at his feet, looted by Marshal Soult from the Escorial, followed them in 1946 to help pay death duties. The scars of the long losing battle against taxation and depreciation of land are seen in the fresh patches on the faded marigold satin walls.

Below their black-and-gilt labels hang the household bells, that once summoned maids from the Crimson attic to Mrs Lucy's room (crimson on geranium flock paper), from the sewing-room to the young ladies' room (strapwork design of buff on white with chintz to match), to the Leather room (kept for bachelors), to the white and gold Boudoir, the Pink Room with its rosy birds, the Green Room (believed to be haunted), and the Ebony dressing-room.

The villages of Charlecote and Hampton Lucy and the outlying cottages supplied the big house with willing girls. The agricultural wage was very low and taking employment outside the neighbourhood was frowned on by the Parson and the Squire. A family tradition of service to the Mansion—not a bad tradition and not, it seems, abused—sent the ten- and twelve-year-olds punctually to the back door, to be interviewed in the Housekeeper's room. After the crowded cottage and a diet of thin broth and flour dumplings, life in the big house held all sorts of attractions. It was mysterious and alarming, ordered by rigid tradition, but exciting: fun even to rise in the black dark of a winter morning and creep down with the other young maids, not daring to whisper on the stairs, chase away the black beetles and rake out the cinders of the oven; fun when promoted to 'doing' the library and the billiard-room fires, where a rich stuffiness of cigar smoke and the dregs of port lingered on the shuttered air; fun to help turn the vast feather mattresses, and run errands to the kitchen garden; but most fun of all to walk across the Park to church in a new bonnet (black stockings were insisted on for maids, but bonnet ribbons were allowed; they must not, of course, be gaudy), side by side with the newest girl but one, and file into a pew at the back, one of an established hierarchy. Many of the little maids had started work in the fields at the age of six scaring crows, had helped their mothers through childbirth, learnt their alphabets at the Hampton Lucy Dame School in Snitterfield Street, where the Dame would slap their faces with a dirty dish-cloth if they made a slip.*

The kitchen which George and Mary Elizabeth built on, part of the south block added in the 1830s, breathes of plenitude, of cheap labour, and strongly of the dignity of domestic service. You could put a small church into its dimensions (length, breadth, *and* height), and the place has known its own form of worship. The black-leading and polishing of the range was a four-hour task; home-killed meat was roasted behind a meat screen and basted with a long-handled ladle, for its heat was intense. The great table was scrubbed white with sand and cold water; no scouring powders could make it more spotless. The kitchen furnishings included a cool marble slab for pasty-making, a block for chopping meat, and a pestle and mortar for pounding the sugar which came in cones (wrapped in blue paper), a *batterie de cuisine* in copper and pewter, all of it immensely heavy and some of it very ancient. And everywhere so much space! A cook and six kitchenmaids could move about in starched print dresses bearing vast tureens, or great china platters with haunches of venison, or a whole tench out of the Avon, without impeding each other.

High up at the top of the house the servants slept in attics

---

* It will not, perhaps, be amiss to mention here Old Phazey, remembered with affection by my husband's generation. He went to work at Charlecote at the age of seven as rabbit boy and graduated to being under-keeper and eventually park ranger. When he was past outdoor work he used to sleep in the Great Hall to frighten off burglars, his arms for a nightly patrol of the shuttered rooms being an antique shot-gun and a pair of handcuffs. No one knew half so well as he how to train gun dogs and cure their ills. He lived to long past eighty, earthy, illiterate, happy, full of memories.

unaltered since the house was built. Through the lozenges of
green and mauve glass they saw below them the gatehouse,
like a child's toy. Moving round the arms of the half H, they
had views on one side of the cedar lawn and the yews of the
North Garden, and on the other of the stable buildings that
were young with Queen Elizabeth. No doubt the maids
preferred the rooms that looked down on the court, where
glimpses of the comings and goings of the young ladies and
gentlemen could be had, and of carriages driving up to the
front door under its high Renaissance porch. In the empty
cells that will never hum again with domestic politics, are
beds (in use till the Second World War) that have survived
from the eighteenth century. Across the frame strong sacking
is stretched, laced through brass eyelet holes with thick cord.
Short turned posts and brass medallions gave a touch of
elegance, and upper servants slept under a tester. It was a
favourite practical joke among the daring young ones to cut
the strings that laced the foundation, so that when Mrs Cook
climbed ponderously on to her feather mattress (the under
servants had straw palliasses only) it collapsed beneath her.

It was all fun. The scoldings, the chilblains, the inadequate
cotton blankets, the caprices of their betters, became part of
a memory honoured and cherished into old age, along with
the pincushion made from a piece of Miss Emily's wedding
gown and the yellow daguerreotypes of shooting parties
posed on the terrace steps.

Having re-edified Charlecote, Mary Elizabeth Lucy sat down
to write the history of the Lucy family. George Lucy had
painstakingly collected the baptismal records of his predecessors and placed them in the hands of the College of
Heralds. A superb pedigree book, its vellum pages thick
with gold leaf, taking the Lucy descent back to St Edmund
King and Martyr, lay on a table in the library. Thomas
Willement, by Royal Appointment Stained-glass Painter to
George IV and Victoria, was commissioned to fill the upper
windows of the new library and dinner-room with ancestral
coats of arms, through which the westering sunlight still

falls in flames of mauve and crimson on to the red carpet woven with a pattern of white luces.

In so long-descended a family one would have expected to find an unbroken series of records. A roomy old house like Charlecote should have had an Evidence Closet piled to the roof with court rolls, deeds, wills, memorandum books, letters, journals—all the sources from which family histories are fed. That the material was always meagre is evident. During a number of short successions, the house had been often left empty in the charge of servants. At one moment, but it is not known precisely when, there was a fire. Some catastrophe had overtaken the Lucy archives long before Mary Elizabeth sat down to work on them. Wisely she leaned, as all Warwickshire historians and antiquarians must, on Dugdale.

In the 1630s Sir William Dugdale with Sir Simon Archer of Umberslade, a distant kinsman of the Charlecote Lucys, visited Charlecote to inspect the Elizabethan roll of Arms. In a wainscoted parlour that faced west across the Avon, the greatest of Warwickshire antiquarians looked over the evidence that he subsequently compressed into four dry pages of his great work. The Lucys had no need to prove long descent or claim to be armigerous, as many country gentlemen were doing who were eagerly investigating their records to establish ancestry.

It was the golden age of historical research. There was no dearth of material. In most cases people were living in the houses their ancestors had always lived in, or that their great-grandfathers had built under the Tudors. There had been no civil wars since the fifteenth century, no raids on private property except on that of Catholics.

Dugdale in a memorandum reminds himself 'to take Sir Thomas Lucye's and Sir Greville Verney's writings with me', on a journey from Umberslade to Warwick. The bulky deeds travelled in an iron-bound, treble-locked chest, still at Charlecote. He used a wash on the Rous Roll of the Earls of Warwick 'for recoveringe of the blinde wordes'. Whether he did the same to the Charlecote Roll we cannot know, since it had disappeared altogether by the end of the seventeenth century. He could be censorious of the carelessness of others, writing to Sir Simon Archer in 1637: 'It did much grieve me to see (and soe would you) the great spoyle of many rare and antient seales, by carelessnesse; the peeces whereof lye mangled like chipps, in a huge trunke, and much of the evidence utterly rotted with wett and raine.'

Sad it is to relate that when the iron-bound chest in which the evidence was preserved was opened in 1947, after being allowed to lie in a flooded ground-floor room of the gatehouse, the contents were found to be almost utterly rotted. The Warwick Archivist and his helpers worked tirelessly and achieved the impossible; lumps of sodden papers, apparently cemented solid, were persuaded to yield their information. Fragments, where a tantalizing sentence or two was still readable, were transcribed, and tattered transparencies that had been important letters and journals were mounted in such a way as to preserve them.

These were the last of the Charlecote archives. Fifty years before, when the house was being made ready for letting, a mass of papers found in a cupboard in the attic had been burnt. The incumbent of Charlecote, The Rev. Mr Tobin, saved what he could from the flames, and to him we owe much. For some time afterwards butter from the farms used to arrive wrapped in torn-off pieces of medieval and Elizabethan parchments.*

Before the nineteenth century was half-way through, in 1845, Richard Monckton Milnes was writing: 'The gradual pauperization of the upper classes is distinct and tangible. I never saw so many houses to let. Barouches turned into flies, chariots into broughams. There are fewer balls, and it is

---

* This has historic precedent. About the middle of the last century an autograph collector bought a piece of fish from a fishmonger near the Tower of London. The wrapping turned out to be a Charter of Edward VI. He bought more fish, and each time found the wrapping was some document of value. The fishmonger admitted to having bought two or three sacks of such papers from an official of the Tower, who, it was discovered, had been disposing of the State Archives to the shops in the neighbourhood, in order to rid himself of the bother of them.

getting rather respectable than not to have little money to
spend.'

Reading Mary Elizabeth's journals of the middle stretch of
the century, it is not apparent that the Lucys were aware of
any such threat of pauperization. It was always possible to
cut down timber—as every generation had been doing since
the seventeenth century.

Wallington, the agent, writing in the early 1840s to his
master abroad, reports: 'I am pleased now to have a good
report to give you of the proceedings of the Rent day, which
went off very well. All regretted your absence but expressed
their best wishes for the health and happiness of you, Mrs
Lucy and all your family. Your Brother took your place and
all enjoy'd themselves, and I am glad to say all paid up;
indeed £4.11.0. in the cottages is only deficient and that
caused by illness in one case and death in another.' (The
annual rental varied very little between £3,000 and £4,000.)
'I have been making all the enquiry I can respecting the
projected railroad across your estate, but cannot find that
any farther steps have been taken; some people consider that
it must be given up as the money market will not allow of
such a speculation.'

The project came to nothing; the strong opposition of
hunting and game-preserving landlords squashed it, in consequence of which the railway from Warwick to Stratford
has to make a considerable detour. There was no need for it,
when coaches thundered into Stratford daily—the *Rocket*,
the *Oxonian*, the *Triumph*, the *Royal Pilot*, the *Paul Pry*, the
Britannia, from London, from Holyhead, from Leicester,
from Birmingham, from Kidderminster and Bath. The
Stratford-on-Avon Canal was the highway for the transport
of heavy and breakable commodities; Pickford's canal boats,
which arrived from London twice a week, brought down
George Lucy's valuable marbles and pictures shipped from
Genoa and Leghorn, insuring them against rough handling
or jolting, and it was probably as satisfactory, if more
leisurely, a method of conveyance as anything we have
today.

Charlecote was so well entrenched with prosperous farms,

so buttressed by woods of splendid timber, that it seemed nothing could threaten it. George Lucy had inherited the house from his father in a dilapidated condition. With care and thought he improved and re-edified it, according to the taste of his time; it was his sole absorption and delight.

The passion was handed on, but not the discrimination. Lavish spending had become a habit difficult to break. The stone gateway on the Stratford road is out of its context, as it were, lacking the arcading and pavilions that should balance it; equally ill at ease are the stone boars and the municipal-gardens effect of the gates at the main entrance.

'[In 1853] the North Wing of Charlecote was finished,' wrote Mary Elizabeth, 'that part of the house had not been touched since the time of Elizabeth, and the walls were quite crumbling away. Spencer not only restored it, but made the additional improvement of throwing out Oriels to both wings and restored the stone mullions which had been taken out about a hundred years [ago] and replaced by Grecian [*sic*] ones.' (This was Francis Smith of Warwick's work, done in Dr William Lucy's time.) 'Gibson was the architect and designed the *much admired ceilings* in the Drawing and Billiard rooms. Trollope of Parliament St, London, did the gilding and painting entirely after my taste and directions, with Spencer's approval. The amber-coloured Chinese Silk on the walls of the Drawing room, and the Crimson Chinese Silk Curtains, was bought many long years before by my husband and for which he gave a guinea a yard.' (George Lucy, who had died in 1786, had refused permission for the cornices to be touched up with silver. Nothing now remains of *his* improvements to the house.)

The grass slope to the river from the windows of the library that had been part of Capability Brown's plan, was too informal for the taste of the 1800s; and after submitting a number of designs Gibson produced the present arrangement of steps and terraces. His first idea that the river should have its course slightly altered so as to flow directly beneath the library windows, the house to rise from it like a Venetian palazzo with moorings for boats in alcoves below, was turned down as being likely to make the rooms damp. The north wing having been made to match the rest, there was nothing left to do but to loop in the croquet lawn with a gimcrack imitation of the gatehouse balustrading. This conceit was found so pleasing that the same balustrading was introduced between each of the gables, and in fact wherever space could be found for it. The knack had been lost, but the spending went on, until by the 1870s it was impossible any longer to ignore the fact that Charlecote, improved in an ampler age, was too big, and cost too much to keep up.

The seventies and eighties were years of severe agricultural depression. The old woman, Mary Elizabeth, who had been born when George III was on the throne and was nearing her end, wrote in her journal: '. . . What with war, bad trade, and worse harvests, few things, social or agricultural, can be said to have prospered. Spencer was most unfortunate in having about 50 acres of Hay entirely spoiled by Floods . . . there was frequently 20 and 30 degrees of Frost and it set in after, or very shortly after, a very protracted and wretchedly bad Harvest. Farmers in despair were throwing up their Farms—and Spencer has had notices from 5 of his Tenants to quit at Lady Day. . . . Alas, the year 1881 has been still less prosperous, weather so severe, such rain and floods destroying the Hay . . . Spencer had about £700 worth washed away. The Corn Harvest was better, but so late, not finished here till the end of October, in which month we had the highest flood in the memory of the oldest inhabitant of Charlecote. . . .'

And again: 'Lady Day! [1885] a *sad* one for Spencer, many of his Tenants coming to ask for a still further reduction of Rent, and to which he was obliged to accede, fearing to have more farms on his hands, as he now has nine—seven in Hampton Parish and two in Charlecote. . . . In fact his income is not one half what it was a few years back.' (This was the year that saw the breaking-up of the picture collection.)

Edward Fitzgerald wrote to Fanny Kemble in the summer of 1881: 'If still at Leamington, you will look upon a sight which I used to like well; that is, the blue Avon (as in this weather it will be) roaming through buttercup meadows all the way to Warwick; unless these meadows are all built over since I saw them some forty years ago.' Forty years before, William Howitt had been dismayed to find the country haunts of Shakespeare's youth desecrated—near to Anne Hathaway's dwelling at Shottery a farmer, he tells us, 'has already pulled down some of the neighbouring cottages and built up a row of staring red ones in their places.'

The process of growth and change as it affects the country-side has two aspects. For centuries, while taste ruled with expediency as its servant, all was well. When expediency rules alone it makes use of shoddy workmanship and inferior material. It has never been found satisfactory to allow a servant to command.

The word 'improvement', current through the last century, has been replaced by 'development', with its uneasy suggestion of arbitrary powers. Standardization and development go hand in hand nowadays, and an ugly-looking couple they are. The other face of change is averted from us; only its true lovers know the look it wears. From what the *Oxford Dictionary* calls 'a latent or elementary condition'—the five hides of land cultivated by a Saxon freeman—there grew very slowly the Charlecote we know. This is the true process of development which the *Dictionary* defines as 'a gradual unfolding'; it is the subject of the following chronicle.

The human race, not being dowered with second sight, and being born optimistic, desires to believe that everything is working out for the best; those possessing the sour gift of divination are generally prevented from using it—the optimist and the pessimist travel the same road to the same end. No amount of foresight could have done more for Charlecote than postpone the inevitable. After a long span of retrenchment, during which land, furniture and pictures were sold to maintain its existence, it was recalled to life in 1946, though to a very different life to that visualized by Mary Elizabeth Lucy when she penned the dedication to her eldest son: '. . . may God through you prolong the line of the Lucys till time itself shall end'. Never had it been imagined that the day would come when Charlecote would no longer pass from one generation to another.

But on 6 June 1946 it happened: Charlecote with its deer park, furniture, and pictures was presented to the National Trust by its owner, Sir Montgomerie Fairfax-Lucy.* There was a short formal ceremony in which the keys of the gateway passed from the hands of Sir Barry Jackson, Director of the Shakespeare Memorial Theatre, into those of Dr George Macaulay Trevelyan, OM, representing the Trust. Thus happily were the muses of drama and history involved to grace the occasion, and there were some smiling allusions to William Shakespeare, not only as a poacher of other men's deer, but as a stealer of other men's plots.

It was my husband's task in his brother's absence abroad to preside over an occasion that might have been melancholy had not all present taken the determinedly civilized attitude that preservation in the public interest is the happiest fate that can befall such a place.

The small crowd of strangers round the gatehouse archway stood with bowed heads while my husband spoke of his family's tradition of responsibility for tenants and villagers, and voiced what only those who have had a like upbringing can appreciate, the affection and gratitude felt for its old servants, those arteries of a house's life without which its life stream stops. . . . 'Charlecote is as much a memorial to the uncounted generations of servants who worked loyally and faithfully for the preservation of this place, as it is to my own ancestors.'

The flag on the gatehouse roof bearing the 'three luces hauriant' flapped in the wind. It had seen torchlight and crowds welcoming young brides to Charlecote, and coffins carried out smothered in the Gloire de Dijon roses that still grow on the gatehouse wall. In the short, restrained ceremony of relinquishment there was implicit a strong sense of the dissolving moment mingling with the living past.

---

* Grandson of Henry Spencer Lucy and great-great-great-grandson of Admiral Sir William Fairfax, who commanded HMS *Venerable* at the Battle of Camperdown.

Charles Lamb wrote of a house he loved whose glories had passed away: 'I sometimes think that as men, when they die, do not die all, so of their extinguished habitations there may be a hope—a germ to be revivified.' Where there are old bricks and old trees that have stood so long that they have the weathered look and feel of rocks; where sunlight warming a faded fabric into a moment of vivid life warms the heart, too, with the knowledge that a loving hand placed that curtain to fall in such a way; where an outdoor clock's striking lets drop into the noon-day silence its reminder that every hour, every minute, every second is slipping away from the present, which is already gone, into the past which cannot die—here is to be found not the coldness of death but the freshness of immortality.

CHAPTER 2

Knights of the Shire

'O eloquent, just and mightie Death . . . thou hast drawn
together all the far stretchéd greatness, all the pride, crueltie, and
ambition of man, and covered it all over with these two narrow
words: *Hic jacet!*'

Historie of the World: Sir Walter Raleigh.

In the twelfth and thirteenth centuries there were Lucys
living all over England, Anglo-Normans who had acquired
estates by marriage. Of these, the Lucys of Cockermouth in
Cumberland and the Lucys of Lesnes Abbey in Kent were
historically the most important. There were plenty of others
in Hertfordshire, Norfolk and Essex who all carried the three
pike *hauriant* (coming to the surface for air), but with a
difference, some being white on a red field, some gold on
blue. Lesnes Abbey, built and endowed by Richard de Lucy,
Henry II's Justiciar (the Lucy motto, '*By truth and diligence*',
might have been invented for him), fell into ruin with the
wreck of the rest of the great abbeys. The Lucys of Egremont
and Cockermouth, a grim race, castellans of fortified keeps,
devolved in the end on one woman, the daughter and sole
heiress of Thomas, Lord Lucy, who, marrying a Percy, took
the two baronies of Cockermouth and Egremont with her
so that the Dukes of Northumberland to this day quarter
their arms with the three white pike. By the end of the
fifteenth century there were practically no Lucys left anywhere but those of 'Cherlcot' on the Avon. Leland making
his itinerary of England in about 1550 learnt, probably from
the knight of Charlecote himself, that the Warwickshire
Lucys believed themselves to have stemmed from the baronial house of Lucy of Cumberland, lords of the high-
sounding liberties of Cockermouth, Papcastle, Broughton,

Brettby, Crosby, Ullendale, Aspatric, Caldbeck, and Loweswater, long since dispersed. So strong was this tradition that when a new house was built at Charlecote in about 1558 the bay of the Great Hall was filled with armorial glass bearing the arms of these northern Lords Lucy.

Dugdale, who pieced together the first three hundred years of Charlecote history from material that had survived the demolition of the medieval demesne house, preferred to reserve judgement. The College of Heralds in the nineteenth century had not freed itself from Elizabethan influence, as may be seen in the pedigree taking the Warwickshire Lucys back to St Edmund the Martyr, compiled by Bluemantle in 1822. Dugdale was much ahead of his time in that, though he was himself a Herald, he ignored the previous findings of the Herald's Visitations, and went into the individual merit of every claim. Like Professor Round in our own day, he viewed alleged descent from a cadet line with reserve.

The earliest discoverable document that refers to Charlecote is a deed of gift (of about 1187) by which one Thurstan de Cherlcot confers on Cecilia, his son's wife, some land in Cherlcot 'which Ailfric held of him'. Not in itself interesting, it is important because it confirms that Walter, who was the son of Thurstan, had married a lady called Cecily and that the land in Cherlcot came to him from the de Montfort family. We know from Domesday Book that Cerlecot was taken from a free Saxon called Saxi and given to the Norman Count of Meulan, along with a great many other properties in Warwickshire; that the Count of Meulan passed it to his brother Henry de Newburgh, the new Earl of Warwick, who was finding it necessary to buttress his new status in the shire with as many fiefs as he could acquire; and that it was held under the lordship of Warwick by Thurstan de Montfort, lord of Beldesert, near Henley-in-Arden, a branch of a great Norman house whose only claim to fame is that one of its line fell fighting beside his greater kinsman on the bloody battlefield of Evesham.

The sons of Cecily and Walter were to hold Cherlcot in fee to Roger de Cherlcot, who appears to have been the deceased Walter's brother, by the yearly payment of a pound of cummin at Michaelmas. The land was to descend to the one of Cecily's two sons whom she chose to make her heir. The charter was witnessed by men of some local standing: William, Abbot of Stoneleigh, Stephen the cellarer of Bordesley, Jordan, Dean of Warwick, and others. "Tis not unlike', says Dugdale, but without giving his reasons, 'but that the said Thurstan de Cherlcote was a younger son of the before specified Thurstan de Montfort. . . . From this Walter de Cherlcote (who was a Kt.) by Cecily his wife descended William that assumed the name of Lucy; which makes me think that he was an heir to some branch of that family; for it hath antiently been usual enough with the descendants of great heirs to relinquish their paternal name and take the Mother's.'

William the Norman's desire to be regarded as the lawful successor to Edward the Confessor did not make him so in the hearts of Englishmen, who were still tribal in outlook. The Saxon bowed his head and settled his shoulders to bear the yoke of bondage, to find the bondage no harsher under the new aristocracy than under the old overlords. Habits that have evolved out of primitive needs have a way of passively resisting change, and what has been called the 'peasant substructure' quietly persisted. It was as if the huge, mailed grasp of the Conqueror, closing greedily on Anglo-Saxon England, was not big enough to hold all it seized; the little people wriggled out, and, with a watchful eye on their new masters, went steadily on in their former ways.

But the Conquest can also be likened to a great wind that raised a cloud of blinding dust; when it settled, the personality of English society had altogether changed. In all departments of public life, in the King's household, in the Church, in the administration of the King's justice, foreigners replaced Englishmen. The old manors changed hands, and all disputes had to be referred to and judged by an alien mind, vigorous, unreactionary, bewildering to the slower mental processes of the Anglo-Saxon.

Though many Saxon freemen were ruined and sank to the level of serfs, their work lived after them. The hides of land which Saxi and his kind wrested from bog and waste are the cornfields and buttercup meadows of Charlecote today. At a point where the river plunges into deep shade, a steep, scarred bank, crowned with trees still bears the name of Old Town. The water here is over forty feet deep and fed with secret springs. Here may have stood the reed and clay huts of Saxi's *vill*, or the name, like a tenacious root, may burrow even deeper into the deep past. Charlecote, Cherlecote, Cerlecote, Ceorlcote; it dwindles with distance to a vanishing point, and Saxi, who made it and was a free man, swings his plough round and guides his oxen out of sight.

The Conqueror's grantee, the Count of Meulan, one of the lively, angular lords of the Bayeux Tapestry, does not come into this story. To his bailiff the people of Cherlcot brought their rents in kind, eggs, poultry, and milk, carried and stacked his hay and threshed his crops, receiving at harvest time a rye-bread loaf, rough cider and the Warwickshire cheeses that are made to this day. It is all so small and far away from us now that the Count of Meulan and his vassals are like the little figures looped into the burnished initial letter of a missal. Secure as squirrels burying their winter store, the hedger, the woodcutter, and the swineherd went about their work as they had always done, built their brushwood fires, cut turf for roofing and poles for fencing, snared ground game for the pot, indifferent as to who presided over the shire at Warwick. But to Walter, the son of Thurstan, the fact was of the first importance; Roger de Newburgh, who succeeded his father Henry as Earl of Warwick in 1123, showed him some favour, perhaps recommended him for the knighthood by which the poorest landowner, with no more than a timber farmhouse to shelter him and a handful of inarticulate peasants for a following, was assumed equal in honour with the greatest in the shire. For the next three hundred years the Lucys in their rustic manor moved in the orbit of the Earls of Warwick and Leicester. William's grandson Fulc followed his mesne-lord,*

---

* The middle lordship; de Montfort at Beldesert could call on his kinsman at Cherlecote for forty days' military service. In a time of national emergency the mesne-lord, de Montfort, had to turn out to support his liege-lord, Warwick. It paid to be a mesne-lord, but knight-service, though aristocratic, could be a heavy liability for a poor gentleman.

Peter de Montfort, to fight for his kinsman, Simon de Montfort, Earl of Leicester, against the King and the barons. Fulc's grandson was in the retinue of Warwick at the Battle of Crécy. So little is known of them that they seem to have almost no independent existence. Yet, generation by generation, they were putting down roots into Warwickshire and becoming part of the England of their ancestors' adoption. The genesis of the de Cherlecotes, who were by blood de Montforts and who at some time near the end of the twelfth century assumed the name of de Lucy, is as slow as the growth of a tree that seems to acquire no visible girth or spread of branches till it begins to be perceived that its leaves cast a substantial shade.

Though the landscape of the early Middle Ages must have appeared darker than it does today, being much more wooded and overgrown, the cultivated fields had a cheerful patchwork appearance, it having always been the custom in England to cultivate land in strips running parallel, partitioned by grassy ridges. Traces of this early strip cultivation can still be seen: England has been slow to depart from agricultural tradition. In the early nineteenth century Warwickshire fields were described as being tilled in 'large crooked ridges gathered very high, with a small one between', and even at so late a date it was recommended that a better system of rotation of crops would improve the land. Round the common pound were the hovels or one-roomed houses of the villagers, each with its cap of reeds, and its yard, or cultivated patch, which grew a few sackfuls of corn or barley for the holder. There was a church in Cherlecote by 1187, for in Thurstan's deed of gift to his daughter-in-law it is mentioned;* it was dedicated to St Leonard, a saint for whom the de Montforts had particular veneration. A much later deed (5 Edward III) speaks of William de Lucy's garden which bordered the common way leading to Brocmulne or Brookmill—in fact, the same way that leads today

---

* This Cecily de Lucie, about whom nothing is known, granted half a yard land to the church of St Leonard at Charlecote to be used as a burial ground. Of her grave, and Walter her husband's, there is no trace.

from the present Charlecote stables to the Warwick road, where, instead of the bridge over the Wellesbourne brook built in the mid-eighteenth century, there stood one of the two mills mentioned in Domesday.

The demesne of the lord of Cherlecote was set low by the river with the wasteland (spongy ground drained by ditching) all about it. Later the warren of scrub oak and elder grew up over the wasteland and obscured the little demesne-house with its barbican and outer trench. It was never a house of importance. Nothing about it could arouse the envy or displeasure of the overlord, as did nearby Fulbroke in the next century, that 'praty castle' of brick and stone which, according to Leland, was such an eyesore to the Earls of Warwick.

Later Lucys may have made walled garden enclosures with seats of banked turf and espaliered fruit trees, but when William, the son of Walter, succeeded his father the place was still primitive. Licences to build fortified manor-houses were not easy to get; the Conqueror and his sons were never forgetful of the anarchic strain in their Norman followers. The house would be half of stone, its upper storey of timber with a roofed-in gallery running round it. The autumn freshets that brought down great catches of eels flooded the guardroom under the hall and retired leaving a high-water mark of scum on the west side. Indoors a craving for beauty and order was beginning to be felt, and finding expression in a more formal way of life. The fire no longer blinded the inmates with smoke, but burnt in a hollow shaft or flue cut in the wall, with an outlet to the sky. In rainy or windy weather it still smoked. Hangings disguised the bare walls; there was everywhere an impulse to decorate. The stone surrounds of the windows were pierced in the simplest leaf and flower forms. By the reign of Henry III, glass, very dim, and thick, was in use in the King's palaces and in churches, but in humbler dwelling-houses wooden shutters had to serve, though in summer linen was sometimes stretched tightly across wooden frames and fitted into the windows. In the upper rooms there were floors of pale waxed wood and stone walls thinly washed with plaster. Even though candle-smoke blackened everything, though tables and benches grew greasy with use, and rushes, so fresh smelling when cut, withered underfoot, life had moved a long step forward.

To the Earl's castle at Warwick each young Lucy was sent to learn how to balance a lance and how to buckle on, without fumbling, the component parts of a suit of armour, and heave its wearer into the saddle without tipping him over on the other side.

William had received his polite education in the household of Earl William,★ and this perhaps influenced him to take the Sign when the Pope called the faithful to subsidize a Fifth Crusade. Whether he made the hazardous journey is not known. It seems unlikely; the vow to follow a Crusade so often wilted under the weight of the practical problems it presented. The Sign was eagerly taken by young Englishmen who yearned to leave their bleak stone castles where draughts billowed the hangings, only to die of typhoid and dysentery in the burning desert under an unpitying sun.

To be signed with the Cross conferred the right to wear a red cross on the shoulder of a surcoat (the thin linen tunic worn to keep the sun off armour). Being so signed, but unable for reasons not known to join a Crusade, William de Lucy decided to endow a religious house at nearby Theles-ford, a mile away across the fields. Nothing is left of Thelesford but the name; not one stone has remained upon another of the House of the Holy Trinity which stood here till the Dissolution. Only the little stream that once watered the Prior's garden still runs under the Warwick road, where once there was a ford.

Tanner believed there had been a religious foundation, most probably of the Order of the Holy Sepulchre, an order formed to ransom prisoners in the hands of the infidel, established at 'Theulisford' as early as 1200. William de Lucy added to his grant of land the advowson of St Leonard's church in Charlecote, which his father had built, and with it

---

★ This pious Earl founded two hospitals in Warwick and himself died in the Holy Land on the Third Crusade.

the piece of land his mother had granted to it for a burial ground.

The story of Thelesford is one of humility and obscurity. It was a hospice, a little place of hospitality, with a chapel and a dovecot. It was always poor. A document called 'The Thelesford Register', which was among the family archives at the end of the eighteenth century, covered the whole story of the Brotherhood; a few disjointed notes copied in an eighteenth-century hand alone survive. From them we know of a gift from the lord of Cherlecote of a free fishery in his water of Avon on all days except Sundays from the mill of La Ley (in Barford) to the mill pool of Cherlecote. William made a present to the monks of their demesne and villein-age—their dormitory, chapter and cottages—and of a vivar-ium, or fresh-water pond, for rearing fish.

Eight years before their patron's death the Friars were reorganized and Thelesford became a Trinitarian Priory. The Brethren of the Holy Trinity for the Redemption of Captives was placed by Walter de Cantelupe, Bishop of Worcester, under the rule of St Augustine in 1240. Below the field called Thelesford Grove lie buried almost all the Lucys of the Middle Ages, ending with Edmund, who commanded a company for Henry of Richmond at the Battle of Stoke. Before the Dissolution there was a chapel full of brasses and effigies (one stone coffin alone survives). There were cups of silver-gilt and pierced dishes, and embroidered robes and mass books. The monks had their herbarium and a vineyard on the south slope. But no effort of imagination can put back what man has erased and the plough has passed over.

From now on the young Lucys, as well as learning about chivalry and fighting and farm management, received a smatter of education, and could at least sign their names and make out a little Latin. Fulc, the grandson of William, who came into his inheritance in the forty-seventh year of Henry III's long, ineffectual reign, shows a hint of personality through his actions, though, owing to the initiative of Henry VIII's agents at the Dissolution, he has no more features than his predecessors.

His duty to his kinsman and mesne-lord at Beldesert sent

him with a following of picked Cherlecote men to join the
Barons in 1264, to fight for English liberties; Magna Carta
had been rendered ineffectual by the appointment of the
French Queen's Poitevin relations into high offices. English
castles, rents, fees, and wardships were being pocketed by
Frenchmen. That the magnates who protested were nearly
all of them of Norman French extraction, struck no one as
inconsistent.

In Dugdale's *Warwickshire* Peter de Montfort of Beldesert
earns three pages of censure. 'This Peter . . . he even sided
with the rebellious Barons of that age, who, the better to
shadow their disloyal practices first plotted their meetings
under colour of exercising themselves in martial Tourna-
ments which were forbidden by the King, who well foresaw
the danger that might ensue.' In a small and threatened
society, always looking for safeguards, the obligations of
kinship were binding. Fulc was ready to forget that he was a
Lucy, and while de Montfort's insurrection lasted enjoyed,
according to Dugdale, much favour with the Barons' party
for his activeness. He finished up in Kenilworth for the
duration of the King's six months' siege of it.

Peter de Montfort's name invested him with a reflection
of Earl Simon's popularity—he was chosen as one of the
Council of fifteen who were to control the actions of the
King and wrest the government out of the hands of his
Poitevin favourites, and was entrusted by Earl Simon with
the Great Seal. When Fulc de Lucy ran heavily into debt with
a Jew of London, his kinsman procured for him a special
mandate (in May 1265, just when the fortunes of the Earl's
party were on the wane) cancelling the debt.

The year 1265 saw the first English Parliament of its kind
to which each shire, city, and borough sent representatives.
But the dissatisfied of Earl Simon's party were already
melting away to join the King's son, the Lord Edward, a
veteran soldier of twenty-six. Simon's French blood, his
wild temper, his popularity with the people, his extravagance, had made him too many enemies. While his partisans
were holding Kenilworth Castle for him, his small force met
the Prince's well-equipped army in the Vale of Evesham on

an August morning and was cut to pieces. Peter de Montfort died with him. In the years following the insurrection, Beldesert went through many hands, and fell eventually into ruin. Fulc obtained a discharge of his annual service by paying up two hundred pounds in silver. The rent became a mere consideration, a pair of gilt spurs valued at sixpence, until the mesne-lordship was extinguished at the beginning of the next century; and that, as far as Cherlecote was concerned, was the end of the de Montforts of Beldesert.

Under the Dictum of Kenilworth, so called because it was framed during the blockade, in fact under the very walls of the castle where the King's force was encamped, all the estates of those who followed Earl Simon were to be confiscated unless their owners could pay the King five years' revenue on their property. What it amounted to was that all rebels were required to buy back their own lands. If they could only afford to pay the half or a third of the penalty the corresponding amount of land would be retained by the King. It was a harsh dictum, but roughly just. The actual garrison were to be more severely treated. Seven years' annual income was required from them.

The answer from within the castle walls was obstinate silence. The stock of food dwindled, the winter set in bleakly, the supply of firewood ran out. Ten days before Christmas, 1266, the gates of Kenilworth were opened and the defenders were allowed to return to their homes.

Fulc was not able to raise all at once the seven years' annual rents which the Dictum demanded. His estates passed to a King's man, Robert Waleran, and Fulc found himself living as a tenant on his own land. By the time the sum was raised, the country was once more at peace. As had happened in the years immediately after the Conquest, a strong personality had caused a lot of dust to be blown about, and uncovered the withering roots of established institutions. The dust settled. England stretched and relapsed into the habits of ordinary life.

This thirteenth-century lord of the manor, about whose life we know only the barest facts, lived on into a great epoch of reform under a King who bent all his ambitious will and tremendous energy to the formation of a new Constitution, bringing Englishmen of all classes and denominations together, and changing the pattern of English society. Many landowners got into trouble over the findings of the Statute of Winchester, Fulc among them. His wise father and grandfather had taken the precaution of getting their charters from Richard I and John, granting them 'divers privileges and immunities', renewed, but the charters were beginning to be out of date. Fulc was sharply questioned on what authority had he held a Court Leet in his hall at Cherlecote without the presence of the King's Bailiff. It was held that he had overstepped 'the divers privileges and immunities' that the charter allowed.

This brought up a recurring problem of manorial government. With the lordship of a manor went the responsibility for keeping the peace within its boundaries. The manorial court was set up in the name of the lord of the manor, generally in the great hall of his dwelling-house. To this the villeins brought their grievances against the lord's steward, their complaints about their neighbours, their wish to marry or put away unfaithful wives, and asserted under the Saxon laws of *firebote* their right to take brushwood for firing, and of *hedgebote* and *housebote* their right to cut the lord's trees to make their ploughs and repair the timber framework of their hovels. These rights were already very ancient when Fulc became lord of the manor of Cherlecote, and had never been clearly defined. Ignorant as the English peasant was, he was not inarticulate, and the records of manorial courts show the calm persistence with which he stood out for his rights.

Complaints had reached the King's Remembrancers from Shrewley, near Birmingham, which had come to Fulc from his grandmother. To punish a flagrant breach of the manorial peace, Fulc had threatened to put up a gallows there and dispatch the felon out of hand. Hanging was the agreed punishment for theft, but the sentence was not often carried out, and could only take place in the presence of the King's Bailiff. The indignation of Shrewley brought the King's Remembrancers down to Cherlecote, and Fulc had a date assigned to him on which to appear and justify his action.

No more is known except that in the year following and again in 1288 he was constituted one of the Justices for the gaol-delivery at Warwick. Into the county gaol prisoners of both sexes were herded like cattle. Before an Assize could take place, they had to be roughly sorted and their suits given a preliminary hearing. At the Assize the prisoners were brought up in batches before a bench of Justices, whose aim was not so much to see justice done as to clear the place out before the next lot came in.

Fulc presents, from the few known facts of his life, a number of contradictions. His life seems to have been without any more dramatic episodes, but he had enough de Montfort temper in him—the temper of revolt—to make him combative to authority. On more than one occasion he outfaced the King's commissioners and continued to practise certain dubious feudal legalities. In spite of this, in January 1287 he was, according to Dugdale, one of the four Knights of the Shire whose business it was to see that the articles of the Statute of Winchester were carried out. He assumed knighthood by virtue of his landed property.

The Lucys of Cherlecote must have had daughters, but there is no mention of them. In the monotonous records of William succeeding to William, varied by an occasional Thomas, the estates acquired by marriage descend in the male line according to feudal law. Daughters had to be married if they were not inclined to become nuns (even a nun had to be endowed) and were bound to accept their parents' (or, if they were wards, their guardian's) ruling in the matter. Having only such limited opportunities for finding husbands for themselves, they very often had to accept men below their station, landless knights risen from humble beginnings who had had a knightly training in some feudal household, but had no fiefs to support their honours. If no money could be spared for the girl, a father would remit the knight-service of one of his followers as a marriage portion. Heiresses were in a worse position; they were bargained for like cattle. A widow was most valuable, as she brought her late husband's property as well as her own dower lands. It was not till the great Charter of 1215 that women were allowed a voice in the selection of a husband.

We know almost nothing of the early Lucy wives; the apparently dowerless Cecily, who gave her surname to the line, Isabell de Alderminster with her Worcestershire lands, Maud Cotele, with her manor of Broughton in Hampshire, Amicia de la Fourches with her Herefordshire properties of Kyngeston and Bodenham Fourches, and the nameless heiress who brought lands in Gloucestershire and Leicestershire.

Fulc had married a lady called Petronille about whom nothing whatever is known. Waiting at Cherlecote for Fulc to return, or for news of his death in the field, she can never have known a quiet night. Hammering on the postern and shouts might mean a detachment of de Montfort's following needing food (and capable of taking it and leaving the larder swept bare of six months' supply) or the King's men looking for plunder. Useless to lock the doors, hopeless to attempt to hide; the lady of the manor, with as bold a show of firmness as she could summon up, must descend. The shrewd ones would recognize the temper they had to deal with, and use pathos, wifely alarm, or simply affect not to understand anything but French as spoken at the King's Court. The wife of a landed lord had to keep her wits about her if she had only a bailiff and a house-steward to support her whose loyalty she could not count on, and a handful of terrified house-servants ready to beat it for the woods if anyone so much as laid a hand on a sword.

Fulc de Lucie riding home from the siege of Kenilworth along the road to Cherlecote, lean from the blockade, to find his gates hanging open, his cattle straying the roads, is linked with the great reforms of his epoch; his son was one of the legs of the three-legged stool which has supported the Constitution of England ever since, the Baronage, the Clergy, and the Commons.

His son, William the Third, sat in four Parliaments, and received 4s. a day for doing so. He married a wife called Elizabeth, and carried on his seal (the first Cherlecote Lucy to do so) the red shield sown with crosslets upon which the

silver pike swam upwards.* In the Chronicle of Battle
Abbey, Richard de Lucie the Justiciar is recorded to have
said that in the old times, and by that he meant the pre-
Angevin days, it was not the fashion for every small knight-
ling (*militulus*) to own a seal, which was the prerogative of
barons. But fashions were changing. Arms embossed on
seals of brass or bronze were becoming the indispensable
signature to legal documents, being much more difficult to
forge than the rudimentary handwriting of the day.

In 1314 famine touched Cherlecote. The agricultural
depression which produced it was not local; all England felt
it. Below a certain level there was not enough food to go
round. The labourer went to his long day in the fields on a
piece of barley bread. It is a wonder the population increased
at all, for the deadly hazards of medieval life, agues, dysentery, childbed-fever, took toll of bodies dismally undernour-
ished. It was a marvel children ever grew up. Cherlecote by
the Avon had plenty of river fish; but fishing rights were
jealously guarded, and the lord's demesne commanded a
long view of the river, both up and down.

Snail-slow as the growth of the population was, it had at
the beginning of the fourteenth century overreached production. The countryman hoed over his bit of exhausted yard
land which needed manuring (manure was scarce and the
lord had first claim on it) and wondered if the blackened
beans struggling to grow and his dwindling sack of dried
peas would see him and his children through till Lammas
and the harvest.

The fourth William de Lucy fought at Crécy. During the
minority of Edward III a sort of peace prevailed. But war
with France was piling up. William de Lucy saw the beginning of the series of defensive pauses, punctuated by bouts
of fighting, that grew to be known as the Hundred Years'
War.

---

* Only those who had actually been on a Crusade were allowed to wear the
cross as part of their arms. The crosslets on the Lucy coat may have been
adopted in honour of that Aymer de Lucie of the Cumberland line who
accompanied Richard I to the Third Crusade.

In his grandfather Fulc's day, sheep farming in Warwick-shire had increased. Sheep were profitable, not only for their wool, but for their skins, which provided the parchment membranes on which all legal business was inscribed. (The meat was regarded as much inferior to beef.) England's prosperity was carried on the woolly shoulders of its sheep, and forced loans from the rich wool-merchants later became the standing resource of the Plantagenet kings when their coffers were low.

Flanders being too small to support itself by its own internal economy, the astute Flemings turned themselves into the international brokers of Europe, through whose hands flowed all Europe's supplies of corn, wine, oil, silk, furs, salt, and spices. Firstly, though, Flanders was the centre of the weaving industry; its traditions went back to the days when Charlemagne had ordered Frisian cloths as a gift for the Sultan Haroun al Raschid.

The King of France, titular overlord of Flanders, was helpless to prevent the mutually profitable alliance of English and Fleming. In 1331, when Edward III went to France to do homage for his French possessions of Guienne and Gascony, and for his wife's dower of Hainault, he was paying lip-service which did not in the least disguise his intentions. No Plantagenet could endure to be both ruler and subject, inheritors as they were of the restless, despotic temper of the House of Anjou.

Even in remote little Cherlecote the creeping shadow of coming events was seen. At Michaelmas, 1332, we find a subsidy being raised on all taxpayers, which would give a useful idea of the sort of following such places as the manors of Cherlecote and Shrewley could provide for the King in case of need.*

The picture of English rural life had been perceptibly changing; since the upcurve of the wool trade everyone, except the very poorest, owned much more personal prop-erty. On a man's house furnishings, his chests, his dormant tables, his frying-pans, trivets, gridirons, pepper querns, and

* *Lay Subsidy Rolls of Edward III*: Dugdale Society.

farm stock, not only the lord of the manor, but the freeman
too was liable to assessment. William de Lucy (he was not
knighted till 1344) paid 19s. 4d. for Cherlecote, and the
Minister of the House of the Holy Trinity at Thelesford,
15s.*

The expected call to arms came in 1346.

The mustering of all the counties 'citra Trent' was like the
stirring-up of a giant ant-hill. Messengers carrying writs,
sheriffs with their retinues, took the roads at a smart pace.
Expectancy ran high. No Cherlecote man living had seen
any war service, no one on the manor had ever crossed the
sea. In the Pipe Rolls we find that Cherlecote was assessed
for 5 marks—there is a small discrepancy between this and
the findings of the Assessors who compiled the Lay Subsidy
Rolls ten years earlier, but only of a few shillings—but this
had to go toward the cost of the equipping of a hobelar, or
lightly-armed horseman. The rest of the cost came out of
William de Lucy's pocket—on his other manors and properties in Herefordshire, Gloucestershire, Shropshire, and Worcestershire he would have to contribute in the same way. He
would have to have at least two personal attendants to look
after his horse and grease his armour and a mounted bodyservant as well.

With Warwick's men, twelve abreast, William crossed the
River Somme at the passage of Blanche-Taque where the
water ran white over chalk, between the dangerous tides that
came up twice a day, the water churning at knee height. And
in the forest of Crécy he saw his men flex their bows and
settle down to wait for the attack.

The tactics of the French, beautiful in themselves and
formal as a pavane, were powerless against the mobile
infantry of Edward III. The French *gens d'armes* who came
from their farms to fight, and disputed pride of place with
the French crossbowmen because the front rank in battle was
the position of honour, were so closely packed together that
they could not effectively handle their pikes. As those in
front fell, the French horsemen from behind, weighted with

---

* Ten shillings at this time was about equal to £20 previous to 1914.

their armour, rode them down, and fell themselves under the steady rain of English arrows.

The army was in three divisions: the first, nominally under the young Prince Edward, was really commanded by the Earls of Warwick and Oxford. The name of Sir William de Lucy of Cherlecote in the retinue of Warwick is recorded between those of Sir Hugh de Wrottesley and Sir Roger de la Warr. De Lucys other than Sir William of Cherlecote are found in the Muster Rolls: Thomas, Lord Lucy, of the northern family, who stayed behind to keep the Scots in check and joined the King at Calais, and Geoffrey de Lucy, a Kentish squire, who died during the siege of Calais. This followed on the victory of Crécy, and the town surrendered on 4 August 1347 to the now depleted army of the English King. During the year of the siege it had been necessary to allow knights to return home from time to time in order to collect fresh supplies of men and equipment, for dysentery had halved the English forces. Sir William of Cherlecote died of it in France in the year of the siege.

After Crécy and Calais there was a brief illusion of peace, and England's spirits rose. In the modern phrase, there was more money about; even the peasant who sold his cheeses in the nearest town and trudged home with the rain in his face felt it, for he had coins to jingle in his pocket.

Into this lull broke the Black Death, or bubonic plague. In three years it spread over all England and into Wales and Scotland, battening on the dirty and ill-nourished bodies of those unable to protect themselves from it, paralysing the life of the country. No building was done, no manuscripts illuminated, all weaving, embroidery, painting, carving stopped. There has never been a stricture on the national life comparable to it. Boccaccio's elegant ladies and gentlemen, who fled into retreat in the country to escape infection, epitomize the behaviour of the privileged at this time. In cramped, close rooms the deadly plague germs multiplied, and were carried on boots and clothing and on hands that prepared food, till the disease penetrated to all but the remotest moorland hamlets. After three years the infection disappeared, to go underground and reappear intermittently for the next three centuries.

There is no record of a visitation of Black Death at Cherlecote, but the place can hardly have escaped it. The virgates of those who died would stand unweeded and uncut, their hovels derelict, grass growing high at the doors. The bodies would be put into a common pit, which was filled in with clay and turfed over, making a green mound long to be avoided with superstitious dread. Cherlecote men bearing the sturdy-sounding names found in the Lay Subsidy Rolls (Pounts, Clots, Rugges and Fychets) must have sickened and died.

It now became possible for a labourer to ask for and get higher wages. Thomas de Lucy, son of the Sir William who died in France, found himself, no doubt, faced with the need to let out a good deal of his land. If the toll of the plague was heavy locally, he must have been hard put to it to find enough men to work his demesne. On many estates the lord, finding himself unable to pay free labourers the wages they demanded and which they could get elsewhere, enclosed his wastes and common lands, and took to sheep-farming. The open-strip system of farming that had come down from the Saxons was wasteful and laborious, but the new enclosing of the common fields, where the village had from time immemorial pastured its cows and geese, was bitterly resented.

If the Lucys were—as Fulc evidently was—harsh landlords, exigent in their demands for service, greedy about their dues, heavy-handed in dealing out punishment for small offences, then the men about the place who were not bound by family ties would slip off by night and offer their services elsewhere, a thing which could not have happened a hundred or even fifty years earlier.

In a community that had jogged peaceably along on a basis of mutual give and take, adjustments were made which would have seemed revolutionary to Thomas's grandfather.

We have seen Fulc de Lucie commuting his knight-service to his mesne-lord for a sum of money and the consideration of a pair of gilt spurs. In the same way, in the village and on the manor, the natural economy of payment by service was being gradually replaced by commutation in money.

To set out the meagrely documented acts of the Lucys of the Middle Ages, generation by generation, would add little to the picture. They are the faceless men, too far away for us to visualize since none of their works remain; not a vestige of the medieval demesne-house, not one stone left upon another to show where Thelesford stood. Their lives were constricted, their situation precarious. Knowing no others, they endured cold, smoky houses, clothing stiff with dirt that, worn in all weathers, dried to them like old leather, food that was either burnt, raw or maggoty. They accepted pain with fortitude, having no cure. At any moment a small landlord might find himself liable for a heavy fine if his mesne-lord, as happened to William Lucy at the time of the barons' insurrection against King John, went contrary to his feudal overlord. A drought, a wet harvest, a contagious sickness, could mean the ruin of a year's prospects.

The tension of great events, such as a king's ransom, a Crusade, or a royal marriage (as when William, father of Fulc, had to contribute to the aid levied when Henry III's sister married the Emperor Frederick II),★ were felt even in the deep country, running from the head through all the limbs and sinews of the feudal aristocracy.

Lucy sons continued to be sent to Warwick to complete their education. The last de Newburgh of the Conqueror's creation had died childless about half-way through the thirteenth century, and the honours of Warwick eventually devolved on a nephew, a Beauchamp of Elmley Castle in Worcestershire.

At the beginning of the fourteenth century a Thomas Lucy was in the retinue of Richard Beauchamp, Malory's perfect, gentle knight; his son saw the ascendancy of Beauchamp's successor, a Neville from the north. In the struggle in which England was locked during the last half of the fifteenth century, the Cherlecote Lucys are lost, confused with those

★ *Book of Fees*, I, p. 512.

of the Kent, Essex, and Northamptonshire branches,* adhering to their liege lord through a density with only here and there a glint. One, a William, married into the Baronage, his wife being a sister of the Yorkist Lord Grey of Ruthyn, and died in the hour of Warwick's success, believing the war to be well won. His son, another William, more worldly and more wary, after the death of the Kingmaker at Barnet Heath thought it prudent to retire to his estates and busy himself with affairs in the country. He had contracted a marriage to please himself—the girl was not well dowered—and by doing so put himself in an awkward relation to the party in power.

At Edward IV's death the greedy contestants for the throne closed in like a pack of hounds. The man who schooled himself in patience till the dogs should have drunk each other's blood, Henry Tudor, Earl of Richmond, was in exile. William Lucy's wife was brought up in the household of his mother, the widowed Countess of Richmond, granddaughter to John of Gaunt. She was Margaret (called after her patroness and godmother), daughter of John Brecknock the late Earl Treasurer. The Countess, having a great regard for John Brecknock, kept his daughter close to her. It followed that when Margaret married William Lucy of Cherlecote she should, with the Countess's approval, call her first son Edmund.†

Edmund Tudor, who was the son of a French princess and a Welsh squire, lies in St David's Cathedral under a restored stone tomb chest, the cost of the restoration having been borne by the Rev. John Lucy of Hampton Lucy and Charlecote, a nineteenth-century squarson who was as brimful of feudal sentiment as his seventeenth-century forebear,

---

* At the Battle of Northampton, a Yorkist victory, in 1460, 'that good knight Sir William Lucy that dwelled beside Northampton heard the gun shoot and came into the field to have holpen the King, but the field was done before that he came; and some of the Staffords was ware of his coming and loved that knight his wife, and hated him and anon caused his death.' I quote this episode from Gregory's *Chronicles of London* to show how easy it was to confuse Lucys; this story is often told of Sir William of Cherlecote.

† She died young, and William Lucy took to wife Alice Hanbury. Margaret was buried at Thelesford; William and Alice in Stratford Parish Church.

William Lucy, Bishop of St David's, had been lacking in it. Edmund Tudor's son, Henry, lies in effigy in his own matchless chapel in Westminster Abbey. To these two Tudors the Lucys, who up to now had been Yorkists, owed their advancement. John Brecknock's post as Treasurer was filled by Reginald Bray, whose interest with the new King secured the Order of the Bath for Margaret's husband, a command under Lord Oxford for her son Edmund, and eventually preferment for her grandson too.

Like his ancestor, Fulc, Edmund's fighting years were over in his twenties. In the hall of Cherlecote there now hung the banner of a high-ranking officer in the King's army—the knight of Cherlecote was not '*militulus*' any longer. At the battle that took place at Stoke against the Pretender Simnel and his army of German mercenaries, supplied by the late King Edward's sister, the Duchess of Burgundy, a lady of rabid antipathies, Edmund had been in command of a company. Simnel was taken prisoner, and his claim to be the son of the late King's brother, Clarence, on whom the honours of Warwick had devolved, exposed. Henry had been keeping the real Warwick in the Tower all the time, and had only to produce the boy to discredit the story, but with a gardener's thoroughness set himself to root out the pretenders who sprang up in his path like dandelions. Simnel was put in his place, which was the royal kitchen; others were not so leniently used. During the Wars of the Roses the crown of England had been looked on as a prize for him who could get it, ambition and ruthlessness qualifying rather than royal blood. It had passed from one head to another till the day when it rolled from the helmet of the slain Richard at Bosworth and was retrieved from a bramble bush. When Elizabeth of York was crowned Henry's Queen in 1487, the marriage grafted the red rose with the white to conciliate old enmities.

The late civil wars had been going on so long that their origin was almost forgotten. To country gentlemen living on their manors a new King meant only that a new party was in the ascendant; those who had changed their coats in time hoped for compensation. The Lucys were among these, and had, it seems, no reason to complain. For the first time since the days of the great Justiciar of Henry II, the Lucys were *familiares regis* at Court. Feudal tenures in the prosperous midlands were weakening; only the feudal sentiment remained, as we shall see later. The Lucys who saw the fifteenth century out looked back on predecessors who had squandered their whole lives and resources on a dynastic quarrel.

By transferring their allegiance from York to Lancaster the Lucys were only following the examples of countless other small country gentry, who from the accession of Henry Tudor vowed their loyalty solely to the Crown. Here exists a natural watershed; on the one side we have the line stretching back to Domesday of a family of Anglo-Norman descent, farmers, soldiers, lords of the manor, Knights of the Shire, but vassals always of a noble house. With the political collapse and death of the last great Earl of Warwick, all this changes.

No truth is more true than that nothing is final—not wars, nor the fall of governments, nor the end of dynasties. The Wars of the two Roses flickered on after Bosworth Field, the feudal system lingered in pockets, just as the Saxon mode of self-government persisted in spite of the Norman occupation. But in the history of the Lucys of Cherlecote, which is a microcosm of a whole class, a definite, almost an abrupt, change begins to be noticeable; as the great magnates go down the smaller gentry come up.

In October 1494 Edmund was summoned to Court to be installed as a Knight of the Bath with the King's younger son, Henry, but was unable to obey the summons. There were expenses attached to the privilege, though the rich symbolic dress was the King's gift to the new Knight, but it was an honour no one would refuse without grave cause. Something shortened his life, perhaps the dysentery or the sweating sickness that ravaged English armies abroad. He had crossed to France with the King and been with him at the siege of Boulogne, a gesture on Henry's part to remind the King of France that the English still had a footing on French soil, even though the great heritage of the Angevin kings had been lost. (Many English families still owned property in France. The rents of some tenements in Calais that had been awarded to the Sir William who fought at Crécy were the subject of litigation as late as 1437.)

Young as he was, Edmund had buried one wife, Elizabeth Trumpington, and married again, Joan the daughter of Sir Richard Ludlow, by whom he had, certainly, a son, Thomas, and possibly a daughter, Radegunde, called after the patroness of Thelesford. Edmund Lucy, the simple soldier, for soldiers are always presumed simple, was wholly a man of the Middle Ages, and when he made a will before his early death in 1498 gave directions for his body to be buried at Thelesford, and left the Priory a magnificent cross of silver and gilt costing £10, which was no small sum in those days. At his month's mind (the anniversary of his death) he desired that eleven poor men should be given black gowns and hoods and carry tapers in procession; and for the space of twenty-two years after his death 40s. be spent on the masses for his soul and for the relief of the poor of Cherlecote.

As his body was carried to Thelesford for burial, the manorial tenants of all degrees paused at their work. The thought in all minds was of the next lord of the manor; would he instruct his bailiff to be lenient, or enclose fields traditionally open, or evict those who at next rent day could not find their rents? Their forebears had been thinking the same since the time of the Conquest. The elders of the village, who presented defaulters at the manorial court, began to check over the ill-doers due for presentation; those who were guiltily conscious of having disrupted the manorial economy applied themselves with zeal to the work in hand. The ox-brace creaked, the scythe swept its measured arc; life on the manor of Cherlecote was resumed, not to alter its pattern till far into the eighteenth century.

The land hunger of the thirteenth century, when the de Lucys were acquiring properties in the midlands and the west, had given way to a state of affairs when landed gentry found themselves with more land on their hands than they could afford to cultivate. By now the Lucy possessions were widely dispersed. Alice Hugford,* who had married Thomas de Lucy (the one who was in the retinue of Richard Beauchamp, the great Warwick) in the early fifteenth century was the daughter of a Shropshire knight and had inherited from her mother the manor of Carlton or Pabenham in Bedfordshire, and with it the manors of Ravensden, Wilden, Trailly, and Wootton Hoo. Thomas Lucy was holding a manorial court at Pabenham between 1512 and 1517. His father, Edmund, had already sold in 1495 an emparked wooded close called Pabenham in the overlordship of Carlton, 'with free incurse and oute-curse for the falling, carrying, and re-meading of the same wood'.† Re-meading or turning land to pasture was going on everywhere. Reginald Bray's influence got Edmund's son Thomas the position of server at Court, which meant he was in constant attendance at the King's table. A lease exists of the parsonage and garden of St Bride's, Fleet Street, dated 1509 (the same year young Prince Henry married his brother's widow, the Spanish princess, and succeeded his father), and there Thomas lived, and his children were born. He was knighted, and given by Henry VIII a valuable wardship, that of young William Catesby of Ashby St Ledgers, whose mother, Elizabeth, he married.

Elizabeth was the daughter of Henry VII's ablest extortioner, Sir Richard Empson, who, with his colleague, Sir Edmund Dudley, spread alarm through England by their methods of mulcting private property to enrich the Crown. Many gentlemen, because of some flaw in their claim to inheritance, found themselves beggared as a result of Empson and Dudley's researches into legal precedent. They became the best-hated men in the country, and Henry VIII on his accession saw it would be a popular move to eliminate them. Having no compunction about inaugurating his reign

---

* After Thomas's death she married within eight weeks Richard Archer of Umberslade, ancestor of the antiquarian who came to Charlecote with Dugdale in the seventeenth century to study the archives.
† *V. C. H. Bedfordshire.*

with judicial murder, he gave his consent, after a show of reluctance, to Empson's execution.*

Elizabeth Empson had been married to a Leicestershire gentleman, George Catesby of Ashby St Ledgers, and was a widow. Thomas Lucy took her the news of her father's death on Tower Hill and married her a month later. They had six children, William, Thomas, Edward, Anne, who married a Monmouthshire knight, Radegunde, and Barbara, who married Richard Tracy of Stanway in Gloucestershire. Thomas must have returned to live at Charlecote after the deaths of his mother and stepfather in 1514. Edmund's widow had re-married, to Sir John Hungerford, but desired in her will to be laid at Thelesford beside her first husband. Her will gives us for the first time a glimpse of the interior of Charlecote. That it had always had a chapel we know. In the first William de Lucie's day a special dispensation grants it to the founder of Thelesford for the private worship of his family, where Roger the priest of Cherlecote is to celebrate mass on seven of the festival days of the Church's year. The chapel, according to Joan Hungerford's will, was hung with 'red saye and green', a fine cloth of mixed silk and woollen, and had an altar frontal of worked crimson velvet. There was a chapel-chamber adjoining it for the priest's use, the feather bed and hangings of which she left to her daughter Radegunde's children. To her friend John Spencer of Hodnell who had just built himself a fair 'manour place' at Wormleighton, she left an allegorical tapestry of the Nine Worthies. The clothes she distributed among her maids are those worn by the women that Holbein painted; a black gown purffled (trimmed) with looped shanks of gold wire, others furred with mink or ornamented with raised paddings of black velvet lined with satin of Bruges.

Thomas did not die a rich man. There is a clause in his will regarding 'obligations' to the King of £116, probably Wolsey's 'amicable loan' of 1525, which demanded a sixth of

---

* Through all the disruptions of the next three centuries, two relics survived at Charlecote of these dangerous days: a gilt wine cup bearing the initials R.E. and an enamelled ring, the gift of the King to his Treasurer Ward, which was stolen from the house in the 1850 burglary.

all lay property. He divided his Hugford inheritance between his younger sons. His eldest son William was to have the Herefordshire estates that had been the portion of his ancestress Amicia de la Fourches,★ till he should inherit his mother's life interest in Charlecote. A Londoner from choice, he was buried in London in the church of the Grey Friars, Smithfield, long destroyed, of which Dugdale wrote indignantly that you would look in vain there for Sir Thomas Lucy's tombstone.

All this time the monastery of Trinitarian Friars at Thelesford had been deteriorating. It had shrunk in numbers and ceased altogether to be a hospital or place of hospitality. The brothers' interests were now centred wholly on the means of subsistence, since it had no profitable industry to support it, such as a mill for fulling cloth or a tannery. A Papal Indulgence of 1334 had allowed the brothers to collect alms, which was no more than licensed begging. They had been guilty on more than one occasion of evicting tenants in order to enclose land for grazing. Sir William had allowed them the privilege of stallage—the right to erect a stall in a market—and licence to slaughter beasts on their premises, and made over to them the advowson of the church of St Leonard in Charlecote, but all to no purpose. Because it was a house of little importance and described as 'ruinous' it was not dissolved till 1535, five years after the disgrace and death of Wolsey. By then, as Dugdale says, the rest of the lesser houses had 'gone to wrack'.

Writing to Thomas Cromwell in November 1538, his 'visitor' or agent, the notorious Dr London (a Wykehamist and Warden of New College, Oxford), describes almost indulgently a crude fraud perpetrated by the monks, who were not, themselves, much less ignorant than the poor they served.

Thelesford; . . . There was a fond fashion of Idolatry. In the body of the church was an Image at an altar's end called Maiden Cutbrogh and under her foot was a trough of wood descending

---

★ Wife to the second Sir William, who succeeded to Cherlecote in 1247.

under the altar which was hollow. Thither resorted such as were troubled with the head ache, or had any sluttish widows lockes, viz. Hair grown together in a tuft. There must they put in to the trough a peck of oats, and when they were once slidded under the altar the cross friar behind the altar [should] privily steal them out, and the sick persons must give to the friar a penny for a pint of these Maiden Cutbroghe oats and then their heads should ache no more till next time. I have pulled down the Idol with her manger.

The earliest Lucy letter that has survived is dated 18 March 1538. It is from William Lucy, who succeeded in 1525, to his wife's cousin, Hugh Latimer, Bishop of Worcester; written from the clergy house at Hampton in which he was living as a tenant while alterations to the demesne house at Charlecote were going on. Dr London had visited Thelesford, exposed its naked poverty and feeble fraudulence,★ and swept on to deal with other, richer game. Surely, William wrote, since the place was de-valued, there could be no objection to the descendant of those Lucys who had given lands and benefactions to it receiving it back into his hands, always provided that the King was not a loser by the transaction.

The poverty of Thelesford was indeed pitiable. The Valor Ecclesiasticus, the Domesday Book of the Reformation, gave its annual rent as £24. 19s., but Dr London (and he had plenty of experience) thought it could not be worth more than £18 a year. The prior, who was too old to look for new employment, was recommended for a pension of £5.

William's plea to the Bishop ends: 'This thing were very commodious for me being so near unto me, if I might attain it.' Thelesford land was good farmland, but that, he makes clear, is not his only motive for wanting 'this little house, being so near unto me (that) my ancestor's did build. . . .'

Dr London, writing to his master in January 1539, endorsed William's plea to be allowed to re-possess Thelesford:

. . . I have committed the custody of the late Friary of Thelesford unto your assured orator [*suppliant*] Master Lucy, and surely I found it a very poor house, as any that hither to I came to. I have

★ *V. C. H. Warwickshire*, Vol. I, p. 106, for the whole history of Thelesford.

dispatched the brethren all, with the servants and have taken a way for the payment of their debts. The house is in much ruin and the church is but a little thing and not perfectly builded. If I should have defaced the church and the house and sold the whole house and church, I could not have made £20 to the King's use, and standing as it doth it may do Master Lucy, which is a right worshipful gentleman, much pleasure. He is a man of right good learning and much soberness and liveth quietly among his neighbours, wherefore it had been pity to plant any stranger so nigh him. . . . And your Lordship in helping this worshipful man thereunto shall do a right good acte, for he keepeth a right good house and hath many children and bringeth them up in learning and in virtue. He hath also a great many of brothers and sisters upon his hands to bestow and some he had bestowed all ready right honestly to his no small charge. I could no rather [*no better*] dispatch that friary.

But the Vicar-general had other grantees in his mind for Thelesford. It went to a higher bidder* for £648. 19s. 2d., together with the seven acres of woodland called Thelesfordgrove, and some land in Charlecote and nearby Wasperton which had long ages ago been granted to the monastery. William Lucy had to possess himself in patience for four years before he was able to buy it back. By then it was ruined indeed.

William had gone to Northamptonshire for a wife, to Easton Neston near Towcester. Her name was Anne Fermor, and her father was a Merchant of the Staple of Calais, one of the powerful cloth-brokers who lent money to the government. Tradition says that William Lucy and Anne Fermor lived in mutual endearment for thirty-three years, and when she died he followed her before the year was out, it is said of inability to live without her.

William's brothers, Thomas and Edmund, had received the manors of Claybrook in Leicestershire and Bickering and Sharpenhoe in Bedfordshire. As well as his many brothers and sisters, William had ten children of his own, and a good marriage must be secured for his eldest, or how could Elizabeth, Maria, Jane, Martha, and Joyce be dowered?

---

* William Whorwood, the Solicitor General.

His Charlecote property had been enlarged by the acquisition of derelict Thelesford. His great-grandfather, the Sir
William who had married Margaret Brecknock, had obtained
from Edward IV the office of Keeper of Fulbroke in the
parish of Bishop's Hampton on the other side of the river,
and ordered from a timber merchant of Wroxhall six score
oaken posts ten feet long and twelve score rails thirteen feet
long, for the purpose of reinforcing the park fence to keep in
the deer. Seventy years earlier the whole property had been
enclosed, and the village of Fulbroke, half a dozen hovels
down by the brook's edge, depopulated, to make a park for
a royal Duke, John of Bedford, brother to King Henry V,
who built the little castle there, which, according to Leland,
was an eyesore to the Earls that lay at Warwick. Edward IV
had granted it to the Kingmaker. It went with the Warwick
title to Neville's son-in-law, Clarence, on whose attainder it
returned to the Crown. (Thomas Lucy had received the
custody of it from Henry VIII.) The place had a bad name
locally. The enclosing of the park with wooden palings in
old Sir William's day to keep the deer in★ had provided
shelter for thieves, so that no one dared pass that way after
dark. The labourer trudging by the Redway to Hampton
was glad to put Fulbroke behind him. In the same way, the
villagers of Charlecote would go a long way round to avoid
what was left standing of Thelesford Priory. Places thus
abandoned served evil purposes. It is curious in this context
to note that not one carved corbel or spout head survived
from the abandoned chapel that Dr London had not thought
worth pulling down.

The minds of men were changing and opening to new
ideas. It could not have occurred to the humble forebears of
William Lucy's labourers that the monasteries were corrupt.
If the priors were hard, exacting landlords, so was the lord
of the manor. If clerical tithes were heavy, and heavier still
the mortuary dues exacted before a body was allowed the
last rites, at least the religious houses did not depopulate for

---

★ The agreement is dated 16 Edward IV (1477).

the purpose of preserving land for sport, as had happened at Fulbroke.

William Lucy was a man of the New Learning. Young men at Oxford, who attended lectures in Greek, felt a wind blowing from antique civilizations that withered superstition and blew away the shreds of medieval scholasticism. But a critical attitude towards orthodoxy was not general. At Stratford Grammar School, founded a hundred years earlier, the old Catholicism was still taught. From the humble and poorly paid priest of Charlecote William Lucy received the bare rudiments of Latin, a little penmanship, and some elementary arithmetic, but not much more; his leaning toward the new unorthodoxy was fostered by Edward Large, the curate of Bishop's Hampton across the river, who provided in the April of 1537 an example of how the New Learning had power to disrupt a quiet country district. Even to read about it is like poking a wasps' nest from a safe distance with a long stick.

On Easter Monday, which fell on 2 April, a marriage was celebrated between a man of Stratford and the sister of one of the churchwardens of Bishop's Hampton, to which, there being a bride-ale at the church door, a number of Stratford people came, among them Combes, the town's High Bailiff, and Anne Lucy, William's wife—William himself being at the time ill.

The curate mounted the pulpit, but before beginning his sermon begged the congregation to attend to him patiently, as many lies were spoken about him in the country. If it was thought he could not justify his words, they could come to him afterwards and he would set them down in writing, having ink and paper by him for the purpose.*

(It was noted that the Stratford Bailiff, a King's man, was present, and Mistress Lucy, but that William Clopton, a strict Catholic of the old orthodoxy and leader of the anti-Reformation party in Stratford, was absent.)

* This affair is briefly alluded to in the *V. C. H. Warwickshire*, Vol. 3, p. 276. I have taken this account, however, from an article in the *Athenaeum Magazine* of 18 April 1857, the author of which claimed to have copied it verbatim from the then uncalendared State Papers.

The testimony is confused. At one point in the sermon a man of Clopton's, one Richard Cotton, rose and violently protested. He was hustled out of the church and committed to Warwick Gaol. A week later Edward Large was also in prison—or perhaps just in close custody—on a charge of having said in his sermon that all those that use Our Lady's Psalter shall be damned, and for making the extraordinary statement that the Ember Days were named after one Imber, a paramour of a certain Bishop of Rome.

A number of Stratford townspeople, convened by William Clopton, suborned the jury that tried Large. The King's Commissioners, Combes the Bailiff, and William Lucy, haled from his sick bed, among them, examined Cotton, who turned out to be a very poor artisan. No one could be found to corroborate his statement that Large had actually spoken those words during the two hours' sermon from the pulpit. When one Richard Lightfoot, a baker of Stratford, a tenant of Clopton's, asked to hear the indictment, Clopton told him that the priest had said further seditious words, such as: 'Who put Christ to death but the peers of the realm in those days, that were high and learned men, both spiritual and temporal? And if Christ were now alive again He should die as cruel a death, "*as you see how their heads go off now daily*".' Richard Lightfoot said bluntly that he had never heard the priest preach any such thing. When Clopton rounded on him, saying that the reason he would not put his signature to the indictment was because Combes the Bailiff would not make him master of his Guild if he did, Lightfoot turned on his heel, saying he would belie no man falsely.

Cotton was soon induced to confess that he had been put up by Clopton to make a scene in Hampton Church. Clopton angrily told William Lucy that the parishioners of Hampton Lucy dared not speak the truth in front of him. But Hampton was solid behind the lord of Charlecote, no one could be found in it to say a word against Large, and Cotton was dismissed with a caution.

Pleased with his own handling of the business, William Lucy forwarded a long report to the Judge of the Assize, Anthony Fitzherbert, an irascible man, who was not impressed, having had already a long string of complaints of this sort to deal with, and roundly called William a meddler.★

Undiscouraged, William, on several occasions, judicially examined those who found themselves unable to accept the Act of Supremacy. While his wife's cousin, Hugh Latimer— one of the 'bold and heterodox minority' of Cambridge thinkers—occupied the See of Worcester, there was a strong Protestant influence in the diocese. Even after Latimer had resigned the Bishopric, William continued to lean on his guidance, and ten years later was influenced by him in his choice of a tutor for his eldest son, Thomas, then a boy of thirteen.

The previous tutor, John Falkner, had just accepted a Berkshire living. He suggested as his successor an Oxford graduate, a friend of his own University days, and Latimer endorsed the recommendation. This man, John Foxe, had had a strenuous academic career at Magdalen, where he had held a fellowship for seven years. On his refusing to take Holy Orders (on which the degree of Master of Arts was conditional), he was obliged to resign. As he was a hotly outspoken Protestant the College was not sorry to be relieved of him; being a poor man, he had to look about for immediate employment. Latimer offered him shelter, but Foxe did not want charity. It was then that Falkner wrote to him offering him the post of tutor of Charlecote, and Foxe in a letter wrote warmly of William Lucy to whom he had taken an immediate liking: 'Some days ago I was with Lucy and greeted him; but no more than greeted him, for I only stayed with him two days. The talents and character of the man I do not so much approve as admire; never in my life have I seen anything more fine and noble. His family pleases me equally, answering in everything to its head; it is such as I could desire, and in every way matches my wishes and feelings.'

Foxe was an ardent, emotional man—where he liked

★ His book, *The newe book of Justyces of Peas*, is in the Charlecote library today, and was to be a manual for William's son, grandson, and great-grandsons.

he liked wholeheartedly. Unfortunately, this happy first impression did not extend to the place. The letter goes on: 'But you know the lie of the house, how it is deserted on every side, shut off by hills and thickets from almost all light and society of men. Also it has a river by it, whose waters are at all times nearly stagnant, save that once in the year it washes the house itself, as the Nile washes Egypt.'

From this description one would think Charlecote ideally situated to hide a man whose religious views had incurred the displeasure of authority and who wanted to avoid attracting any more notice to himself. It is the first word-picture we have of the house and its surroundings, and in those few lines the scanty visual impressions given in the court rolls and wills, which have been up to now the sole source of reconstruction, draw together and harden into a picture of a real place. Not remotely like the Charlecote of today, with its spaced solitudes of park and pasture land, but small and lonely and dark, swarmed about by thickets, washed by a slow-moving, stagnant stream. Foxe adds dispiritedly: 'Lastly, Falkner has a chamber smelling so strong of the sewer that its occupant needs to have his nose cut off.'

The tutor no doubt fared badly in the matter of a bedchamber, there being not much space into which to fit the growing Lucy family and the necessary house-servants. What had suited Edmund the soldier had been too rustic for his son Thomas the courtier, and was now a tight fit for William the scholar, with his ten children.

Foxe, however, overcame his objections, and his year at Charlecote was sweetened for him by the companionship of his clever pupil and by his marriage with a member of the Lucy household. Her name was Agnes Randall and her father was a man of Coventry. (There have always been, and still are, Randalls at Charlecote.)

Dr London had commended William Lucy to his master as a man of learning and soberness, living quietly among his neighbours. Happy with his books, shut away among his wooded acres, satisfied with family life, William Lucy had nothing to offer John Foxe but asylum. Preaching to the converted had no appeal for a man who was under a fearless compulsion to uproot heresy. After one year's stay, during which time he imparted his love of the classic civilizations and his hatred of Catholicism to young Thomas Lucy, he left the kind if cramped roof, and without thought of personal safety fled with his young wife to London, embracing hunger, poverty, and the probability of death. The waters of the Avon were perhaps too much for a perpetual reminder of the greater danger of stagnation.

The Middle Ages, so rich, murky, and complex, and so difficult for us to understand, had passed. Over the remaining acts of the Lucys of Charlecote the mist shreds and the plain is sunlit, though the ground at our feet is in shadow still. The mist thickens again once or twice—for instance, during the uneasy years of the Interregnum—but on the whole individuals acquire thickness and solidity, and begin to bear relation to their own Warwickshire earth.

'In the heart of England and Wales, the Muse is here entered, that is Warwickshire, her native country; whose territory you might call Middle Engel (for here was that part of Mercland spoken of in Story) for equality of distance from the inarming Ocean.' So wrote the chronicler-poet, Michael Drayton, the contemporary of Shakespeare. In his immense poetic narrative, the *Polyolbion*, he lingers with especial tenderness on the heart of England, for he was born in the neighbourhood of Atherstone and spent much of his life in the houses of Warwickshire gentry; at Polesworth with the Gooderes, in which household he received his education, with the Rainsfords at Clifford Chambers—his 'Muse's quiet port'. He was to be protégé of that Lord Aston, son of Anne Lucy and Sir Edward Aston, whose birth is recorded in the Charlecote baptismal register. His buxom Muse is happiest in his own Warwickshire; the *Polyolbion* unwinds a broad ribbon of narrative verse which ripples through thirty cantos. The weft is shot with the greenery of Arden, the gold bounty of the Vale of the Red Horse, the blue of sky-reflecting Avon and Arrow. Not great poetry, but immensely evocative of the England of the sixteenth century. Drayton's publishers

made him angry by telling him that his stuff was out of date
when the last edition of the *Polyolbion* was brought out in
1619; the Jacobeans were not for nostalgia. The *Polyolbion*
evokes a vanishing England as Camden's *Britannia* does.

Dugdale, drawing on the memories of old people who
would have been young when Shakespeare was setting *As
You Like It* in the Forest of Arden, wrote that the country
north of Avon was known as the Woodland, and that to the
south of it as the Open Country. But the actual geographical
limits of Arden are not clear. By William Lucy's day you
would have had a long walk and a steep climb along the spur
of Ingon before getting a glimpse of the fabled forest.

In Drayton's day the Wealden or Woodland was already
receding. The salt-boiler and the miner were hacking down
pole timber for salt-refining and for pit-props. By his death
the forest's one hand no longer 'touched Trent, the other
Severn's side'. Diana Nemorensis, the goddess of the woods,
was being pressed back through thinning shade. The forest
was in the blood of Englishmen; it had been for so many
centuries their refuge and their livelihood.

Charlecote had always been in the champaign country of
the Felden, the corn and cheese-producing land of Warwickshire, but even the Felden was fairly densely wooded and
not all productive; there were still outcrops of heath and
common land where Camden recorded finding the rare
moonwort (*Osmunda Lunaria*), vervain, nightshade, and
squinancy berries.

The emparking that had been going on all through the
Middle Ages had bitten deep into both woodland and arable.
Under Henry VII three more important parks were enclosed;
Coughton by Sir Robert Throckmorton, Fletchamstead by
the rich mercantile family of Smith, and Pooly by Sir
Thomas Cockayne, who already had two other parks in
Derbyshire. By 1520 Compton Wynyates had been
emparked by Sir William Compton, Weston by the Shel-
dons, and Beauchamp, in the parish of Alcester, by the
Grevilles. By the middle of the next century Sir Thomas
Holt had emparked Aston by Birmingham, and Sir Thomas

Lucy Charlecote and Fulbroke.* This did not, however, rouse such bitter indignation as did the enclosing of land by farmers for grazing purposes. John Hales of Coventry, who was a Chancery official under Henry VIII, and whose brother married one of William Lucy's daughters, was praised by Bishop Latimer for daring to denounce the stealing of the poor man's livelihood. The homeless wandered miserably about the country, begged, starved, or took to evil ways. Fat, profitable sheep browsed where tillage had been; whole villages disappeared, as it seemed, between one week and the next.

After the Dissolution, monastic land was eagerly bought up; even the philanthropic John Hales purchased land belonging to the White Friars in Coventry, though he willed it at his death to the Free School he founded there. The Gooderes acquired the nunnery of Polesworth, the Harringtons the Abbey of Combe, the Burgoynes the Priory of Wroxhall, the Lucys the site of the Trinitarian Priory of Thelesford. But the chief profit on these estates went to the Crown, which drove a hard bargain with the purchasers. Everyone everywhere was busy driving bargains; these were thriving times for speculators.

Edmund Lucy, who fought for Henry of Richmond at Stoke, was the last Lucy to be buried at Thelesford in the faith of his ancestors. His great-grandson, Thomas (known to family tradition as 'the first Sir Thomas', though there had been others before him), knew the relief of professing an established religion. In the churches, hurriedly whitewashed and innocent of images, Foxe's *Book of Martyrs* lay on the reading desk beside the Bible, in order that the horrors of the Marian persecutions should be kept awake in men's minds. Thomas Lucy, Foxe's pupil, was a man at peace with his conscience and with the established Church. His family tree was nearly the longest in Warwickshire, a fact which he found pleasant to reflect on, and there was every prospect of his adding fruitful branches to it. In the year that John Foxe

* In the first decade of our own century there were twelve flourishing deer parks in Warwickshire.

left Charlecote, William Lucy drew up a marriage settlement between his eldest son and Joyce, only child and heiress of a Worcestershire landowner, Thomas Acton of Sutton. They were nearly the same age—he fourteen and she thirteen: so young that, after the ceremony, she returned to her father's house and he to his studies. The marriage was a master stroke that provided for the future of Charlecote, on a scale beyond anything it had previously known.

CHAPTER 3

A Goodly Dwelling

"Fore God, Master Shallow, you have here a goodly dwelling
and a rich—'
Henry IV, Part II: Shakespeare.

Thomas Lucy, the fourteenth Lucy in succession from the
first William, lived on his wife's property of Sutton near
Tenbury for four years before he began to rebuild Charlecote. His father-in-law, Thomas Acton, having died, Joyce's
mother had the place for her lifetime, and the young people
lived with her. She was born a Lacon of Willy and had reared
but this one daughter. The alabaster monument which Joyce
Lucy erected to her parents' memory in Tenbury church,
with fluted pilasters and Ionic capitals supporting a frieze
with dentil cornices, has a strong family resemblance to the
porch of the new Charlecote.

Rebuilding at Charlecote may have begun in the year of
William Lucy's death in 1551 (his wife, Anne, had predeceased him). He had lived long enough to give his blessing
to a grandson, born at Sutton. If the new Charlecote was not
completed till the year of Elizabeth's accession, it must have
taken seven years to build. According to Leland, Sir William
Compton, the Keeper of the royal park at Fulbroke, 'seeing
it [Fulbroke] going to ruin, helped it forward, taking part
of it, as some say, for the buildings of his house at
Compton by Brayles in Warwickshire'. Compton Wynyates
was therefore already in part built, but Charlecote must
come first, or very nearly first, in the list of the great
Elizabethan houses.

Leland's itinerary took him through a changing England.
Along with the spoiling of churches, he saw the destruction

of rustic manor houses whose walls had survived the civil
wars of Stephen and Matilda and the recent wars of the two
Roses. The sixteenth century was no more immune from
fears than the fifteenth century had been, but there was a
new essence in it before which the old superstitions began to
pale their ineffectual fires; an element of immense curiosity,
a growing confidence, immature but bold. Men were intox-
icated with the possibilities of life, with the continents and
empires of the mind, with the poetry and imagery of nature.
They had to express themselves in words and music, in brick
and marble and stone.

The new houses were conspicuous against the pale English
wheatfields and dark, plum-coloured woodlands. Across the
diapered bricks there played the perpetual mutations of
English weather, glooms and gleams that turned them all the
shades from wood ash to claret. The effect was not always
quite what the builders intended; in rainy seasons the new
houses could look bleak. They needed sunlight and sharp
shadows to bring to life the glitter of myriad windows
reaching from floor to ceiling, and the vitality of bold
ornament and fretted skylines.

Inside there was, for the first time, space and daylight
within doors. By the second half of the century the staircase,
instead of being curled round inside a turret, sprang out over
an open well in short flights each with its square landing.

The centre of the house was the Great Hall below stairs,
and upstairs the Great Bed Chamber, where windows on all
sides gave views of newly-emparked land planted with
young trees. The huge Tudor beds of blackest oak, whose
carvings of wild-haired men caught travelling highlights
from sunshine slanting across window-panes of tinted glass,
were encrusted with embroidery and padded with goose-
down. More even than the barrelled and coffered ceilings
with their stalactites of plaster and patterns of grape and rose
and flower de luce, or the tiered chimney-pieces of coloured
marbles (influenced impartially by Italian classicism and
German naturalism), it is the family bed, solid and four-
square, roomy as a cottage, sheltering as a great oak, that
brings the sixteenth century before our eyes.

The Rector of Radwinter in Essex, William Harrison, in his *Description of England*, a piece of trenchant Elizabethan journalism, laments the decline in fine timber, in particular of oak trees—'far unlike that plenty which our ancestors have seen heretofore, when stately building was less in use'. The newly-rich, he says, never tire of altering their houses, but set up, pull down, and enlarge, so that their purses are never shut or their books of account made perfect. The hedge as well as the park oak 'go all one way, and never so much hath been spent in a hundred years before as it is in ten years of our time; for every man almost is his own builder, and he that hath bought any small parcel of ground, be it never so little, will not be quiet till he have pulled down the old house (if any were there standing) and set up a new one after his own device'.

The greater landowners of Warwickshire may have looked on Thomas Lucy as a *parvenu* enriched by monastery loot (not actually true in his case), or, more justly, as typical of the small gentry inflated by having married money, who are never satisfied with what they have got but must hack down sheltering trees and mar the landscape with raw red brick.

Certainly Thomas's first act was to cut down the great oaks of the warren which densely closed in the house. His memories of childhood were gloomy. He would endure no more smoking fires, nor have to be aware of his dinner before it was brought to the table, or sleep in a cupboard in the wall, or crack his head on low lintels. He would have a great hall roofed with timbers of his own Charlecote oaks.

Harrison thought bricks vulgar, and condemned those who did not use the good stones with which God hath blessed this island, but 'do commonly leave these national gifts to mould and cinder in the ground, and take up an artificial brick in burning whereof a great part of the wood of this land is daily consumed . . . .' Thomas Lucy had no such sentiment. If Sir William Compton during his tenure as Keeper of Fulbroke had not pulled down John of Bedford's little castle and removed the bricks and the chimneys to build his house at Compton Wynyates, Thomas would have had them for Charlecote. However, the brickfields at Hampton

were still workable, and the black smoke of the kilns which
Harrison so much disliked was soon seen rising again.

His next consideration, after bricks and timber, was the
pattern of the house to be. When he finally decided on a
'plat' or plan for Charlecote it was plain, as Tudor building
went. Who was the surveyor (there were then few architects)
who provided the finally acceptable plat, and who the master
carver who put the finish on it, we shall never know.

All that *is* known is that Thomas Lucy followed a middle
course in building his house near the site of the old demesne,
but out of reach of flooding from the river, that he chose a
pattern that was handsome but not florid (not for him the
sugary graces of the Italian Renaissance), and that he built
well with local bricks and some imported stone. His foundations were on gravel and sand, his windows faced east and
west as was usual, for Elizabethan gentry feared a south
aspect as much as if they had been brought up in blistering
Italian sunshine instead of in dark and rainy England. The
house he caused to be built was a cautious blend of the old
and the new (and as such typifies its builder) in the mid-
Tudor vernacular.

The plan was half-H, and not, as has so often been said,
an E-shape in compliment to the Queen, who did not accede
to her throne till after the house was finished. At the four
corners were octagonal turrets crowned with leaded cupolas
and gilt weather vanes. The front face of the house has to
this day three gable heads just as when it was built; the wings
that extend forward to enclose a courtyard have two gables
on their inner faces and three on their outer, with a gable at
each end, facing east; the brickwork was all diapered in blue.

About the inside of the new Charlecote we can only
conjecture. The Great Hall, which filled the centre block,
had a roof of timbers and a screen. This screen of Tudor
inspiration stood as late as the beginning of the nineteenth
century, supporting a gallery. It was last seen (in the 1870s)
in the shop of an antique dealer in Warwick. A door opened
from the Great Hall on to the river bank, where the old
manor house had stood. Under Thomas's grandson this
became a formal garden sloping down to the Avon; later a

gravelled courtyard with a ford; much later a balustraded terrace with a flight of steps leading down into the water. The master mason who carved the porch should also have added a great erection rising giddily, tier on tier, over the fireplace of the Great Hall, and florid decoration and elaborate strap-work features everywhere. Why Charlecote is completely without this sort of enrichment cannot be explained.

If in our mind's eye we strip Charlecote of its modern trimmings (the pierced balustrading between the gables, the transomed windows filled with plate glass, the flocks of chimneys, the west block on the river side, and the disproportionate extension to the south), we shall see that it was just a very unpretentious, gable-ended house. The sole touches of elaboration were added during the next twenty years, and they were restrained enough. The gatehouse stands as Thomas Lucy conceived it (helped perhaps by a mason who had got his ideas from Longleat)—a brick box, with a flat roof of lead edged by a pierced stone balustrade. The arch is vaulted in the Gothic manner, but shell-shaped alcoves in the Renaissance idiom seem to have been intended to hold statues. The eye comes to rest on the balance of the balustrading and the windows with a sense of pure relief— no wrenching incongruities here. This simple piece of Tudor domestic architecture was so satisfactory that the Lucys of the nineteenth century felt no need to embellish it further. The gatehouse and the porch have been repeatedly attributed to John of Padua on the strength of a remark in Vertue's notebooks, but I have it on Sir John Summerson's authority that this is an impossibility. The porch was probably finished before 1570, and Thomas's gesture of loyalty on the occasion of the Queen's visit in 1572 was the addition to it of the Royal Arms supported by the lion of England and the dragon of Wales, each with a foot on the initials E.R., which his grandson, the Jacobean Sir Thomas, saw no reason to alter.

The great house of Kirby in Northamptonshire, built for Sir Humphrey Stafford and later the seat of Elizabeth's Lord Chancellor Hatton, begun in 1570, was partly at least the work of a Northamptonshire master mason, Thomas

Thorpe, father of the more celebrated John. Its broken porch, grass-grown and weather-stained, still stands, lovelier if possible in ruin, and has the resemblance to the porch at Charlecote that a peony has to a daisy. The porch at Charlecote, as at Kirby, is two-storeyed; it contains a small room that once opened on to the gallery in the Great Hall and was used as a retiring-room for the musicians. Again as at Kirby, a pair of Ionic pilasters flank the arched doorway, and above them project trusses carved with fishscales, carrying another set of rounded Corinthian columns. Where Kirby soars, Charlecote modestly stops short with a corniced balustrade, surmounted by two heraldic creatures holding standards (now lost at Kirby).

Like his father before him, Thomas Lucy had his hands full with brothers and sisters for whom estates had to be found. The land he had inherited in other counties was a liability that he was anxious to be rid of; he sold one of his Worcestershire manors, Bishampton, and conveyed away Dagnall and Great Loughton (Margaret Brecknock's dowry) part of the Honour of Peverel in Leicestershire, and Carlton in Bedfordshire which had come to the Lucys from the de Pabenhams. He entrenched himself at Charlecote by the acquisition of nearby Sherbourne, a property of the Knights Hospitallers till the Dissolution, which he exchanged for some more of his Bedfordshire lands; and bought the reversion of the manor of Bishop's Hampton* in the demesne house of which he had spent his early childhood. Much of his other outlying proerty must have gone to procure marriages for his brothers and sisters.

In 1565 he was 'dubbed' in his new Great Hall, with his Northamptonshire neighbour and friend, Edmund Brudenell of Dene, and perhaps others, by the hand of Robert Dudley, deputizing for the Queen. The Lucy servants wore on this occasion the livery of Dudley, in token of the Lucys' long allegiance to the Houses of Warwick and Leicester.

Eight years later the Queen herself visited Charlecote. She

---

* Previously the property of the Bishop of Worcester from whom it had its name.

dined at Itchington on 12 August, and from there went to
Warwick to stay with Ambrose Dudley, Earl of Warwick,
Leicester's brother. After making herself affable to the bur-
gesses and people of Warwick, who were given a splendid if
alarming firework display to mark the visit, she went on to
Kenilworth.★

Her love affair with Leicester was then in its happiest
phase; they had only tenderness for each other's foibles; in
public their mutual glances were gay, ironic, intimate—they
might have been married for years. After a strenuous three
days of entertainment at Kenilworth, where every bush
sprouted a nymph primed with a Latin ode, she returned to
Warwick for the week-end, but the soft persuasions of
Robert Dudley drew her back to Kenilworth, where she
rested till the Saturday after, and 'from thence by Charlecote
to the Lord Compton's and so forward'. In the Declared
Accounts (Treasurer of the Chamber) for March 1571 to
March 1572 it is noted what money was allowed to gentlemen ushers whose unenviable task it was to prepare country
houses for a visit from the Queen, soothe fluttered country
ladies, and drill alarmed servants.

Warwick and Kenilworth are named for that two days'
stay in the lovely August of 1572. Symonds Bower, one of
the ordinary gentlemen ushers of the Queen's Chamber, was
instructed to prepare Charlecote, which the Queen was
curious to see. As she intended to stay, there must be a
worthy bed, carpets on the floor, bedding free from fleas, a
kitchen staff capable of producing meals for a large party.
The account reads: 'and also for making ready Sir Thomas
Lucy's house by the space of two days, *mensis Augusti anno
xiiij Regine predicta* as appeared by the bill, signed [by] the L.
Chamberlain, £x. xvs. viid.'

Was the sum of £10 15s. 7d. for necessary embellishments
to her sleeping apartment, or tips to servants and
gamekeepers?

After Kenilworth the Queen would be in a mellow mood;

★ *The Black Book of Warwick*, transcribed and edited by Thomas Kempe in
1898. Other visits have been mentioned, but on no good authority.

small slips might pass unnoticed. But the Maids of Honour, whose spite could be deadly, would be sated with fireworks and pageantry and would hardly find a country knight's quiet establishment entertaining. The Queen's servants, too, had a way of unsettling country households—it was weeks before the place settled back to normal.

Tradition has it that Elizabeth slept in the Great Bed Chamber, which till 1836 was the name by which the present drawing-room was known. (In an account book of 1664 there are entries of sums paid to Nicholas Paris for locks and hinges for the Queen's Chamber.)

The Queen was so well pleased by her entertainment that she presented Anne Lucy, the daughter of the house, with a curious jewel, a flower of gold, enamelled, with an amethyst lozenge or pendant, and two daisies, in one of them a ruby and in the other a diamond, with a butterfly in between. It had been a New Year gift to Her Majesty from the Lady Cheake.★

Thomas Lucy was now a Justice of the Peace and a Commissioner of Musters. The year before the Queen's visit, 1571, he had been elected to Parliament. The chief concern of this Parliament was to put through anti-Catholic measures. One biographer has said of Thomas Lucy that he put his Puritan principles in his pocket under Mary Tudor, and pretended, under Elizabeth, to favour the Church 'as by law established'. But through the five angry years of Queen Mary's reign, when the glow of the martyr fires staining the sky could be seen all over England and the hot wind fanned the sparks as far even as remote Charlecote, Sir Thomas was occupied with blameless domestic preoccupations.

The only rap Charlecote took was at the beginning of the new reign, when the incumbent was dismissed for refusing, on his Bishop's orders, to take the Oath of Supremacy which made Elizabeth head of the Church, as her father had been. A later vicar, Richard Southam (appointed to the living in the 1580s), admitted at a Bishop's visitation that he had taken no degree at school, 'Neither in Oxford or Cambridge. I

★ Nichols, *Progresses of Queen Elizabeth*, Vol. I.

have no licence to preach, neither am I any preacher.' He is described in the Minutes of the Stratford Corporation as dumb and unlearned. He could make shift, however, to read the new Prayer Book to his scanty congregation. He received wages from his patron of eleven shillings quarterly, and twelve shillings and threepence from the suppressed Priory of Thelesford.

Sir Thomas's scholarly father had eagerly embraced the New Learning because it opened intellectual vistas. Thomas Lucy's Puritanism was chiefly political. It has often been said that his anti-Catholic activities were the fruit of the seed implanted in him by his tutor. He was in fact simply ambitious. He had made a bold bid for prestige in Warwickshire by building a finer house than his ancestors had enjoyed. As a Commissioner of Musters, Deputy Lieutenant, Justice of the Peace, and finally as Sheriff of his county, he established himself as a personage. As an ardent raker-in of recusants he earned the approval of the Privy Council and enjoyed the exhilaration of being feared and placated. One cannot help wondering if this did not come his way very often at home. (Of his son so little is known that it can only be assumed that his Puritanism was of the same political brand as his father's.)

Thomas Lucy's Parliamentary activities are on record; he sat busily on a number of committees to impose penalties for saying and hearing mass, and for the prohibition of the practice by priests of disguising themselves as serving-men by wearing the badges of the noblemen who employed them.

In the Parliament of 1571, in which he sat as Knight of the Shire for Warwickshire, he made no particular mark. To see it through his eyes one must open Simonds D'Ewes' *Journal of Parliament* at the page where he describes the Judges and their learned Council sitting on their woolsacks, and the Knights, Citizens and Burgesses all standing below the Bar, their faces turned expectantly toward the Queen's chair: '. . . Her Majesty then stood up in her Regal Seat, and with a Princely Grace and singular good Countenance, after a long stay, spake a few words to this effect. . . .' (How effective that long pause must have been before the simple words were spoken.) 'My right loving Lords, and you, our own right faithful and obedient subjects, we, in the name of God, for His service and the safety of the State, are here now assembled to His glory; I hope and pray that it may be to your comfort, and the common quiet of ours, yours, and all ours forever.'

The *Journal* has the same soporific effect on the mind as *Hansard*; the speeches on perjury, on privilege, on con- science, go on and on through the quiet afternoon sittings. Private Members' Bills come up to the surface and subside, either to sink without a ripple, or to be dragged up again, debated, referred to committees, amended, and in most cases shelved. Such a Bill was one proffered by Sir Thomas in the Parliament of 1584 'on the better preservation of Grain and Game'. It came under those described by Simonds D'Ewes as 'bills of no great moment'. On its second reading it was committed to the charge of Sir Edward Hoby, Sir John Tracy, and others, who were already sitting on a Bill for the increase of Pheasants and Partridges brought in by Sir Henry Cocks. The preservation of Grain and Game seems to have petered out; the Pheasants and Partridges, however, were brought to the vote and passed. One can almost hear the scratching of the clerk's pen and the drone of a single voice through the drowsy summer afternoon session.

By 1581 Thomas Lucy was thought useful enough to be appointed to a commission with 'truly inquisitorial powers'.* Country gentlemen who had grown rich through judicious marriages or by the acquisition of monastic lands were not allowed to stagnate; those of ability were picked out by the Privy Council for administrative work in which their special knowledge of the locality and of the private affairs of their neighbours would come in useful.

There is a sinister memorandum to the State Papers of October 1583 after the inquisition of a lunatic Catholic gentleman of Warwickshire, John Somerville of Edstone,

---

* The commission was composed of forty-four, twelve of whom were in Holy Orders. It was later pronounced unconstitutional by Sir Edward Coke.

who in his uneasy dreams had been overheard calling the
Queen a viper and saying he wished he could shoot her.
Under torture he implicated others. The memorandum
recommends that Edward Arden of Park Hall, Somerville's
father-in-law, and his family, shall be sent for trial and their
houses searched.

An agent and clerk of the Privy Council, Thomas Wilkes,
was despatched to Warwickshire with clear instructions for
Sir Thomas Lucy. Wilkes stayed for a fortnight at Charlecote. On 3 November a party set out on the long ride for
Park Hall, twenty miles the other side of Warwick, and
ransacked it from garret to cellar.

By the 7th the Ardens were in the Tower, with their
daughter, Somerville's wife, and their massing priest, Hugh
Hall. At the same time as the trial in London—that is, early
in December—a jury sat on the Somerville-Arden case in
Warwick, one of the members of which was Sir Thomas's
brother, Timothy Lucy, a BA of Oxford.

While Wilkes was at Charlecote, late and secret discussions
took place with other Puritan justices, Fulke Greville,★ the
Recorder of Warwick, Edward Aglionby, Robert Burgoyne
of Wroxhall, and Rafe Griffin, Master of the Leicester
Hospital, as to how far the net should be thrown that should
draw in a batch of recusants. Much nearer to Charlecote than
Park Hall was Northbroke, only four miles away on the
other side of Fulbroke, whose Catholic owner, Edward
Grant, had married a Somerville; and Idlicote, eight miles to
the south-east, home of the Catholic Underhills, where
lodged the priest Hall.

In these raids the Justices ransacked the places without
finding much in the way of mass books or vestments. Wilkes
admitted as much in a long private letter to Walsingham
written from Charlecote '. . . unless you can charge them
with matter from the mouths of your prisoners [Arden and

★ Father of Sir Philip Sydney's 'loving and beloved Achates', afterwards Lord
Brooke. He inherited Beauchamp's Court, near Alcester (his mother's property), in 1559. He sat on almost every commission with Thomas Lucy, whom
he outlived by six years.

Somerville], look not to wring anything from them, by finding matter of suspicion in their houses'.

According to Dugdale, Arden had already damned himself by disdaining to wear Leicester's livery. He had no feudal sentiment, as Thomas Lucy had. Leicester meant to have his life, not for his own Catholic sympathies, but for the hauteur with which he looked down on two generations of ennobled Dudleys, both tainted with the block. Arden was executed at Smithfield; Somerville was found strangled in his cell; the priest Hall died in prison. Wilkes was allowed to return to London, and Charlecote returned to its everyday routine.

Arden of Park Hall was an ancient name, though not more ancient than Lucy of Charlecote; yet a smear of the *parvenu* sticks to Thomas Lucy, while Edward Arden, poor, proud, defenceless, goes to the scaffold like a gentleman.

The Privy Council rewarded discretion; Sir Thomas, being already a Justice, got only the four shillings a day allowed for attendance at the Quarter Sessions, but his servants, Thomas Paynter and William Mann, were well paid. William Mann appears in the Charlecote Account Book as a liveried servant and received from the Council thirteen pounds, six shillings and eightpence for himself and two others, for bringing the prisoner with four horses from Park Hall (presumably only as far as Warwick or Stratford where they changed escorts for the long ride to London).

The Arden affair made Thomas Lucy feared; he was already respected. The Catholic strongholds in the neighbourhood, Eddeston, Lapworth, Idlicote, Coughton, Clopton, Northbroke, held haughtily aloof from county politics.* Their women prayed in secret, kept Catholic priests disguised as serving-men, or hid them in a cupboard or among the trunks in the lumber-room. The master of the house paid

---

* Though Warwickshire was predominantly Puritan, there were a number of these families: Olneys of Tachebroke, Skinners at Rowington, Smiths of Wootton Warren, Greswolds of Solihull, Middlemores of Edgbaston, Knotfords of Studley. George Catesby of Lapworth was sent to the Fleet for harbouring Campion's Jesuit missioners in his house in 1581, though the year before he had been on a Commission for Musters with Thomas Lucy and other Protestants.

the heavy fine exacted for recusancy and went alone to the
village church to hear the new form of service read, fingering
the sacred image on his heart. If he passed Thomas Lucy or
Fulke Greville riding into Stratford to a meeting of the Town
Council, and had caps doffed to him by their servants, he
did not speak or smile.

The See of Worcester till 1583 was held by the zealous
John Whitgift, who in 1579 wrote to Burleigh saying: 'Two
kinds of men delight to molest and trouble; the contentious
Protestant and the obstinate Papist.'

'Massing priests' often posed successfully as vagrants and
begged their way from village to village and from one house
of known Catholic sympathies to another. The Commissioners complained to the Privy Council that the priests
were hard to catch; that they performed marriages and
christenings, were heard of lurking in this place and that,
making converts, but were not to be found. But not many
slipped through the meshes of the Commissioners' net.

In the Domestic State Papers for 1584 Thomas Lucy is
officially thanked for sending up to justice the Habington
brothers, recusants from Hindlip in Worcestershire, one of
whom he found starving in a hay-stack. He petitioned
Parliament for the execution of a Welsh lawyer, Dr Parry,
who had had the courage to protest against the Bill that
penalized Jesuits, seminary priests, 'and such like disobedient
persons', and set a premium on betrayal, as being full of
blood, danger, despair, terror, and a threat to the English
way of life. Parry was executed after torture.

The same Parliament passed a Private Bill for the assurance
of certain lands (not defined), to Sir Thomas Lucy and
others, which coincided with the Bill dispossessing Catholic
landlords living in exile of their lands (Englefield and Clopton were the two contingent on Charlecote). Fulbroke then
became, if not actually his by purchase, his in all but title.

By now Sir Thomas Lucy presented to the outside world
a formidable front; men hurried to placate him, on his
progress up the crowded High Street of Stratford on his way
to a Guildhall dinner. Charlecote, for so long so obscure,
was for the first (and last) time in its history in constant

touch with Westminster. The agents of the dreaded Privy Council—that inhuman body from whose decisions there was no appeal, which crushed the marrow out of men's bones under torture, stayed at Charlecote to confer with its owner.

In the Armada year of 1588 we find Sir Thomas, as one of the Deputy Lieutenants of Warwickshire, writing to the Earl of Warwick to complain of the difficulty of equipping a hundred horsemen to be sent to Tilbury against a Spanish landing. The letter is signed also by Fulke Greville and Sir John Harrington of Combe, and points out that the Earl must take what they can muster in the way of horses and armed men, it being so late in the season. This, with the extreme want of money, 'since nothing can be uttered [published] that will bring it in, hath in part been cause that this service is not so well perfected as we desire. . . .'

Either 1585 or 1587 was The Year, the Annus Mirabilis in which young William Shakespeare left Stratford—left, not fled—to join a cry of players on its way to London.

In Sir Thomas Lucy's Account Book,* written in his own hand, there is an earlier entry of wages paid to Robert Mathews, 'one of my keepers', and to another keeper, Humfry Ashorn (a native of Ashorne, a mile away across the fields from Charlecote, but apparently a keeper at Sutton; perhaps they were sent to Sutton for part of the year to gain experience with deer, and then changed over). Two years later 'Antony my keeper' and 'Humfry my keeper' are getting twelve shillings and threepence a quarter. George Cox, 'keeper of my coney warren', seems to have been dropped by 1585, though George Scales, the falconer, goes on drawing his wages.

The word must have gone round the alehouses of Stratford that the property of the absentee Sir Francis Englefield had been appropriated by Lucy; it was covertly said that Sir Thomas dared not empark his own warren because it would involve demolishing cottages and denying grazing rights to

---

* A stout notebook sewn into white vellum covers; still at Charlecote.

the villagers, but had seized Fulbroke and put palings round it so that Stratford lads might no longer enjoy it. Fulbroke had always been enclosed, more or less; probably Sir Thomas did no more than put the fence in repair. The rest is silence, and pure conjecture. Whether the deer was taken from Fulbroke covers or Charlecote warren is unimportant; what matters is that for once it was not 'borne cleanly past the keeper's nose'.

Malone, in defence of the legend (by his day the story had taken roots too firm to dislodge), quotes, not accurately, from an Act repealed in the first year of Edward VI, by which any person 'with his face hid with hood or visor, or with a painted face . . .' who should attempt to steal deer or rabbits in a park or warren by day or night stood in danger of death. This was amended in the fifth year of Elizabeth to damages, three months' imprisonment, and a seven-year guarantee of good behaviour. Anyone caught with a dead deer within a paling or fence must appear before the local Justice.

The Merry Wives, in which Sir Thomas was supposed to have been revengefully caricatured, was not written for another twelve or fourteen years. The piece was put together in a hurry and was a knock-about romp. Almost every character in it is a figure of farce, but none surely the object of long-hoarded spite?

I think it most likely that when he began hurriedly to cast together *The Merry Wives of Windsor*, having been given fourteen days in which to have it ready for production, his thoughts turned back to where they were most at home: the little town of Windsor, with snow-piled roofs and miry roads, had a family resemblance to the Stratford of his boyhood. The flooded fields round Windsor, where Dr Caius was to attempt to fight a duel with the Welsh parson, were the meadows of Alveston, candied with ice where in winter Stratford boys were fond of sliding. Falstaff sends Master Page a piece of venison, but it is 'ill killed' (wounded and pulled down by dogs). A doe with a black scut, not thought of since boyhood, serves its turn; and a bribe-buck, or present of venison presented by someone to the Corporation in his father's time.

The Queen's taste was not at all subtle or finicking, and the humour of the Gloucestershire Justice and his friends had to be broadened. The grey stone Gloucestershire manor house in which Robert Shallow, Esq., dwelt reminiscently on wild nights in Clement's Inn, while peaceably grafting pippins in his orchard, belonged to another dream; his eager questioning about ewes and bullocks at Stamford Fair, and the greyhound coursing on Cotsall, was the Warwickshire market-day talk of Shakespeare's boyhood, lifted straight from memory. In order to raise a laugh from the Court, there must be jokes whose point no one could miss about gentility, high venison, bear-baiting, old cheese, cuckoldry, and dirty linen. And every comedy must have a play on words (*luce* and *louse* was a tried standby).

Thomas Lucy had his Achilles' heel; he worshipped his ancient descent, and had filled the panes of the oriel window in his Great Hall with the arms of his ancestors. There was then at Charlecote (Dugdale saw it) a parchment Roll of Arms, comparable to the Rous Roll of the Earls of Warwick, taking the Lucy pedigree back to the Conquest. It may be that Thomas Lucy was smiled at behind his back in Stratford for his family piety, though why he should have been it is hard to say, since every other landed family in England shared the sentiment, which was considered highly praiseworthy. Perhaps he was over-anxious to assert the superiority of Charlecote over his wife's property of Sutton in Worcestershire, and received edged looks from her in public. His domestic life was known to be not harmonious. So, perhaps, without conscious intention of dredging in the past, the poet put out his hand and pulled out an old memory, gilded it with an ancient pun, and made immortal Robert Shallow, 'in the county of Gloster justice of the peace and coram . . .', a gentleman born, one who wrote himself *armiger*, as his forebears had done for 300 years before him.

Slender: All his successors gone before him hath done't; and all his
      ancestors that come after him may: they may give the dozen
      white luces in their coat.

Shallow: It is an old coat.
Sir Hugh: The dozen white louses do become an old coat well . . .'

We can make what we will of it. It is doubtful that many people in the audience caught the slight allusion, unless they were Warwickshire born. In a certain highly private circle in London, Thomas Lucy's name had once been well known, but by 1599, when *The Merry Wives* was produced before the Queen and Court, he was beginning to be infirm, and had in fact taken very little part in public life since his wife's death four years earlier.

There are many evidences that Sir Thomas was a kindly, and, at home, a diffident man. The few letters from his hand are just; one to the Registrar of the Diocese of Worcester, 1583, certifies that Joan Hitchcock, living in Charlecote, is of honest and good conversation and fit to be the wife of that weak prop of the Protestant faith, Richard Southam. Another to Robert Dudley recommends an old servant, Burnell, once a notable archer, but fallen into a long sickness, whereby his shooting is much hindered. His lordship must take care to see that he is not placed too far back or his arrow will fall short, for his strength is greatly decayed.

He appears in an amiable light settling a lawsuit between Hamnet Sadler, an Alderman of Stratford, and Ananias Nason (baptized in Charlecote church in 1552 and probably the son of a Charlecote servant, Thomas Nason, who first appears in the Account Book as a retainer in 1573, but who had been in Lucy service long before that). On this occasion, January 1583, the Corporation of Stratford broached a bottle of wine. Eight years earlier Sir Thomas had attended the wedding of the daughter of the Stratford Bailiff, Richard Hill, to Abraham Sturley, a Cambridge scholar who is mentioned as being a retainer at Charlecote in March 1573. He is spoken of as a good Latinist and a devout Puritan, and is found again in the service of Sir Thomas in 1580, not this time as a retainer, but, one cannot help thinking, as an informer about suspected Catholics in Stratford.

A man called Clark, who held the living of Woodstone in

the Diocese of Lichfield and Coventry, humbly prayed God to forgive the Queen her sins. His Bishop tried to have him on a charge of sedition, but Clark was known for his good and devout life, and the matter coming up before the Bench, who occasionally dealt with cases of sedition, Sir Thomas stood up for him and roundly said that before Master Clark should have any wrong he would kneel to the Queen for him. (Clark was acquitted.)

Charlecote was a roomy house. The hearth-tax returns for Warwickshire do not begin before 1663, and the number of hearths in Charlecote House was then forty-two—this was after Thomas Lucy's grandson had made some improvements to the house so that it had the greatest number of hearths of any house in the country, after Warwick Castle and Stoneleigh.

If it was smaller in the Elizabethan Sir Thomas's day, it was still big enough to accommodate two families. In the Charlecote Register is the notice of a marriage between Thomas Lucy, Esq., and Dorothea Arnold, described as 'sonne' of Sir Nicholas Arnold,* Knight, 27 January 1574 (the omission being the words 'daughter of' the son, etc.). She was in fact the only daughter of Roland, Sir Nicholas's son, who died before his father. This young couple were living at Charlecote in the seventies and early eighties, in the same way as Thomas and Joyce Lucy had spent their early married life at Sutton.

Anne Lucy, Sir Thomas's sole daughter, was married at Charlecote in the April of 1580 to Edward Aston of Tixhall, Staffs.† They owned Blythe Hall in Warwickshire and later sold it to Sir William Dugdale. Thomas Lucy, being of the Peace, was obliged to entertain his fellow Justices a good deal and would be glad occasionally to be able to bid someone of Sir Edward Aston's aristocratic birth to dine. 'It was the custom of the cultured and civilized Lucys to sneer

---

* Harrison complained (he was always harking back to the good old days) of the importing of foreign blood-stock, saying 'Sir Nicholas Arnold of late hath bred the best horses in England'.
† 'Trent by Tixhall grac't, the Astons' ancient seat', as Drayton calls it.

at the old-fashioned Shallows, who, for want of better company, filled their halls with yeoman neighbours.'* Perhaps. At all events Edward Aston, a disconsolate widower at twenty-nine (his first wife had been a Spencer of Althorp), was welcomed at Charlecote and agreed to take Sir Thomas's daughter, with a fair jointure, as his second wife.

The marriage was most unhappy. An undated letter among the Bagot papers,† from Edward Aston to his cousin and neighbour Richard Bagot, gives such a lively picture of the family circle at Charlecote, that those who discredit 'the bitter ballad', with its lines, '*At home a poore scarecrow, at London an asse*', on the grounds that these could not conceivably be applicable to a member of the Privy Council's Commission on Recusancy, have preferred to ignore it.

Edward Aston did not come in to Tixhall till 1589, and while his father, Sir Walter Aston, lived, spent much of his early married life at Charlecote. At the long table in the Great Hall there assembled daily Sir Thomas and his wife Joyce, young Thomas and his wife Dorothy, and, after 1580, Anne and her husband. Dorothy Lucy became the heiress of Highnam in Gloucestershire.and died soon afterwards, perhaps by 1582. But there must have been a time when they were all together at Charlecote, waited on by those servants in livery whose wages are recorded in the Account Book, in a seething ferment of tight-lipped disapproval and covert revolt.

To his cousin Bagot‡ the son-in-law unburdened himself forcefully; but it is clear that he did not dare to be so forceful to his wife. 'My discontentments', he says (the spelling as well as the punctuation I have modernized), 'are infinite, and such as if you knew them, I know you could not but pity

---

* D. H. Madden: *The Diary of Master William Silence*.
† Now in the Folger Shakespeare Library in Washington, with whose kind permission I quote from it.
‡ Richard Bagot of Blythefield and Sir Walter Aston of Tixhall were the two most strenuous Protestants in Staffordshire. Both were concerned in the humiliation and ruin of Mary Queen of Scots, and they hunted Papist sympathizers with zeal and success.

me, proceeding from the mother and daughter; the which I
have drunk up with silence and endured with great patience.'
He has, he says, mentioned only a few of his wrongs,
'having forgotten infinite'.

The Lucys had thought Edward Aston a handsome match
for their daughter, and Joyce Lucy had persuaded her husband to bait the marriage with land which she afterwards
accused her son-in-law of having 'fraudulently and cozen-
ingly' wheedled out of his future father-in-law. 'I need not
wonder that my lady Lucy doth malise me, for that it is and
always has been her custom to malise her husband's kindred,
her son's wives,* and her daughter's husband, and that in
so high a degree that the devil himself could not devise
matter of more high despite than she will.'

(Yet Sir Thomas, in his carefully worded epitaph on his
wife's tomb, used such words to describe her as 'constant',
'rare' and 'singular', and says that she was 'misliked by none
unless of the envious'.)

It was the injustice of his mother-in-law's dislike of him
that hurt Sir Edward Aston: 'Whilst I did lie at Charlecot no
man living would have endured with patience the hard usage
I had there, and yet she hath often said that she never saw
gentleman in her life that would give less cause [of] offence
than I. . . .' He could not go hawking with the Charlecote
falconer, George Scales, for the outdoor servants were
forbidden to obey him. Joyce Lucy had the cool upper
chamber that formed the end of the north wing, and from
this point of vantage could see what went on in the court
and the yard beyond at the back of the servants' quarters.

He could not escape her even at Tixhall. 'She came to
Tixhall in my father's time only to complain to me that I
would not suffer my wife to go to London, and yet I had
gone up twice with her, having no business in the world
[and] having spent 200£. at a time, and yet was driven to let
her go again, where her journey cost me 220£ for no cause
but to give the Queen a hat.'

* Gentle Dorothea Arnold was dead by the time this letter was written and
son Thomas had re-married. The letter, undated, is written from Tixhall, to
which Sir Edward must have succeeded.

The stuff of legend and a popular subject for Victorian engravers: the young Shakespeare, accused of poaching deer, is brought before Justice Thomas Lucy in the Great Hall at Charlecote.

Bust of the first Sir Thomas Lucy. Shakespeare caricatured him in *The Merry Wives of Windsor* as Justice Shallow.

The Great Hall as it is today. Over the fireplace is Cornelius Jansen's portrait of the third Sir Thomas, his wife Alice Spencer and seven of their 13 children.

The Lucy coat of arms, featuring three 'luces hauriant' or pike coming up for air, confirmed to the third Sir Thomas in 1619.

Richard Lucy, puritan and member of Oliver Cromwell's 1653 Parliament. He collected most of the rare books now in the Library at Charlecote.

The west prospect of Charlecote, painted c. 1695, showing the elaborate Dutch-style water gardens installed by Captain Lucy. The village houses in the distance are almost identical in appearance today.

Captain Thomas Lucy, painted by Kneller c. 1670.

These portraits show (*top*) Colonel George Lucy, (*left*) his first wife
Mary Bohun, and (*right*) Jane Bohun. Jane was Mary's cousin and
George's second wife; they married in 1708. She was 25 years his
junior.

George Lucy had this fine portrait painted by Pompeo Battoni in Rome in 1758 while on the Grand Tour.

Charlecote prior to its nineteenth-century restoration.

These busts by Behnes, c. 1830, are of George Hammond Lucy and
his wife Mary Elizabeth, who married in 1823. In later life she wrote
her memoirs, which were published as *Mistress of Charlecote* in 1983.

Alice Fairfax–Lucy, pictured in the grounds of Charlecote by John
Morley in 1972.

Sir Edward was a mild man and a stay-at-home. All this extravagant going to London upset the routine of country-house life and made the servants discontented. Anne's temper was frayed by miscarriages; there were factions in the household that led to whispering behind doors and black looks and sulks at meals. When Lady Lucy arrived to stay with Tomson, her coachman, and Mrs Jennings, her waiting gentlewoman, trouble came in at the front door of Tixhall.

Anne flew to her with complaints of her husband's penni-less cousin, Jane Aston, whom Sir Edward refused to turn out of his house, and who conducted a brisk feud with Lane, the body-woman. But it was worse when Anne went home: 'Truly my lady Lucy herself is the cause of my wife's discontentment, for she never goeth either to Sutton or Charlecote, but she is the worse one quarter of a year after, for there is no talk but that I must go lie at London and brave it out; it is base lying in the country, I must sell land and spend it lustily there, which will win that credit which is better than land. I must labour either the [Earl] of Rutland or Bedford for her daughter, all which humour I may not contrary, but dissemble a show of liking as I may.'

One can see that Sir Thomas was not guiltless of urging his son-in-law to make the sort of show at Court that he himself was perhaps too mean or too timid to venture, and that Joyce Lucy would have been proud to see her daughter attending on a Countess. Anne was not robust enough to stand up to her parents, and her husband was helpless between the lot of them, for in his own household his wife insisted on keeping five servants, against his expressed wishes, to one of his own choosing. 'I hold one, mine own cousin-germane; she [my wife] holdeth a priest's wife, a frenchman and a sea-captain's widdow and others against my liking.' One, he darkly hints, 'desireth to close up mine eyes'. The letter, as his feelings gain in momentum, runs out in incoherent lament: '. . . truly, cousin, there is no indiffer-ence that I should make myself so very a child, a fool, a poopee [doll], and a subject to my lady Lucy's malice. There is no cross like to have an enemy in a man's own house, in his own chamber, in his own bed, and therefore better for a

man to remove his grief at once than to live in continual
torment.'

The postscript of the letter holds a whole history of
domestic discontent: '*I pray you let me know what Sir Thomas
whispered in your ear when he parted from you.*'

The counter-charge to this is now in the Lucy archives.
Sir Thomas is writing from Sutton to Richard Bagot on 10
July 1591. The letter, modernized, goes:

Good Master Bagot, I have occasion to send to see how my
daughter doth, thought good to write and signify unto you that
my son Aston and I departed nothing in friendly manner; I
requesting him, in all good sort to remove that wicked woman out
of his house that hath bred all the unkindness betwixt him and his
wife.

This was the poor relation, 'mine own cousin germane',
whom Sir Edward refused to turn out of his house, having
promised her father to support her. Frustration was making
Anne ill (she died five years later). Her husband's refusal to
make the change in his household that would restore peace
strikes Sir Thomas as suspicious. 'I can not conceive or think
that he hath any other intent or meaning than to hasten the
death of his wife, the which, it appeareth he so much
thirsteth after.' Would his friend Bagot act as intermediary?
'One other notion now on the sudden came into my mind,
knowing him to be weary of his wife, and that he would
separate from her, as by the drift of his dealing doth too
manifestly appear; let him give her a portion to maintain her
and her children . . . and a convenient house to dwell in.'

Sir Edward solved his difficulties by giving in. To London
he and Anne removed with their surviving children, and the
shutters were put up at Tixhall. The marriage was patched,
Anne was satisfied, and his mother-in-law in Warwickshire
ceased to be a menace to his peace. Having stirred up enough
trouble at Tixhall to provide talk for the servants' hall for
months, Joyce Lucy returned to Charlecote, to make sure
that her household and her husband had not idled in her
absence.

The Account Book shows that the households of Charlecote and Sutton averaged about forty-two servants between

them; in the first half of the book the office as well as the name of the recipient is given, the second half, which is in Sir Thomas's own hand, being less detailed. It is noticeable that there are never more than two gardeners mentioned, that no dairy work appears, though outdoor workers, such as a shepherd and a pigherd, do. The bailiff probably had his own wage list and paid the husbandmen himself.

The servants, according to the compiler of the first half, were paid in the following order: 'My Lady's woman, Mrs Anne Brudenell [a poor relation of the Northamptonshire Brudenells], Mr Thomas Lucy's attendant for the languages, the Vicar, the Clerk of the Kitchen, the yeoman of the chamber and wardrobe, the yeoman of the house, who was also usher of the hall, the butler, Mr Thomas Lucy's man, Mrs Anne Lucy's man, bailiffs at Charlecote and Sutton, the keepers before mentioned, two cooks, a stableman, a keeper of the horse, a falconer, millers both at Charlecote and Sutton, a baker and brewer [and an under-brewer of the kitchen], a carter, a gardener, and some maids.'

The keeper of 'Mr Lucy his great horse' was called just John Welshman, and Welsh names recur.* John Challoner, who attended young Thomas Lucy for the languages, did not stay long, nor did Lady Lucy's personal attendants till Joan Jennings became waiting gentlewoman in 1578. When Sir Thomas took over the accounts in 1587, he moved the Vicar up into first place; before that his quarterly wage had come second to the thirteen shillings paid to my lady's gentlewoman. The list was augmented as the years went on by 'an attendant on your mastership in your Chamber', a yeoman of the pantry, a second and third falconer (young Thomas had evidently given up the study of the humanities in favour of hawking), an extra keeper of the park at Sutton, a fisherman, and a market man. Keeping all these servants busy must have been hard work for the lady of the house, rustling round in her stiff petticoats, heels tapping, keys

---

* An ancient drift road starts just north of Charlecote village and continues over the fields by Newbold Pacey in the direction of Southam. This was the route along which Welsh cattle were driven to the London markets. Many Welsh cattle-drovers returned and settled in the neighbourhood.

jangling, pouncing on flirtatious maids, running a finger
along grooves in the wainscoting for dust: a tireless woman,
one, according to her epitaph, '*so furnished and garnished with
virtue as not to be bettered and hardly to be equalled by any*',
stiffened by a narrow faith and a sense of privilege, strong in
Elizabethan ladies, which she would not have bartered for
any so-called rights.

Firm and arbitrary was her rule over her maids. Only the
waiting gentlewoman, generally of as good birth as her
mistress though poor, had licence to be free of speech. The
housekeeper kept to her own quarters, the maids, who were
roused by their mistress at five-thirty, were never seen about
on the stairs or in the passages. At night such menservants as
slept in the house retired to the attics above the wing where
the master slept and the maidservants to those above the
housekeeper's quarters in the other. Both were locked in,
and the mistress kept the keys; this custom was still in use at
the end of the nineteenth century. The outdoor menservants
had pallets above the stables or in the long room over the
brewhouse. A vast amount of beer was drunk by the
household. There was a brewer, an under-brewer, and a
malt-maker, Agnes Eaton, who walked up from Hunscot
daily (most of the maids were daily workers from the
village).

Joyce Lucy had her hop-yard on the other side of the
Wellesbourne brook. (Sir Edward Aston, after complaining
about his wife's debts to tailors, periwig-makers, and such-
like, says he allowed her ten acres to make a hop-yard, like
the one at Charlecote, which clearly she had been importun-
ing for.) Hospitality must be maintained; beer was not drunk
at the Justice's table, but each servant had his due of it and
visiting servants theirs.

There was a huge bread oven and a miller to grind flour
for it, two men cooks, one to make pastries and cakes only,
and a slaughterman for the kitchen. Owing to the curious
knack the Victorians had for reducing space while adding to
bulk, it is difficult to see how this great kitchen can have
looked, for a complication of pantries and passages now
covers the site.

It was the master of the house's business to control the outside menservants, to inspect daily the stew-ponds, the duck decoys, the eel traps and the mews where the hawks sat hooded on their perches. But Joyce Lucy during her husband's absences in London must have had to take over all this, with the result that there are changes among the outdoor men during the sessions of Parliament. There is no record that she brewed medicines for the household from herbal receipts handed down to her, but it would have been expected of her, and seems so much in character that one can almost taste the bitter black draughts she made them swallow.

Perhaps, like Sir John Harington, she kept her household in order by fines; twopence for not attending prayers, a penny for a bed unmade, a penny for swearing, and sixpence for a tardy meal. The humbler maidservants, whose chapped hands were not allowed to touch the silk- and tinsel-embroidered covers of the Great Bed, carded thread (which could make their hands no rougher), scoured pots, washed out floor-cloths and cheese-clouts in cold water, and endlessly carried in wood to feed the ovens. Busily the ladies of the house pattered about, bottling and picking and sealing the bottles with hot candle-grease, making sweets of boiled sugar flavoured with aniseed and coriander (good for coughs), and distilling roses and eglantine for scented face-washes. A good life, never dull, and sustained with a sense of moral rectitude which made the preserving, pickling, and distilling into acts of piety.

Joyce Lucy died on 10 February 1595, and was given a great funeral. According to a document once in the Lucy archives but no longer extant, she was not buried till the tenth day of March following, the chief mourners being her grand-daughter, Joyce Lucy, Fulke Greville's wife, and Jane Verney (her sister-in-law). The Astons were not present.* The tomb, intended to carry two life-sized effigies of painted stone, was executed by Gerard Johnson† (it suffered some

* Anne Aston died the following year.
† Who sculpted the memorial to William Shakespeare in Stratford Church.

damage at the demolition of the old church in 1854, and the effigy of Joyce Lucy now rests on a modern plinth). Below the recumbent pair are the two kneeling figures of Thomas the Second in armour and his sister Joyce, and, above, on a black marble tablet in letters of gold, the eulogy by Sir Thomas of his wife, 'signed like an affidavit'. '*Never detected of any crime or vice . . . to what was in trust committed to her most secret. . . .*' She might rail and scold in the family circle, but when agents of the Privy Council came to Charlecote and were closeted with Sir Thomas, she tightened her lips, locked the doors, drove off the servants and possessed herself in rigid patience, for hours dragging the needle through the canvas on her embroidery frame. Sir Thomas did not stint his tribute to her discretion: '*Set down by him that best did know what hath been written to be true.*'

The portrait effigy of the first Sir Thomas is unrevealing. The firmness of the square jaw is contradicted by the weakness of the mouth. A small spade beard gives him an Elizabethan look; otherwise it is not an impressive head. He outlived Joyce by five years, dying in the summer of 1600, and the great Camden, then Clarenceux King at Arms, conducted his funeral. He had been the friend at Oxford of Sir Thomas's young brother, Edward. The funeral certificate says that the preacher on this occasion was Mr Hill, the parson of Hampton. The standard, 'the old coat' with the three white luces enlaced, was borne by a Mr Edward Newport, gent., the pennon by Mr William Walter; the Windsor Herald, Thomas Lant, deputizing for the Chester Herald, carried the helmet which is to this day in Charlecote Great Hall. The Lancaster Herald carried the sword and shield.

The chief mourner was the eldest child and only son, and behind him walked his cousins Richard Fiennes and Jerome Fermor and his uncle, Timothy Lucy.* It was a seemly and fitting closure for the old knight, whose greatest pleasure in life, since he had begun to grow infirm, had been to spread out and pore over the armorial roll of the Lucys.

*

* MP for Warwick in 1571 and 1584. Buried at Bitterly, Salop.

He and Joyce had scarcely thought themselves blessed with but one son and one daughter, but these two had striven to make amends with numerous grandchildren. If the name of Lucy had spelled trouble at Tixhall in Joyce Lucy's lifetime, the name of Aston set Charlecote humming like an over-turned hive a few months before Sir Thomas's death in the July of 1600. The old man was not to be allowed peace of mind at the end of his life; his heraldic preoccupations were rudely broken into by the news of a grand-daughter's headstrong intention to marry one of his servants (described in the complaint he was forced to lodge with the Star Chamber as 'a mean mercenary serving-man without other means to live').

Sir Edward Coke, the Attorney-General, who had the wardship of Walter Aston, the girl's elder brother, framed the complaint in strong terms. The Knight of Charlecote had been duped by a trusted member of his household—Stratford and the neighbourhood buzzed with the scandal of it.

Anne Aston being dead, her harassed widower had con-fided his children to the care of his brother-in-law, Thomas Lucy the younger, who was himself the father of a rapidly expanding family and now living in London. At Charlecote there was a great empty house and only one old man to fill it; it was thought expedient to commit the five younger Aston children to their grandfather's care (four of them, Walter,* Edward, Joyce, and Elizabeth, had been born there, as the Charlecote Parish Registers show).

The grandfather engaged a tutor called Bartholomew Griffin, thought in the light of recent research to have been the son of that Ralph Griffin who was Master of the Leicester Hospital in Warwick, and as a fellow Justice had been associated with Sir Thomas Lucy's anti-Catholic activities. The young man had just been ordained. The Aston children, Edward, Joyce, and Elizabeth, were to do lessons with him up in the gallery above the Great Hall, on one side of which slept the menservants and on the other the maids. It was lit by windows set in deep bays and had views of the court on

---

* Afterwards created Lord Aston of Forfar, the patron of Michael Drayton.

one hand and of the river on the other. In wet weather
rowdy games could be enjoyed up there without disturbing
the master of Charlecote in his bedroom below in the south
wing. It was altogether too private, and became the scene of
a clandestine courtship between Elizabeth Aston and a man-
servant called Sambach, with the active connivance of the
tutor, Griffin.

The affair as set down in the bill of complaint emerges as
a sordid conspiracy between a mean serving-man and a
newly-ordained priest to force a young girl's consent and
divide her dowry. But in fact Sambach, being kin to the
Sheldons at Beoley and Broadway, was of quite respectable
ancient family, and the girl, like Bianca, was delighted to
find amorous messages between the pages of her Latin
grammar. After a tempestuous night when Sambach's
friends, all more or less drunk, tried to storm the gatehouse,
Sir Thomas took action; but to no avail. Elizabeth went very
much of her own accord to her humble lover from her
brother-in-law's house at Chipping Norton, to which her
alarmed grandfather had sent her in disgrace.

Old Sir Thomas did not know how to deal with the
headstrong girl, who refused all the respectable suitors
suggested for her (who was her own mother all over again,
though no doubt he blamed the Aston, not the Lucy, strain
for her waywardness). He died suddenly at the outset of the
affair, perhaps of an apoplexy, the concerns of the outside
world grown meaningless and faint as voices outside a closed
window, till they fell silent altogether one July morning with
the last stroke of noon from the gatehouse clock.

A fortnight after her grandfather's death, Elizabeth Aston
and John Sambach were wedded without asking of banns
(but they never got her dowry), and the priest Bartholomew
Griffin discreetly absented himself from Warwickshire.

During the last years of the old century the locally slightly
discredited name of Shakespeare had become respectable,
even illustrious, in the eyes of Stratford. The playwright,
now a shareholder in the successful theatrical venture of the
Globe on Bankside, had bought New Place from the Underhills in the pleasant leafy suburb of Old Town. Through

Camden's intervention he received a grant from the College of Arms of a coat of arms, bearing on a bend sable 'a spear of the first, the point stiled proper' (very easy to mistake for a pen, which would have been much more appropriate). Wisely, the family of Shakespeare decided not to impale their arms with those of Arden of Park Hall.

Plays were falling from that pen in the years 1599 to 1603. *Troilus and Cressida* was cast together a year after the Aston-Sambach lawsuit had been finally dropped. The scandal soon ceased to be matter for Stratford ale-house talk; if it came up it was only to cause a reminiscent smile for the formidable old knight of Charlecote who had sent Edward Arden to his death and yet had been unable in his dotage to control his own grand-daughter. The imagination to which all human foibles were grist, laid the amorous girl and the pander Griffin away on a shelf in its vast shadowy storehouse, until time should ripen them and give the world a Cressida and a Pandarus.

CHAPTER 4

The Third Sir Thomas

. . . the things that do attain
The happy life be these, I find;
The riches left, not got with pain,
The fruitful ground, the quiet minde;
The equal friend, no grudge, no strife,
Nor change of rule or governance,
Without disease the healthful life,
The household of continuance. . . .
                    Henry Howard, Earl of Surrey.

In the year of the defeat of the Armada the Avon flooded its
banks at seven o'clock in the morning. No one could
remember a worse flood—even 'old father Porter of the mill
. . . being then a hundred and nine years of age', never knew
it so high in his long lifetime. A miller's wife was so amazed
to see the water rising all about her 'that she sat till she was
almost drowned'. Past Charlecote the yellow tide swept
down, carrying pots and pans, broken chairs, cheeses, legs
of mutton. Below Stratford it even collected a woman who
was making a haycock, and who on seeing the flood coming
'had no shift but to get upon the top of the haycock and was
carried there upon the water a quarter of a mile well nigh'.
The flood took ten carts out of one village, smashing and
splintering the shafts and axles, and three heavy wains 'with
the furniture of Sir Thomas Lucies'. This is the first and one
of the few things known of the second Sir Thomas.

His monument in Charlecote Church lacks a tablet of
commemoration. He outlived his father by five years, dying
in 1605. Their two plaster busts flank Maximilian Colt's
portrait effigy of the Queen in Charlecote's Great Hall.*

* Originally made to go in the church. The late Mrs Esdaile thought that
these three portrait busts, owing to the thickness of the plaster used, were near
contemporary.

Identically alike, father and son gaze at their changed hall
with a duplicated air of anxiety. Such close proximity to
their royal mistress is something that neither would have
chosen.

The second Sir Thomas was knighted, according to Met-
calfe, in 1592, in his father's lifetime. His first wife, Dorothea
Arnold, had died in 1580 after six years of wedlock, one
month after giving birth to a son, Thomas. The boy did not
live long, but long enough for litigation to be started about
the lands which Sir Thomas insisted should have come to
him through Dorothea from her grandfather, Sir Nicholas
Arnold, the Monmouthshire estates of Llanthony and Red-
castle. The lawsuit dragged on for eighteen years; it is to be
found in the *Star Chamber Proceedings* and runs to many
pages. This Thomas Lucy was an ardent litigator and,
according to some, 'a verie hard dealer with his tenants'. He
had cut down so much timber on his wife's Gloucestershire
property of Highnam that the value of the place had been
much reduced. His only surviving child, Joyce, became
engaged to a Gloucestershire gentleman, William Cooke
(later created a baronet by James I), who tried to stop his
future father-in-law from taking money out of Highnam. Sir
Thomas was most unwilling to relinquish the Highnam rents
and assets, and tried to convince Joyce that William Cooke
only wanted her for her inheritance. Joyce knew better; and
for the sake of peace and the happiness of his marriage, her
William said no more. But he bided his time, and after Sir
Thomas's death a case was taken through Chancery in which
the executors of Sir Thomas's estate were asked to pay for
the waste and damage done at Highnam and to give up all
claim to leases on the property.

In the course of the long litigation about the Monmouth-
shire property there were free accusations of corruption and
perjury on both sides; but it came to nothing in the end, and
Thomas had to borrow money to pay the costs. Constance
Kingsmill, his second wife, was the ward of the Queen's
Secretary, Sir Francis Walsingham, and brought £40,000
with her. Her father, Richard Kingsmill, had been first
Attorney, and then Surveyor, of the Court of Wards and

Liveries, which dealt with the revenues of estates inherited by minors. The Crown sold the right of administration to a guardian, who received the yearly revenues of the estate, and he, in his turn, sold his ward's hand in marriage to the highest bidder. By the time the estates had been freed and all concerned had taken their profit, the inheritance was generally much depleted.

Richard Kingsmill had bought the Hampshire property of Burghclere and Highclere from the Fitzwilliams. He was the son of Sir John Kingsmill of Sydmonton and had married the heiress of Richard Falconer of Hurstbourne Priors. After his first wife's death, he married again and sold the wardship of his daughter and sole heiress to the Crown. Wards could be very unhappy; they were bought and sold, taken very young away from home to be brought up with strangers. The motherless Constance was not, however, unhappy. At the end of her life she told a grand-daughter of her upbringing in the household of Sir Francis Walsingham, where she was 'extraordinarily kindly used'.

The Lucy-Arnold Chancery suit used up a lot of the profits of Highnam. Thomas was, in her own words, 'much in debt' when he married Constance Kingsmill. From the very little we know of her, she would seem to have been a kind woman, a loving mother and a doting grandmother, with a good head for business inherited from her father, the Surveyor of the Court of Wards and Liveries.

Thomas the Second is more of a worldling than any of his forebears; the old Knight his father was proud to have a son with so many friends at Court. He was the friend both of Francis Bacon and of Bacon's lifelong rival, Sir Edward Coke. When William Cooke, Bacon's kinsman, proposed for the hand of Joyce, Sir Thomas's daughter by his first marriage to Dorothea Arnold, Bacon wrote to him assuring him 'that this bond of alliance shall on my part tie me to give all the tribute to your good fortune, upon all occasions, that my poor strength can yield'. Bacon's hopes had been set on the Attorney-Generalship, which Coke had snatched from him. With a generous extravagance typical of him, he continues, after having set out his kinsman's assets: 'Out of this what he will assure in jointure I leave it to his own kindness; for I love not to measure affection. To conclude, I doubt not that your daughter might have married to a better living, but never to a better life; having chosen a gentleman bred to all honesty, virtue, and worth, with an estate convenient. And if my brother and myself were either thrivers or fortunate in the Queen's service, I would hope there should be left as great a house of the Cookes in this gentleman as in your good friend, Mr Attorney-General. But sure I am, if the Scriptures fail not, it will have as much of God's blessing, and sufficiency is ever the best feast.' Thomas Lucy thought so, too: but he had his own notions of sufficiency. After his second marriage he took up the Chancery suit against the Arnolds with renewed vigour. In November 1595 he was living in the Tower Ward in London, styled a Knight of Gloucestershire, in his first wife's right.

Queen Elizabeth had been induced to purchase as an overflow for the Tower, then in a ruinous condition, its medieval timbers collapsing under the weight of ordnance stored in it, an enclave near the Tower called the Minories, once a Convent of the Minoresses of St Clare. A number of Puritan families had lodgings there, among them the Astons of Tixhall. Having at last succeeded in persuading the unwilling Sir Edward to remove to London, Anne Aston ended her short, querulous life there and was buried in the church in 1596. Sir Edward survived her by only two years, and kind Constance, whose motherly heart had always room for more, took the young Astons into her care. As we have seen already, he tried to induce his brother-in-law to become their guardian, and that Sir Thomas refused. The children played in the nuns' garden, but the convent buildings were already disappearing fast to make way for the premises of gun-makers, smiths, and wheelwrights, who for several centuries were to have the monopoly of this quarter of the city. The embalmed body of Sir Philip Sidney lay in state for over three months in the restored church of the dissolved convent, before he was laid to rest in St Paul's. Half the community who swarmed in the honeycomb of medieval dwellings in and about the Minories was foreign, German craftsmen and Italian musicians. They were its parishioners. The aristocratic families who lodged there came only when the Court was at Westminster, or when their great houses in the country were being spring-cleaned or rebuilt.

In 1595 the Lucys' fifth son Robert was baptized in the Church of Holy Trinity, Minories, and a little sister, Constantia, was buried there in the February of the year following, in whose memory a marble slab was placed in the church with a brass of a mourning female figure on it. The inscription to this much-missed child ran:

> *Nascimur et morimur; non exorabile Fatum*
> *Vita fugax, fragilis, lunica, vana, brevis,*
> *Ocius in campis flos formosissimus aret*
> *Optima praetereunt deteriora manent . . .*

We are born and we die; by inexorable fate life is fleeting and frail, crazed, brief and vain; the fairest flower of the fields perishes the sooner, the best passes away, the worst is left. . . . The touching epitaph goes on to say that this little child 'shone constant beyond her years; patient and modest; a delicate Paphian who in the springtime of her age had felt the cold blast of untimely winter', and concludes: 'thus indeed falls fruit ripe before its time'. There survived Thomas, Richard, George, William, Robert, Francis, Elizabeth, Anne, Brigid, Susanna, and two daughters unidentified, who cannot have married, or who died young.

Richard Kingsmill died in September 1590, two months after old Sir Thomas, and Camden the Clarenceux Herald conducted his funeral.

The same hand is traceable in the tombs of both Richard Kingsmill and his son-in-law. Round the Highclere tomb chest eight Lucy children are shown kneeling in profile. At the head of the recumbent figure of the late Surveyor of the Court of Wards, Thomas and Constance kneel, dwarf-sized, as was the fashion in representing survivors. The tomb chest, the detail of the panels, the heraldic coats and crests, and the *memento mori* generally of the tomb at Highclere bear strong family resemblance to Sir Thomas's tomb at Charlecote. We know now that the sculptors of the Kingsmill tomb were

'Bartholomew Attye of London, tombe maker' and Isaak
James of the parish of St Martin's in the Fields. It was usual
for at least three monumental sculptors to have a hand in the
work. Isaak James was 'my old master' to Nicholas Stone,
Senior, but about 'the unknown Bartholomew Attye', as
Mrs Esdaile calls him, nothing has been proved till now.*

Both tombs are of 'Tatternall' stone, black and white
alabaster, and raunce, a mottled red marble. On both there
are identical Corinthian pillars of black marble with gilded
capitals supporting the two wings of the entablature, which
carry, in the case of Kingsmill, black marble obelisks, and,
in that of Lucy, cartouches of the coats of arms (Lucy
impaling Kingsmill). Round the base of the Lucy tomb is a
shelf bearing two alabaster obelisks which have so little part
in the design that they have the air of having been put down
there temporarily and forgotten. An inscription to the virtues
of the second Sir Thomas as a husband and father was clearly
intended to go in the two bays in the entablature which are
blank. Constance, on the Charlecote tomb, kneels not on
but in front of it, nearly extinguished by an enormous
widow's hood.

A letter from the Privy Council to the second Sir Thomas
as High Sheriff of Warwickshire, in October 1601, takes a
grave view of an attempt on his part to manipulate in some
way the election of Knights of the Shire to his own advantage. He had deferred the election, pretending he could
deliver good cause. 'We cannot hold ourselves satisfied . . .
you are taking upon you very strangely and disorderly to
order and govern by your own concept that which is exactly
prescribed unto you as your duty . . . If we were not
informed of your evil health at this time, we would not
forbear to call you presently before us to make answer for so
great a contempt.'

Nothing that has survived about the second Sir Thomas
shows him up in a particularly good light. But Constance
loved him and for her son's sake refused honourable offers

* The agreement for the Kingsmill tomb has recently come to light at the
Public Record Office: State Papers Supplement, Vol. 25.

of marriage after his death. To her, his entirely beloved wife, he left the house at Charlecote and as much copse wood out of Hampton Woods as is yearly cut for fuel. (The amount of wood burnt in those great houses with their huge bread-ovens and chilly stone-floored halls was enormous.) Constance was also to have all his plate and chattels for her lifetime, but not the gold plate—'the gilt basin and ewer which was my father's, the two gilded livery pots (presents from the Corporation of Stratford), the nest of gilded bowls with a cover, and the great gilt salt', all of which were to go to the eldest son, along with all the furniture from Sutton, his father's best horse, and all his French and Italian books (the 'attendant for the languages' had taught well).

Provision was made for natural daughters, two in number. There was no need to provide for the second son, Richard, as his grandfather Kingsmill had already assured to him the manor of Hurstbourne Falconer in Hampshire. He was, however, to have his father's second-best horse. There is a lot about horses, perhaps those from the famous stud of Sir Nicholas Arnold at Highnam. George, the third son, is alleged by Burke to have been slain in France. The fourth son, William, a lively and contumacious character, must very early have shown a vocation for the Church; his father left him the revenues of several livings and some ecclesiastical property belonging to the Dean and Chapter of Gloucester. He became Rector of Highclere, which was in his mother's gift, before flailing his way to a bishopric. The two younger sons were to have the manor of Cherington, with its associations with the Lucy who fought at Crécy,* and some Shropshire property. All his daughters were to have £100 apiece for a jewel to wear in memory of their kind father, and Thomas Gwillim, his trusted Welsh bodyservant, was to have 'my best trotting gelding' and £40 of current English money.

The curtain must be lowered while the stage is swept and cleared of lumber for the entry of the new century. Sir Thomas the Second, a born supporting actor if ever there

---

* See Lucy Chronology, p. 296.

was one, lived under Elizabeth and died under James yet was neither an Elizabethan nor a Jacobean, but one of those lesser players who occupy the stage through the whispers and fidgets of the audience while the principals get ready for their entrance.

Constance divided her life between Charlecote and High-clere till about 1609, when she removed to a house in London in the leafy district of Blackfriars with an unmarried son, Robert. This part of London had the highest death rate of the city, and two of her grandchildren died while staying with her of the typhoid that broke out there periodically. Dugdale was impressed by the monuments in St Giles' Church, Cripplegate, put up to these two girls by their heartbroken grandmother.*

She had her share of trouble. One daughter, Elizabeth, who had married Sir Anthony Hungerford of Down Ampney in Gloucestershire, had been turned out of doors by her father-in-law, who had promised to support the young couple and now repudiated his promise. But worse was to come. Her youngest daughter, Susan, formed an attachment for a man called Robert Chamberlain, a Clerk in the Court of Wards. It was the Aston-Sambach affair all over again, only Chamberlain was the more unscrupulous rogue. Having got the girl's affections, he abducted her from her mother's house in Blackfriars and went through a form of marriage with her at Chelsea. He hid her in Southwark, in the house of one Sparrowhawk, a waterman, while the hue and cry was on, and thence conveyed her to Blackwall by the docks, to the house of a carpenter. The girl was a minor, and the man's intention was quite simply to blackmail her mother for money. He had a mistress, Eleanore Littlebury, to whom he wrote vowing that his pretended marriage with Susan Lucy was not undertaken for love, but to enable him to maintain himself and be more bountiful to Eleanore. He was confident that Lady Lucy would not wish for an open scandal and that he would get her daughter's portion. He

* Constance Whitney, daughter of Anne Lucy and Sir Robert Whitney, and Margaret, daughter of the third Sir Thomas Lucy.

induced Susan to go with him to the Littleburys' house in
Mincing Lane, where she was made to scour dishes while he
bedded with Eleanore. He swore on the Bible that Eleanore
was his true and lawful wife before God, and that he would
never bed with Susan unless Eleanore joined them there. The
sordid story tails off; the bill of complaint taken to Chancery
is incomplete. Susan was recovered by her mother. Chamberlain threatened to blow up the house in Blackfriars with
gunpowder; he followed the coach in which the girl was
being hurried down to Highclere, and tried to pull her out
of it in the market-place at Maidenhead.*

Though her doctors certified her, in 1624, as too ill to be
moved from her residence in the parish of St Giles, Cripplegate, Constance in fact returned to Highclere for the last
years of her life, and, dying there, was taken with a splendid
cortège to lie beside her husband.

One of the grand-daughters, Lady Eyre, daughter of the
youngest son, Francis Lucy, preserved an account of her
grandmother's death which came into the possession of
George Lucy of Charlecote in 1831. On being asked whether
the Queen's doctor, Sir Theodore Mayerne, 'upon the taking
of whose physic she felt so ill', should be sent for, Constance
said she preferred to submit herself to God. Mayerne was
called, however, 'but the Queen being near her time he
could not come'.

To this grand-daughter Constance related how she many
times importuned her husband to make a will leaving
provision for his younger children. The will was made in
haste, and it was afterwards found that the education of the
younger children had not been properly provided for. This
she made her own charge, 'and yet left her Eldest Son a
greater Estate and freer from Incumbrances than it was left
to her. . . .'

Remembering her childhood, Constance told those about
her that she thought it the best duty belonging to her sex,
and the hardest to do well, to be a good mother-in-law
(stepmother), and how she had tried to treat Dorothea

* Star Chamber Proceedings.

Arnold's child with as much kindness as if the girl had been her own. At the end she rambled of her kind father, and of her upbringing at Sir Francis Walsingham's, that courteous gentleman 'who would put off his hat to her as often as she passed by him, what, or with whomsoever his business was'.

Young Thomas Lucy had left Oxford before 1602, aged fifteen or sixteen, which seems to us an early age at which to consider one's education complete. But boys learnt very early to take part in the wrangles about logic and philosophy which were a feature of university life, and which were often so heated that they ended in blows. Cambridge would have been the more obvious choice for the son of a distinguished Puritan, for Cambridge had been the nursery of the Reformation. Oxford was in slight temporary eclipse. The Queen's education, which enabled her to scintillate like the Arabian phoenix, had come from Cambridge scholars, and indeed most of her ministers were from that University.

But Lucys had always gone to Oxford, and were to continue to do so. Thomas Lucy was probably about thirteen, the age at which boys now to go to Eton, when he left Charlecote one winter day to become a student at Magdalen, where John Foxe, his grandfather's tutor, had been a student three-quarters of a century earlier. He entered the walled city of the Middle Ages, rising out of an inland sea of floodwater, from the west along the high road from Banbury. An Oxford without ignoble brick skirts, of white and yellow stone, a feast for the eye and the imagination, from Magdalen with its river lawns boldly set down by Bishop Waynflete outside the east gate of the city, to Christ Church, where Wolsey's halted dream sketched the outlines of something so grandiose that it challenged comparison with the great foundations of learning abroad.

Young men whose fathers paid for their education, and who took a servant to wait on them, were in the minority. The University was in the main made up of the sons of tradesmen, clerks, and poor gentlemen, who worked for their privileges by waiting on the richer ones. Thirty odd years later, when Thomas Lucy's Oxford days were only a

memory, a young Welshman of Jesus College shivered
through the unhealthy, dripping autumns of the Thames
Valley while the cloudy patterns forming and dissolving in
his head took the shapes of poetry that have placed Henry
Vaughan among the immortals.

Sir Thomas's father insisted that his son should spend two
or three years at one of the great Inns of Court in order to
acquire a knowledge of Common Law, without which a
country landlord would have been at a disadvantage in the
management of a great estate. So to Lincoln's Inn in either
1601 or 1602, the year before the Queen's death, the year
which saw the first production of *Hamlet*, went Thomas
Lucy, the more readily since Oxford had a little lost its
savour for him once his friend, Edward Herbert, had left it.

When domestic cares and the duties of a country gentleman had entirely absorbed the grave-faced man of Cornelius
Jansen's family picture, he must sometimes have stared at
the merry young men of Larkin's two portraits—himself
and Edward, afterwards Lord Herbert of Cherbury, painted
in London during their middle twenties—as if they were
revenants from another world.

It was a very different world into which his friendship
with the Montgomeryshire family of Herbert drew the quiet
boy who was pursuing his lonely studies at Magdalen.*

According to Izaak Walton (who wrote a life of Lord
Herbert's younger brother, George, the poet), their mother,
Magdalen Herbert, on becoming a widow, removed her
household of ten children from Montgomeryshire to Oxford
in order that she might keep an eye on her eldest son when

* There is some confusion here as to the dates. Edward Herbert was born in
1583, one year before Thomas Lucy. According to the University Register
quoted by Sir Sydney Lee in his preface to the autobiography, he matriculated
in 1596 at fourteen. In his autobiography he makes himself out as having been
married at fifteen while still at Oxford. Most probably he and Thomas Lucy
went to Oxford within a year of each other. On the tomb in Charlecote
Church it is stated that Sir Thomas was fifty-six in 1640, and was therefore
born in 1584. But the Students' Register makes him matriculate from Magdalen
in 1601, aged fifteen. At the Herald Visitation of Warwickshire in 1619 his age
was given as thirty-three, which makes him three years younger than Lord
Herbert. I have followed the age given on the tomb.

he entered University College. She arranged a marriage between him and his cousin, Mary Herbert of St Julian's, an heiress who was six years his senior. The marriage took place during an Oxford vacation, and the wife was added to the Oxford household.

When he came to write his autobiography many years later, Lord Herbert had a great deal to say about the importance of keeping young men out of mischief during the formative years that they might devote their minds to study only. By then he probably believed it; he tells us that he had no inclination when at Oxford to sow wild oats, 'having a due remedy for that lasciviousness to which youth is naturally inclined'. Instead, he bent his inquiring mind and lively talents to the study of three languages, botany, medicine, fencing, and the lute—'my intention in learning languages being to make myself a citizen of the world as far as possible.'

Magdalen Herbert was a charmer, according to Walton, 'of great and harmless wit and of a cheerful gravity'. John Donne wrote of her much later:

> *Nor Spring nor Summer beauty hath such grace*
> *As I have seen in one Autumnal face. . . .*

A man's woman, as the saying goes, whose femininity, though never forgotten, does not obtrude, in whose presence men feel themselves enabled to rise to their full stature. Probably Thomas fell in love with her as an impressionable boy. Certainly he continued to frequent her house in London as one of the circle that included Donne.

Walton in his *Life* says that Mrs Herbert managed her eldest son so cleverly 'and with such a sweetness and compliance with the recreations and pleasures of youth as did incline him willingly to spend much of his time in the company of his dear and careful mother, which was to her great content. . . .'

With these charming friends young Thomas found himself persuaded away from his books to ride out into the country towards Islip and Brill, whose small hills rise and subside into the sea-blue plain of Otmoor where the redshank nests, further to Shabington Forest, or westward to Eynsham, where the water meadows are full of fritillaries in spring. Riding home at dusk they would see, from Cumnor uplands, Oxford lying at their feet like a crown, its jewels the festal lights in college halls.

All this maternal watchfulness was likely to have only one end. Edward Herbert went to court in about 1600, while his friend, on leaving Oxford, returned to Warwickshire. The Queen clapped the ardently handsome dark youth on the cheek twice, and said it was a pity he had been married so young. He thought so too. His vanity inclined to make him think that more ladies sighed for him than actually did. But with all his follies, which became, sadly, so much less endearing as he grew older, he was insatiably eager for knowledge and experience, which made their friendship a liberal education for Thomas Lucy.

Thomas's training for the law at Lincoln's Inn turned out to be an extension of Oxford. The *malaise du fin de siècle* which inclines young men to dress strangely, profess a moody cynicism, and dwell emotionally on death and the decay of love, found expression in *Hamlet*, which had its first performance at the Globe in Thomas's first year at Lincoln's Inn (and possibly earlier by a touring company at Oxford), and the two friends had no difficulty in recognizing themselves in *fin de siècle* disguise. Poetry inflamed all hearts; all men of education tried their hands at it. Melancholy was the mode. Edward Herbert had the vanity and the mercurial temperament for the part of Hamlet, but not Hamlet's views on the futility of heroic action and the debasing effects of human love. He was all for heroic zest and knight-errantry. Of Thomas Lucy we know so little that we can only conjecture. In Larkin's lively portrait he has more the liveliness of Laertes; but the melancholy was latent in him, as Cornelius Jansen later perceived.

Lincoln's Inn was one of the four great Law schools where scholars lodged round shady quadrangles much like an Oxford college. Not only Law was learnt within its walls. Gentlemen's sons were given an all-round education, with an emphasis on dancing, singing, and play-acting.

It was a wonderful London to be young in, the London of the early sixteen-hundreds. The plays of Shakespeare were filling the Globe on five nights out of the seven, even when the nights were rainy, the groundlings spreading sacks over their heads rather than miss a moment of Malvolio or Dogberry. Puritans of the middle-of-the-road sort, like Thomas Lucy, saw no objection to stage plays, which were in fact strongly moral in intention under King James. The new Queen loved being entertained, and the King allowed the players to wear his livery. Not till the end of the nineteenth century was it ever again so rewarding to be a popular actor.

Thomas's fondness of the theatre has a footnote in the State Papers Domestic for 1633-4. The Mayor and Justices of Banbury were in judgement upon two strolling players— Bartholomew Jones and Richard Whitinge—for some petty breach of the peace. Jones 'being examined saith that he hath gone with this Company up and down the Country these two years and that he hath acted his parts in divers places' . . . among others at Sir Thomas Lucy's. Whitinge 'hath acted a part with this Company of players lately at Leicester, Stratford, Meriden, Solihull, at Sir William Spencer's, Sir Thomas Lucy's, etc.' . . .

It has been traditionally held by the Lucys that friendship grew up between Shakespeare and the third Sir Thomas, at whose board, according to his epitaph, any good man was welcome, especially if his talk was of theology or poetry. If this is true, as we should like to think it is, the acquaintance could have begun about this time at Lincoln's Inn, where the students at Christmas hired professional actors in order that they might themselves have the fun of making an appreciative and uproarious audience.*

* That Thomas Lucy never became the patron of any poet of substance was due to the dearth of poets in Warwickshire in his day. The blaze died with Shakespeare and Drayton, never to be rekindled. Patronage was an expensive luxury—it cost a lot to keep even the smallest taper twinkling. Sir Thomas was indeed the subject of some doggerel by a Mr John Davis of Hereford, written in 1610, in which he was called a 'Bright spark of wit and courage', and likened to a gem in the court's brow. No doubt the poet was paid; but not, it seems, encouraged to write more.

According to Dugdale, Sir Thomas the Second died after his son had been a year at Lincoln's Inn, in 1603; but the Charlecote Registers have the date 1605. In either case his son must have paid his respects to the ageing Queen and again to the new King. But when he was knighted is not known, though it was almost certainly at the Coronation of King James, when knighthoods were scattered as lavishly as rice at a wedding.

The Herberts would not let Thomas bury himself in the country so young. At her house in Charing Cross, Magdalen Herbert recreated the Oxford atmosphere, the flashing talk, the laughter, the fingers straying on the lute seducing the company from talk to song, yet all kept within the bounds of modesty and sobriety:

> —*here where still evening is, not noon, nor night;*
> *Where no voluptuousness, yet all delight.* . . .

As householders sleepily unbarred their doors of a morning, the young men of the Inns came singing back to their lodgings, the starch wilting in their ruffs, night's candles having been fairly burnt out.

During Thomas's years in London Dowland published the third edition of his *Songs and Ayres in four parts with Tablature for the lute*. Young men of education were expected to be able to read music at sight. The parts of a madrigal were arranged on the page in such a way that four people could sing from the same song-book, one holding it and one performing on the lute, the tablature for which was printed below the cantos. (The virginals were only for ladies, whose fingers were small enough to hop over the keys.) Young Thomas must have heard sung, for the very first time, *Flow not so fast ye fountains* with its crystal fall, dying away on a sigh:

> *Freshly your salt tears*
> *Must still fall dropping, dropping, dropping,*
> *Dropping from their spheres.* . . .

One to whom friendship was a second religion, John Donne, had already made Thomas's acquaintance at Sir

Henry Goodyer's London house, and followed it up with Mrs Herbert's encouragement.* His friendship with the Herberts was pushing Sir Thomas in the direction of marriage; he met his future wife through his friendship with Donne. For four years the poet was secretary to the Lord Keeper of England under Elizabeth and James I, Sir Thomas Egerton, later Lord Ellesmere, the friend of Bacon and Whitgift, the patron of Ben Jonson, whose clever and determined wife had been Lady Derby, and was a granddaughter of Sir John Spencer of Althorp.† An invitation to York House, the splendid official residence of the Lord Keeper, was sought for many reasons, among which were Lady Egerton's three black-browed Stanley daughters, and a host of lively cousins, who helped to fill the great rooms with the stir of silks and flash of pretty smiles. Handsome Edward Herbert was always welcome there; and it was there, under the alarmingly intelligent glances of Lady Egerton and the Ladies Frances, Anne, and Elizabeth Stanley, that Sir Thomas Lucy was introduced to a Warwickshire neighbour, his hostess's little niece, Alice Spencer. She was the only child of Lady Egerton's brother, Thomas Spencer of Claverdon. She was just eleven, but looked older in the stiff, middle-aged fashions of the time. Thomas Lucy, for all his acquired sophistication, meant to follow in the footsteps of his father and grandfather. He knew he must marry well to secure the future of Charlecote. Little Alice Spencer, gentle as a dove, much in awe of her accomplished cousins, was the sort of girl his mother would strongly approve.‡

* Edmund Gosse, in his *Life and Letters of John Donne*, says (p. 173): 'It is possible that Donne had been employed to read with Sir Thomas Lucy, who was intimate with the Herberts . . .' but does not give reasons for thinking this possible. There is a reference to Thomas Lucy in a later letter of Donne's to Sir Henry Goodyer in 1612, but the long letter addressed directly to him printed in Gosse's life (p. 173) is now thought to have been written to Goodyer. I am indebted to Mr I. A. Shapiro of Birmingham University for pointing this out to me.
† On her tomb in Harefield Church she lies under a marble tester with knotted-back curtains, looking at once girlish and matriarchial, her long hair flowing over her shoulder, and round her kneel her daughters, Lady Chandos, Lady Bridgewater, and Lady Huntingdon, the later patroness of Donne.
‡ Sir Thomas, delighted at the project, sent Lord Keeper Egerton a buck from Charlecote.

In July 1605 the second Sir Thomas died. What was left of that summer passed in readjusting the tempo of life at Charlecote. The widow and daughters sorted out the late master's clothes, gave away what was beyond re-furbishing, and cut up good sarsenet and brocatelle stuffs for cushions and foot-stools. It was a hot, dry summer, and the elms of the warren showed bright patches of yellow leaf as early as August. Afterwards all sorts of portents were remembered, and how the sunsets made the river seem to run with blood.

In the small room in London where the Privy Council debated matters of high secrecy, Burleigh's son, Salisbury, read the notes brought in by his secret service. The events of 5 November had been anticipated; Tresham's frantic, scribbled warning to his brother-in-law, Lord Monteagle, '. . . devise some excuse to shift of your attendance at the Parliament, for God and man hath concurred to punish the wickedness of the times', which led to the discovery of piled-up barrels of gunpowder and a fuse ready to be lit in the vault below the House of Commons, was no surprise to the Secretary of State and his agents. The group of Catholic gentlemen led by a Leicestershire squire, George Catesby, who so trustfully plotted (with touching belief in the co-operation of such imponderables as time and opportunity) to blow up the Parliament House, thus disposing of the leaders of the three estates and the King in one purifying explosion, were destined for more terrible ends than they planned for their victims. The hopelessly idealistic aspect of the Gunpowder Plot robs it of sordidness, and invests it with pathos.

The mourning household of Charlecote, turned in upon itself by the presence of death, took very little notice of the whispers going round the neighbourhood. There had been a connexion back at the beginning of the sixteenth century with the family of Catesby (it will be remembered that Thomas Lucy, the one who was a server to Henry VIII, married Empson's daughter, who was widow to a George Catesby, and received the wardship of her son, William). George Catesby, the instigator of this new Catholic plot, had sold his Warwickshire estate of Lapworth and was now the squire of Ashby St Ledgers. But Warwickshire, not

Leicestershire, was the theatre of the conspiracy. Catholic Coughton, that dark secret house where recusant priests could lie long hidden, had been rented from its Throckmorton owner (who was discreetly spending a few months on the Continent), by another conspirator, Sir Everard Digby. At Northbroke, on the border of Fulbroke and Sherbourne, the Catholic Grants* were deeply in the conspiracy. For a long time now these Catholic gentry had paid their fines for recusancy and enjoyed the negative state of being unmolested if they drew no attention to themselves. They were mostly desperately poor, and all proud. Of the conspirators, the few who had money were Ambrose Rookwood (who some time round about Michaelmas, 1605, rented Clopton House just outside Stratford in order to be near his fellow conspirators), and Francis Tresham, who was the indirect means of bringing his fellow conspirators to justice. The Grants lived in their dilapidated mansion like labourers.

There was horse-racing at Rugby on the 4th and at Dunsmore Heath on the 5th. In the same innocent spirit that saw the crazy plot as a perfectly sane plan capable of being carried to a logical conclusion, a number of Catholic gentlemen attended these races in order that when the word came from London that Parliament had roared up in flames they might be assembled in readiness toact; no one had any very clear idea of what exactly they would be called upon to do.

They were not prepared for failure. The short day of 5 November darkened, and at Coughton the women waited and prayed, not daring to light the candles. In inns and at cross-roads knots of men hung about whispering, the horses stamping and blowing with the cold. Everard Digby was there, and John Grant of Northbroke, with Robert Winter, who had married his sister, and two other Winter brothers, John and Thomas, all cousins of Catesby's.

It was midnight before Catesby with thirteen others arrived from London with the news that the plot had been discovered. In the alarm that followed a few sympathizers

---

* John Grant was the grandson of the Edward Grant who had married Anne Somerville, the sister of John Somerville of Edstone.

slipped prudently away. It was decided to ride for the Winters' house at Huddington in Worcestershire, pausing at Northbroke to pick up arms that had been hoarded there for some time past. By the time the party arrived at Northbroke it was only thirty strong—at best they could only hope to make a desperate stand. The wind of the flight, and the chase that followed, just touched Charlecote. On passing through Warwick the conspirators stole horses from the Castle stables. People in the villages round bolted their doors that night, and for many nights following, with extra care. But there was no more violence to come. The conspirators were rounded up. Silence fell on Coughton and Clopton and Northbroke after the Sheriff's officers had torn up the floor boards and flung from windows such incriminating material as could be found. At Northbroke, mass books, a chalice, and an embroidered cope were fished up, a dripping sodden bundle, from the duck pond. Not many years after the house became a tenement. By the end of the century it was demolished.

It was a restless age; young men set off abroad laughingly complaining that England was grown too small for them. Curiosity was in the air. Edward Herbert told his wife that, as he had been too young to go beyond the sea when he married her, he meant to do so now. (He gives the date as 1608, the year of his mother's remarriage to Sir John Danvers, to which he never once alludes.) Poor Mrs Herbert had no choice but to let him go, which he did, congratulating himself that he left her with child. He must have written to Thomas Lucy describing the delight of staying with the Montmorencys at Chantilly, 'that incomparable place' from whose windows one could look down into deep water where carp, pike, and trout glided. In Paris he took up lute-playing and singing again, and practised sword-play. At some point Sir Thomas joined him there and shared his studies, for Edward Herbert says that he was twice second to him in France 'against two cavaliers of our nation, who were yet hindered to fight with us in the field where we attended them'. This uncharacteristic belligerence in Thomas Lucy must have been an ardent imitation of his gallant friend, who was always involving himself in fracas provoked by some real or fancied slight to a lady.

In January 1609 the two turned their faces for England. The story of the shipwreck, from Lord Herbert's memoirs, has often been quoted, but it reads so freshly that I set it down again.

They left Dieppe in a storm and tossed at sea all night:

The Master of our ship lost both the use of his compass and his reason; for not knowing whither he was carried by the tempest, all the help he had was by the lightnings. . . . And now, towards day, we found ourselves, by the great providence of God, within view of Dover, to which the master of our ship did make. The men of Dover, rising betimes in the morning to see whether any ships were coming towards them, were in great numbers upon the shore, as believing the tempest which had thrown down barns and trees near the town, might give them the benefit of some wreck, if perchance any ship were driven thitherwards. We were coming thus in extreme danger straight upon the pier of Dover, which stands out in the sea. . . .

The vessel which had apparently carried only these two and one other as passengers with their servants and horses, as well as a crew, split upon the pier, and the master of the ship called out, '*Mes amis, nous sommes perdus*,' which Lord Herbert obligingly translates:

When myself who heard the ship crack against the pier, and then found by the master's words it was time for everyone to save themselves if they could [I] got out of my cabin (though very sea-sick) and climbing up the mast a little way, drew my sword and flourished it; they at Dover having this sign given them, adventured in a shallop of six oars to relieve us, which being come with great danger to the side of our ship, I got into first with my sword in my hand, and called for Sir Thomas Lucy, saying that if any man offered to get in before him I should resist him with my sword. . . .

There was a heavy sea running and the water must have been pouring into the sides of the split barque. But the gallant Edward, maintaining a precarious balance in the rocking shallop, fended off the attempts of the ship's crew to escape:

whereupon a faithful servant of his taking Sir Thomas Lucy out of the cabin who was half dead of sea-sickness, put him into my arms, whom after I had received, I bid the shallop make away for the shore, and the rather that I saw another shallop coming to relieve us.

The other passenger, a messenger from France bearing letters to England, jumped in after them. Sir Thomas's additional weight had nearly swamped the boat. The Frenchman's temerity in leaping down upon them all but overset it:

I must confess myself, as also the seamen who were in the shallop thought once to have killed him for this desperate attempt, but finding no harm followed we escaped together unto the land, from whence we sent more shallops, and so made means to save both men and horses that were in the ship, which yet itself was wholly split and cast away, insomuch that in pity to the master, Sir Thomas Lucy and myself gave thirty pounds towards his loss, which yet was not so great as we thought, since the tide now ebbing, he recovered the broken parts of his ship.

Almost as important to Edward Herbert as his friend's life was his jennet (a light riding horse) that he had bought in France, 'whose love I had so gotten that he would suffer none else to ride him, nor indeed any man to come near when I was upon him, as being in his nature a most furious horse. . . .'

All that is recorded of the third Sir Thomas testifies to his great love of horses. He offered his friend two hundred pounds for this remarkable animal, who, Lord Herbert goes on to say: '. . . as soon as ever I came into the stables would neigh, and when I drew nearer him would lick my hand and (when I suffered him) my cheek, yet would permit nobody to come near his heels at the same time.' Sir Thomas got him as a loan the year following, when his master had found an excuse to go abroad again, this time to the Low Countries, where England had promised support to the Protestants against the Emperor. The horse pined for its master and died at Charlecote.

Thomas was too innately serious to dangle for long on the edge of a literary coterie. He meant to marry. The little girl he had met at York House, Alice Spencer, had been quietly waiting to grow up, and for him to decide to settle down.

She was dark, with a little, demure face, large eyes and a round, dimpled chin. Small as she was, she fitted into Charlecote as neatly as a bird fits its nest. Where Joyce Acton had pounced and scolded, tapping about on her red heels, Alice Spencer gently rustled and murmured. These Jacobean women recede, where their predecessors briskly assert themselves. In spite of the box-like ugliness of the fashions set by Queen Anne, the women of the period begin to display femininity, though not to the extent of the Caroline ladies who flow in billows of pearly satin. In the supposititious mystery created by dark stuffs set off by collars and cuffs of thinnest lawn and snowflake lace, they turn great hare's eyes on the beholder. Alice Spencer owned a blue enamelled pendant which she brought with her from Claverdon and apparently always wore on a gold chain looped to one side of her bodice. She set off her round forehead by wearing a half-hoop of matched pearls on her head after the fashion that King James's daughter, the Princess Elizabeth, made her own, and sometimes added a white osprey's feather.

There is no record that I can discover of the date of this marriage, which must have taken place in about 1611 or 1612, in London, arranged by the bride's aunt, Lady Ellesmere, since the bride was motherless.

Alice Spencer has always been spoken of as an heiress and in so far as she was her father's sole child, she was. But the Lucy money, of which there seems to have been such plenty in the first half of the seventeenth century, came chiefly from the Kingsmill and Aston marriages, and from the other considerable Lucy estates in Herefordshire, Shropshire, Bedfordshire, and Buckinghamshire. The Spencers were rich and influential, but Claverdon and Yarnton were the portions of younger sons and entailed on the heirs male.

The oval portrait on copper that is a pair to that which Lord Herbert got 'one Larkin, a painter' to draw for him, 'the original whereof I intended before my departure to the

Low Countries for Sir Thomas Lucy',* is of the student of Lincoln's Inn in the first years of the new century. Both these portraits have been attributed to Isaac Oliver. Indeed, the style and the miniature-like fineness of the brushwork is very much Oliver's, who painted Lord Herbert in miniature more than once. With his red hair blown back from his forehead, a small red beard and a low necked toga carelessly thrown on in the Roman manner, Thomas Lucy has the self-consciously dashing and mannered air assumed by gallants, while Edward (a black Herbert) very much aware of his conquering looks, glances sidelong with brilliant black eyes over a satin tunic embroidered with starfish in gold thread.

The friendship cooled and re-shaped itself as youthful friendships do; and in the years to come after Thomas's marriage, they can only occasionally have met, as the slippery career of diplomacy on which Edward embarked (he had always wanted to be a citizen of the world) took him more and more out of England.

As life went on, Lord Herbert's vanity led him into endless trouble. He was so touchy that he would call a man out for a fancied slight. In 1615–16 we find him in trouble and committed to temporary imprisonment in Lyons for off-hand (he does not call it insulting) behaviour to the Governor of that town. One of the very few letters that have survived from the third Sir Thomas is written to him, in the care of Lady Danvers at her house in Charing Cross:

To my most honoured friend, Sir Edward Herbert, this. . . . Sir, when I heard you were under holds at Lyons the knowledge I had [of] how ill you can digest the least indignity, made me in all companies prophecy how honourably you would come off with the Governor, in which methinks I have such a part [sympathy] as I cannot but congratulate with you for it.

(By this time Sir Thomas was a Member of Parliament. While in London he visited Sir John and Lady Danvers, and was welcome at Lord Chancellor Ellesmere's house and at that of Donne's patroness, Lady Huntingdon. The words 'in

* Both portraits now hang in the Great Hall at Charlecote.

all companies' refers to this circle of old friends, though it suggests a highly uncharacteristic garrulity on the part of Sir Thomas.)

The letter goes on:

I hear of no wars at this time worthy you, which makes me hope you have grown so good a husband of yourself as you will prefer your friend's society here before unnecessary dangers abroad; you could not find greater variety abroad than you will at your return find alterations at home, the face of the Court being so changed as you will discuss with yourself whether you are not in some other place or no. It is shortly expected the King will make a scrambling (as boys call it) of the many places he has hitherto hoarded in my Lord of Somerset* and so the poor bird will prove as naked of feathers as he is already of friends—so Sir, most humbly kissing your hands, assuring you it is my greatest glory to know myself your true friend and most faithful servant, Thomas Lucy.†

Among the family papers at Charlecote that accidents and neglect have sifted away, there must have been letters from the poet Donne. A Mr John Pory, who made himself indispensable by carrying letter-packets from gentlemen in England to friends abroad, and vice versa, was later employed by Thomas Lucy‡ as newsletter writer. He carried letters from Donne to England during the poet's travels in France with Sir Robert Drury in 1612. One to Sir Henry Goodyer§ contains this passage:

* This was King James's favourite, Robert Ker, created Viscount Rochester and later Earl of Somerset. Rochester's intrigue with Lady Essex involved him in a frightful scandal. Sir Thomas Overbury, who opposed the nullity suit which Lady Essex tried to bring against her first husband, was poisoned in the Tower under suspicious circumstances three months before the scandalous marriage took place. The pair were brought to book in 1616. Bacon prosecuted and they were found guilty, but eventually pardoned. Rochester was stripped of his high appointments—Lord Treasurer of Scotland, private secretary to the King, Lord Chamberlain—and was indeed a poor bird naked of feathers at the time when this letter was written.
† Printed as from Sir Thomas Lucy in the *Collections Historical and Archaeological relating to Montgomeryshire issued by the Powys-land Club*, Vol. XX, p. 86. Mr Shapiro has examined the letter and assures me that there is no doubt that it is in Sir Thomas Lucy's hand, as it is in his style of expression.
‡ See Birch's *Court and Times of Charles I*.
§ Misprinted by Gosse as 'George Garrard'. Other letters in Gosse headed 'Sir Thomas Lucy' are mistakes for Sir Henry Goodyer.

Sir Thomas Lucy's business, and perchance sadness, forbid me writing now. I have written to him . . . by another way; and if my poor letters were any degree of service, I should do it often, and rather be mine own post, than leave anything undone to which he would give such an interpretation as that it were an argument of my devotion to him.

This could refer to the too common death of a first-born son. Only two of Thomas and Alice's children are entered in the Charlecote Register of Baptism and those the two youngest of the family. It is thought that Spencer, the eldest surviving son, was twenty-four at the time of his father's death in 1640, which makes him not born till 1614.

Vertue, making a survey of English portraits more than a hundred years later, says this in connexion with the Lucy family picture: 'At Charlcot house Sir Tho. Lucy Kt. half length and his Lady. His Family piece in the Hall a copy; a small sketch of the original at large painted by Cornelius Jansen, destroyed by fire formerly.' The small sketch from which the big picture was done is still in existence.

In the Jansen portrait, chairs, a table, family pets, and a view of the garden had been brought together like the unrelated furnishings of a photographer's studio to make the sitters feel at home. The family is sitting in a garden summer-house, with an Eastern carpet on the floor, and books on a table at Sir Thomas's elbow. But there is a hawk in the picture too, and two dogs, to show that his tastes were not exclusively literary. Over the threshold steps Spencer, the eldest son, dressed in a replica of his father's black clothes, bringing a china dish of peaches. The girls' dresses seem all to have been cut out of the same piece of expensive but uninteresting material. Margaret (the one who died in London in her grandmother's care) is the liveliest. Constance, her elder, with a matronly air, hands a saucer full of cherries to her mother. Bridget, it appears, is still young enough to play with a miniature bow; though encased, as they all seem to have been from birth, in starched lace, outdoor sports cannot have been easy for them.*

---

* There is an earlier piece, also attributed to Jansen, of these three girls and their baby brother, painted in 1619.

The chairs are upholstered in silk of the clear red of a carnation, but the clothes are sober; good black for Sir Thomas, with gauze ribbons tied below the knee, and rosettes of gauze on his white leather shoes. Elegance, but of a sad, Hamlet-like sort. Alice Lucy is blacker still, in satin which spills darkness from its folds. Still round-chinned, her little face on its crimped lace plate looks no older than that of her eldest daughter. The baby in the nurse's arms is already a little woman, with wings of pale hair showing under a tight white cap, cherries in her tiny fingers. Outside there is a parterre with formal box-edged beds, reaching to a low horizon with trees under a gloomy lowering sky.

Puritanism in its extreme form could be as blighting as an east wind. Where there was granite in the human composition the discipline of incessant self-examination revealed it, as the stripped and stony hillside is bleached by the winds that blow on it. In Thomas Lucy there was no such rock. His early friendship with the Herberts and with the poet-saint George Herbert, Edward's younger brother, inclined him to the easy, middle-of-the-road Puritanism that is no enemy to natural gaiety. The exercise of tireless discussion with his contemporaries at Oxford cleared his head of the cloudy metaphysics so attractive to youth. By the time the Jansen portrait was painted he had settled in responsible middle age, a grave man, but one who still delighted in clever talk.

There exists also, but not at Charlecote, a portrait of Thomas's next brother, Richard Lucy, painted by an unknown artist a few years earlier, on his wedding day.* In it family likeness to the Larkin portrait of Sir Thomas is strong; there is the same tossed-back red hair, the same long, pointed chin. Richard's attitude, one hand at his hip, a cloak lined with deep-piled velvet over the arm, and the other stretched out to take that of his bride, is all ease and confidence. His doublet and long, full breeches are of a

* It was empanelled in the wall of Broxbournebury House, which was in the possession of the Monson family till the end of the eighteenth century. Richard Lucy married Elizabeth, widow of Sir Robert Oxenbridge, who married a Monson as her third husband.

delicate silver-grey, embossed and braided with gold and silver, and buttoned with crystal and pearls. Knotted across the doublet he wears a scarf embroidered with symbolic devices, a sun, an anchor, a crowned heart, the winged wand of Mercury. Mercurial indeed he looks, as if he took his Puritanism lightly, while Thomas (only so very little older), is set already in the mould of sober middle age.

The house was forty years old in 1608 and the plaster no longer sweated in rainy springs; the trees old Sir Thomas had planted were as tall as a man, even the limes, which are the slowest growing of all, leading to the Stratford bridle road.

The third Sir Thomas found he could not continue to be an absentee landlord indefinitely. If Charlecote and Sutton were to run smoothly he had to travel constantly between the two places. By now (1610) his brothers were growing up and would have to be settled in life. Richard mentioned above, so like him in looks, had been sent to Oxford on their father's death, to Magdalen, where he was confided to the care of his elder brother's old tutor. In 1610 he was a student of Exeter College and bound for a year or two at Lincoln's Inn to complete his education. About George, the third brother, we know nothing; but the fourth, William, already in possession of the curacy of Hurstbourne, had just gone up to Trinity, Oxford. Robert and Francis were still young enough to have a tutor at home. Three of his sisters were married: Bridget to Sir Richard Knightley of Fawsley in Leicestershire; Elizabeth to Anthony Hungerford of Down Ampney in Gloucestershire; and Anne to a Herefordshire knight, Sir Robert Whitney.

His mother spent most of her time at Highclere, where she maintained a house-full of Kingsmill poor relations. At Charlecote he supported an old great-uncle, who kept to his room, but there was no one to whom he could delegate authority. He was at this date contemplating buying, from the nephew of the recusant Sir Francis Englefield, the messuage and lands of Fulbroke, 20 acres of meadow, over 300 acres of pasture, and 100 acres of woodland, intending to enclose the old royal park and complete it by the purchase of

Hampton Woods. The land so long neglected was rank with weeds, the buildings ruinous. If he hoped to get it cheap on this score, he was to be disappointed. The negotiations dragged on for five years and in the end he had to pay £1,850 for it. But all this was still in the air in 1610.

In the July of the previous year armed poachers had broken into his park at Sutton, bragging afterwards in the local ale-houses of what they had done. The case, which was taken to the Star Chamber for redress, is reported at length. By a statute of the first year of King James's reign, it was unlawful to enter into any forest, park, chase or warren to destroy deer or game, by means of dogs, guns, or nets. Yet a party of gentlemen who should have known better, a Mr William Wall of Rook in Worcestershire, a gentleman with preten-sions to long descent, a Mr Rowland Harnage of Kinlet, in Shropshire, and a Mr Gerald Lawley of the same, with others, 'being all of them men of barbarous and uncivil disposition', met together after dark at an alehouse at Sousnet in the parish of Mamble which stood where the roads from Rook and Kinlet join the Tenbury road—'. . . and there being so met together did conspire and combine themselves to hunt Deer, that night following, in your subject's said Park, and . . . to the intent that they would not be hindered but would have full and free passage and progress in their said purpose and designs, they armed and arrayed themselves with guns, fowling pieces, crossbows, swords, rapiers, dag-gers, falchions, pyke staves and such like weapons, as well invasive as defensive. . . .'

It was not hunting; it was butchery. The appeal described how they 'did ride amongst the deer, then in the said Park feeding', with greyhounds trained to leap and pull down the wounded creatures, and 'with the said greyhounds then and there did kill, take, and destroy divers and sundry of the said deer, not respecting whether they were deer in season or out of season. . . .'

Sir Thomas's feelings were exacerbated by the unnecessary brutality with which his deer had been hacked to death, and by the insolence of the marauders in 'giving out that they would come again, at their pleasure, come and hunt in your subject's said park, in despite of your subject's keepers'. Which they did, more than once during that summer of 1609, with perhaps some connivance from the servants at Sutton.

The phraseology of the appeal is not Sir Thomas's style at all, but the bitterness underlying it is that of a young man whose position and authority have been mocked at.

At the beginning of the century Sir Charles Percy had written from remote Dumbleton in Gloucestershire to Dudley Carleton in London:

I am so pestered with country business that I cannot come to London. If I stay here long in this fashion you will find me so dull that I shall be taken for Justice Silence or Justice Shallow; therefore take pity on me, and send me news from time to time, the knowledge of which, though perhaps it will not exempt me from the opinion of a Justice Shallow in London, yet will make me pass for a very sufficient gentleman in Gloucestershire.*

Justice Shallow had caught the public's veering fancy. The little Justice's futile threat that he would make a Star Chamber matter of the stealing of his deer was the popular catch-phrase at the turn of the century. The third Sir Thomas has this alone in common with Shakespeare's Justice—that he actually made a Star Chamber matter of a ruffianly escapade. Whether he received satisfaction is not known. Otherwise the tall, quiet, responsible youth of bookish tastes, whose behaviour at Oxford and at Lincoln's Inn had never verged on wildness, is more like the enigmatic Silence, who speaks but rarely and always to the point. If this Star Chamber matter had happened twenty years earlier, in his grandfather's time, the Lucy-Shallow contention would have ample proof.†

He now bent his energies to the real business of a country gentleman, that of local government. Justices of the Peace have been called 'the backbone of county officialdom', but their duties evade definition. They were the instruments of the central government at Westminster, but they brought to their task a lively individuality which frequently baulked the policies of the Privy Council and the Exchequer. They were almost always drawn from the landed gentry, and as such had inherited notions of privilege. They carried out their orders, but interpreted them in their own way.

Poor relief, the mending of highways, the repair of bridges, indictments of recusancy, not always applied to Catholics (itemized as failure to attend church, refusal to receive the Sacrament, and the uttering in public of subversive sentiments), punishment of vagrancy, drunkenness, assault, adultery, and poaching, were all part of the work of the Justices, who must have been kept busy. 'Nuisances' that are always cropping up in the reports of the Quarter Sessions of this time could mean a variety of things, as, for instance, keepers of disorderly inns, night-walkers (persons who, having no means of subsistence, 'sleep by day and walk abroad by night'), obstruction of the highway by fallen trees, or the fouling of rivers by soaking hides, hemp, and flax, in them. This last recurs continually in the court rolls of the manors of Charlecote and Bishop's Hampton for the years 1626 to 1646.

The manorial court of frankpledge,* which had survived intact in its medieval form, was presided over by Sir Thomas Lucy's bailiff, James Prescott, a trusted servant who was to be one of the overseers of his will. Offenders were presented and judged. From the court's knowlege of their circumstances it was ordered that they should mend their ways, and individually or collectively pay for damage done. 'Every man shall keep his trenches in the tenant's field scoured by All Hallows Day that the water may pass [flooding was a perpetual threat to early crops and young animals]—for every default 5s.' Charlecote was presented for a fine of 12d. for being without a 'Dookestoole, a pillorie and a tumbril',

---

* At which each member of the manorial community was answerable for the good conduct of, or the damage done by, its other members.

and for 8*d*. for the archery butts being in need of repair.
Fines up to 2*s*. 6*d*. were imposed for allowing bows and
arrows to spoil by disuse, and for not practising archery,
'according to the Statute'. But watering of hemp and flax is
by far the commonest offence, followed closely by such
breaches of the manorial economy as allowing beasts to
wander in the lanes and streets, assaulting the hayward when
he impounded stray cattle, or taking dogs into a field where
the sheep were being penned. These were the day-to-day
backslidings of a village community. This system patched
up with a minimum of trouble a lot of minor breaches of the
peace; only the serious offences—murder, rape, robbery
with violence—were sent on to Quarter Sessions.

In November 1632 Sir George Gresley wrote from London
to Sir Thomas Puckering in Warwickshire: 'That Sir Thomas
Lucy is your new Sheriff will, I conceive, be no news to
you. . . .'

The Quarter Sessions were held in the ruinous old Shire
Hall at Warwick, which was partly used as a most unsavoury
gaol. It was Sir Thomas's privilege as High Sheriff to pay
for these gentlemen's entertainment during the week of the
Sessions (a later Sheriff refused absolutely to foot the bill,
and after that the county funds had to produce the money to
pay for the entertainments at the Great Swan at Warwick,
the Red Lion at Kenilworth, and the Bear at Henley-in-
Arden).

He went back after this to being a Justice. He had already
sat in the Parliament of 1614, the Addled Parliament, that
only lasted a year; and in that of 1621, at which Bacon was
impeached and deprived of the Great Seal achieved after a
lifetime of frustration and disappointment, and at which the
Commons protested their right to freedom of speech.

James I died in the early spring of 1625, saying that when
he was dead 'they should have more wars than they knew
how to manage'. It had been on the whole a good reign.
Peace with Spain had been precariously maintained, embroil-
ment in the imbecility of the Thirty Years' War avoided,
poetry and the theatre had been nurtured. James had detested
intolerance, having had bitter experience of it in youth, and

thought nothing was ever gained for good by violence. In spite of the grotesqueness of his appearance and habits, and his liking for playing the pedagogue to foolish young men, he commands respect. London gave him a superb funeral (designed by Inigo Jones) in pouring rain, after which an outbreak of the plague emptied the city and the new King's coronation had to be put off until the following year.

Thomas did not live to see the outbreak of civil war, but all straws were blowing in one direction. The tolerance of James I, of which the worst result had been laxity of behaviour at Court, was replaced by an inflexible idealism. James had thought he could redress the balance of religious difference by lightening the strictures on Catholics. He instinctively feared the principle of 'strenuous liberty' of thought, containing (though he could not know it) the germ of democracy, and from the point of view of a Renaissance ruler he was right.

If Thomas Lucy sat, as has been claimed for him, in the Parliament of 1628–9, he heard during a morning session of the House (the afternoons were given up to committee work) a short, halting speech, delivered in country accents, by a Huntingdonshire member, one Oliver Cromwell. He must have observed the changing temper of the House; seen the mounting of emotion to the crest of hysteria when members overturned their chairs in their haste to hold the Speaker down on his, that he might not rise to adjourn the House before a resolution was passed that they who make innovations in religion, or exact subsidies not granted by Parliament, are the enemies of the Kingdom. It was open defiance. But the skies did not fall; not that time. Thomas Lucy went back to Warwickshire to the duties of the Bench.

Life went on much as usual for the next six or seven years. The Huntingdonshire farmer, now Parliament had been indefinitely prorogued, was back among his domestic concerns.

But Charles, whose narrow skull housed a brain incapable of compromise, was moving with caution but with implacable singlemindedness toward absolute monarchy. At a meeting of the Star Chamber in 1636 where the judges

unwillingly gave it as their opinion that a King without a
Parliament could do pretty well what he liked in the matter
of ship-money,* he found himself in such good humour
that he merely sentenced a Sir William Russell to the mild
deterrent of the Fleet for opposing a scheme to make the
River Avon navigable through those parts of the counties of
Warwick, Gloucestershire, and Worcestershire whose roads
were impassable to carts in bad weather. It was a good
scheme, and most people concerned, like Sir Thomas Lucy,
had supported it. It was abandoned when in 1639 orders
were sent down from London for a mustering of men to
accompany the King to Scotland, to coerce his northern
subjects to obedience.

Scotland had startlingly taken a stand. The King and
Archbishop Laud had overreached themselves, and the
country, always disparagingly thought of by the comfortable
squires of the midlands as barbarous and irreclaimable, had
shown itself strong for the Faith. It was a shock to the
middle-of-the-road Puritans.

In April of that year Thomas Lucy was again a Deputy
Lieutenant with Sir Thomas Leigh, Sir Thomas Holt, and
William Boughton, with orders to press two hundred and
thirty men and equip them to join the King's army at Selby
in Yorkshire.

The Justices dispatched their business, without lingering
to exchange local news, when they met for the Trinity
Quarter Sessions of 1640, where Sir Thomas was in trouble
for having failed to repair a muddy lane running north from
Fulbroke toward Stratford. (Once in a way someone new to
the neighbourhood tried to take a horse and cart along it,
and complained about its condition. It was part of the estate
of Fulbroke, which had not turned out to be a profitable
investment.)

---

* Charles revived an ancient tax levied on ports and maritime counties for
defence of the country in time of war, and extended it to the inland counties.
Charlecote had been part of the ship-soke of Kington when Henry II had done
the same. There had been a lot of trouble in Warwickshire over ship-money,
the towns pleading poverty and petitioning that their trade had fallen off.
There were vehement protests against the assessment and the Sheriff's men
could not persuade people to pay.

Division was in the air; Fulke Brooke at Warwick had refused to obey His Majesty's behest that he render to the King the knight-service which the Crown had always counted on from the owner of Warwick Castle,* but Lord Northampton at Compton Wynyates, who had accompanied Charles, when Prince of Wales, to Spain, had raised a troop of horse. The Justices, no man knowing what was in the other's mind, avoiding each other's glances, gave brief goodbyes and rode their several ways home.

Two of the Lucy children, Margaret and William, were already gone; the last born, Theophila, died aged six in 1638. The death of this child was the more poignant because the clouds of dissension threatening the coming storm tightened the bonds of family tenderness. Sir Thomas spent more time alone in his library and was indeed seldom seen without a book in his hand. He rode alone to Hunscot, to Thelesford, across the ford to Hampton, toward Fulbroke and Sher-bourne. He wrote to his two eldest sons, now travelling abroad, and received newsletters from John Pory in London. It was a longer ride to visit the Hales at Snitterfield, but he liked to go there, particularly if John Hales from Coventry was making them a visit. Sometimes his brother William, who had been chaplain to the Duke of Buckingham, and was now the incumbent of Highclere, came to stay and they sat up late over books, for William was a book lover, too.

A much-admired preacher, Robert Harris, Vicar of Han-well in Oxfordshire, later President of Trinity, Oxford, was a frequent guest; so were Sir Henry Goodyer from Poles-worth, the nephew of Drayton's early patron, and Sir Greville Verney, a kinsman with antiquarian interests from Compton Verney.

I like to think his library was in an upstairs room and looked out on to the stable yard, where, by glancing up from the printed page, he could see The Hobby or Mignon

---

* The title of Warwick had died with Ambrose Dudley. It was revived by James I for Robert Rich, already possessed of estates in Essex where he preferred to live. James presented the Castle to Sir Fulke Greville, Lord Brooke, whose descendants lived there until, at the failure of the Rich male line, the title was revived in their favour.

being lunged in the flat meadow by the Wellesbourne brook
that formed the boundary of the park. In March 1640 he
received a command from the Privy Council to go to
London. His answer is addressed to Secretary Vane* and
runs:

. . . The truth is for this ten weeks I have been so indisposed that I
have scarcely peeped out of my chamber, and a short journey of
four miles on Monday last to Warwick completely distempered
me, so that I find, without much danger, I shall not be able to
endure so long a journey. I pray you, therefore, if occasion be
offered, to move the Board that I may be dispensed with until I
may undertake the journey with probable safety; but if I must
come, it is fit, though I had a hundred lives, I should hazard them
all to testify my obedience.

In September he had begun to fail. There is a letter to him
among the Lucy archives from his physicians, Samuel Pawe
and William Lapworth, giving him some simple rules of
health to follow, with exhortations to keep up his spirits:

Keep up a good diet, make choice of such things as are of easy
digestion and breed good blood, such as mutton, chickens, partridges, quails, new-laid eggs, and broths, caudles, and such like.
Exercise yourself daily and that moderately, for so will you make
up natural heat to the furthering of condition, without puffing
yourself to breathlessness.

Banish all passions of the mind, let not your meditations be too
long bent upon one subject. Labour to be cheerful. . . .

Loss of appetite and heaviness of mind had long troubled
him. The times were not conducive to cheerfulness. When
this was written the King's army was moving northward.
The germ of estrangement was in every family; cheerfulness
at this time was 'in inverse proportion to a man's intellectual
stature'.†
Following the doctors' advice, he rode out every day. He
was interested in medicine, had studied the curative powers

* Sir Henry Vane, Treasurer of the Household and later Secretary of State.
Calendared State Papers Domestic, 1639–1640.
† John Buchan: *Oliver Cromwell.*

of herbs, and was in the habit of doctoring his servants when they fell ill. But one day early in December, when frost had put iron in the ground, his horse stumbled with him. He was found lying where he had fallen, and taken up to his chamber, where, according to the Charlecote Register, he died, conscious to the last and welcoming his end—*'placide dormivit in Christo'*—on the tenth day of December 1640. He was, if we are to believe his epitaph, aged fifty-six, and looked much less.

Robert Harris hurried over from Hanwell to deliver a funeral oration, later published under the title *Abner's funeral*, unreadable now, though no doubt it was perfectly lucid to his hearers. His delivery was at times impeded by his grief: '. . . Certainly if greatness of wit, of learning, of spirit, of riches, of friends, of allies; if greatness of care in servants, of attendance in yoke-fellows, of skill in physicians, of affection in all, would have kept off Death—we had not been thus overcast and clouded this day. But no outward greatness will do it. Death knows no measures, no degrees, no differences, but sweeps away all. This noble gentleman is gone from us. But he lives in his posterity. Charlecote is Charlecote still'— thus he rambled on.

Not all the family were present to hear it, for the two eldest boys, Spencer and Robert, were on their way home from beyond the seas. But the sorrowing widow was there, with Richard, Thomas, and Fulke, Constance, now Lady Spencer (she had married her cousin, Sir William Spencer of Yarnton in Oxfordshire), little Bridget, Robert's twin (who had married a Staffordshire squire, Bryan Broughton), Mary, Ann, Elizabeth, and Alice—as yet unmarried.*

Behind the hearse was led his grey Barbary ambling horse,† which he loved dearly and had been riding on the day of his fatal fall. It was a safe ride if the rider were not a

---

* Mary married Sir Matthew Herbert, Alice, Sir William Underhill of Idlicote, and Elizabeth, Sir John Walcot.
† 'The word "amble" did not then, as now, denote a slow and easy trot. It was an artificial pace. . . . Some horses took more naturally to this pace than others, notably your Irish hobby, which was therefore in much request for an "ambling gelding".' Madden: *The Diary of Master William Silence.*

sick man, and he left it to his brother William, as being suitable in every way for a clergyman's needs. His brother Francis got his 'little roan ambling horse'. No one whom Sir Thomas had reason to love, or be grateful to, was over-looked in his will. One interesting point is that all the lands of Fulbroke outside the newly-empaled park are to be sold for annuities for old servants. The horses are scrupulously left where they will have good homes and be of value. The books go to his third son, Richard, of all the boys the one most like him, who was a Member of Parliament by this time and had sat on the Bench with his father in 1637. Spencer is to have the house at Highclere, and Robert all the household stuff from Sutton. The executors as well as his wife 'are my worthy kinsman, Mr John Hales,★ of the Priory in Coventry, and my approved and loving friend, Mr James Prescott' (his bailiff).

Alice Lucy, who had loved him all her life, gave way after his death to the ill-health she had quietly endured in conse-quence of thirteen babies and several miscarriages. She took to her bed and was looked after devotedly by an unmarried sister-in-law. A legend tenaciously held by the Lucys has it that she sent Jansen's two half-length portraits of herself and her husband to Rome for Bernini to make marble copies of them. This is a clear impossibility, as Bernini, the official sculptor of the Vatican, would never have been permitted by the Pope to undertake commissions of this sort; but it is thought possible that Bushnell, Schurman's pupil, who ran away from him to Rome to study under Bernini, may have had a hand in hers. The effigies were polished in Stone's workshop, and for two centuries shone white in the chancel of old Charlecote Church, where green mould was creeping up the walls, and where there was nothing to detract from the awesome effect of three generations of Lucys in life-sized effigy. When the church was rebuilt in 1856 the tombs were dragged out into the churchyard; exposed to frost and sunlight, their plinths got cracked, and details of the carving were chipped off. Reverently re-housed in a chapel of their

★ To whom he left a diamond ring.

own, they have never recovered their original impressiveness. But the monument raised by Alice Lucy is still immensely evocative of the third Sir Thomas.* Raised on one elbow, he looks sadly over her head where she lies a little below him in grateful resignation to sleep. In the two bays behind him are carved some shelves from his library with the Latin authors he particularly loved, and a book of songs called *Winters Ayres*; and in shallow relief, a foreshortened representation of himself riding his grey, ambling horse in a field with a barn in the background. Black marble pillars with Corinthian capitals carry a pediment with *memento mori*, and the scutcheon with the arms of Lucy impaled with the fretty coat of Spencer. His epitaph, probably from the pen of Dr Harris, who preached the funeral sermon, recites his long descent, his generous nature, his public service, his good governance of his household and family, his well-kept table where good men were ever welcome, but most especially those who were learned in theology and had drunk of the Muses.

The epitome of the seventeenth century's idea of a country gentleman of cultivated tastes, he leans on his elbow in the company of his loved edition of Horace's *De arte poetica* (still in the Charlecote library), and the music book of tunes he liked to have played to him. He is in armour, though in life he can seldom have worn it.

It is all in the key of gentle melancholy, like the Jansen portrait of the Puritan squire in a domestic setting: Hamlet, if he had lived to marry and settle down.

Recalling his years of public service, his grave pleasure in the talk of other men, his tenderness for horses, his love of the woods and fields round Charlecote, one thinks of those words of Falstaff's, spoken in a very different context: 'Good Master Silence, it well befits you should be of the Peace.'

* Mrs Esdaile says it is first in date and interest of its class of sepulchral monuments.

CHAPTER 5

The Uneasy Years

> Our Constitution is in actual operation; everything appears to promise that it will last; but in this world nothing is certain but death and taxes.
>
> Benjamin Franklin.

It was well for Sir Thomas that he died when he did, in the last years of the uneasy peace. The fact that he left Charlecote entailed on the heirs male of five younger sons in succession, but not on the heirs male of the eldest son Spencer, show that a rift had already occurred.★

Alice Lady Lucy was bedridden; she had her household in to her room on Sundays to hear the Scriptures expounded, thus keeping up the Puritan tradition of Bible-searching, which was such a source of uneasiness to the Established Church. She had been a happy wife and was a most disconsolate widow, the more so as she felt her children were being estranged from her and she could do nothing to prevent it. Like dry grass where a spark has fallen, the youth and ardour of the country flared up for the King. At this time of tension, when one supposes tempers were on edge and quarrels broke out continually, she could only use her authority to try to unite them in prayer.†

Spencer was with the King when the Royal Standard was raised at Nottingham in 1642. His second brother, Robert,

---

★ Spencer had married the daughter of a Court official, Mary Brett; after his death in 1649 she remarried one of the Catholic Sheldons of Broadway in Worcestershire.

† A life of her, written perhaps a hundred years later, by one Gibbons, says: 'Every day she reached out her hands to the needy . . . and gave charge to her porter at the gateway in the court that when any aged or poor came there, in those dismal times of our civil wars, that he should come and acquaint her that she might enlarge her charity. . . .'

must have decided to live at Sutton, as nothing more is heard of him. Richard, the third brother, bookish, serious, sandy-haired like his father, had the most Lucy in him. He succeeded his uncle, Francis Lucy,★ as Member for War-wick town in 1639, while his father was one of the Members for the county.

The two younger ones—Thomas and George—had gone on to the Inns, after matriculating from Queen's College, Oxford. They died in the King's service, but where or when is not recorded. Thomas married while he was lodging in the parish of St Martin's-in-the-Fields, studying law. His widow† made one of the sad little household at Charlecote during the war years.

In July of that fatal year of 1642, civil war on a small scale broke out in Warwick town, the rival deputy-lieutenants of both parties distributing ribbons for their followers to wear in their hats. Spencer Compton, Lord Northampton, encir-cled the Castle in the King's name; but its Puritan garrison hung out a Bible and a winding-sheet to indicate willingness to die in defence of Holy Writ. The falsifying of moral values began to be seen as early as this, and a struggle for political ascendancy was cloaked as a righteous war against profligacy in high places, though the King was, in fact, most moral, fastidious, and devout, far more puritanical in his private life than many who professed the Puritan creed.

In August of the same year there was a skirmish at Southam, too far off to affect Charlecote except by rumour. But in September the Parliament force passed by way of Barford and Aston Cantlow to Alcester. Charlecote's first sight of armed men marching with purpose was on this occasion, when the soldiers took the short cut across the ford by the house. The Avon was not as broad as it is now, and deep enough to be passable only at the ford below the

---

★ Francis was the sixth son of the second Sir Thomas and Constance Kingsmill. He had a fine house in College Place, Hammersmith—pulled down in 1770—and was buried, aged ninety, in 1697 in the vault of old Hammer-smith Church. He married Elizabeth Molesworth of Hoddesdon, Herts.
† She was Susan, daughter of Robert Dacres, Esq., of Hartingfordbury, Herts.

kitchen garden. In Spencer's day the Great Meadow that lay
westward across the water was partly cultivated, but a right
of way led across it through an avenue of trees, blown down
in the great storm of 1658 (the year Cromwell died), which
never grew thrivingly again.*

In October the King, coming from the Marches of Wales,
lodged at Sir Thomas Holt's great house, Aston, near
Birmingham, avoided Coventry, which was fervently for
Parliament, and pushed on to Edgecott overlooking the Vale
of the Red Horse, with the Parliamentary general Essex
closing in on him. The King's following had plumes and
bright scarves in plenty, but a shortage of serviceable arms.
The King had, besides his mounted gentry, 5,000 untrained,
unarmed Welshmen, who had joined in order to receive
boots and a coat apiece.

The battle that took place at Edgehill was the dress
rehearsal for the war, and, like most rehearsals, was chaotic.
Men lay out in the frosty fields all that night, and having
died of their wounds, were taken up frozen stiff, and buried
with difficulty, young Thomas and George Lucy† perhaps
among them. If the outcome of the battle was indecisive, it
was because the Ironsides, who were to win the war with
Bible phrases on their lips and religious fervour in their
hearts, had not yet been created to match the young chivalry
that Charles could command.

After Edgehill, Rupert was much in Warwickshire, thun-
dering about in all directions, keeping open the roads from
Oxford, to which the King had removed his Court, and the
north. The summer of 1643 also saw Queen Henrietta Maria
in Warwickshire; she had sold her jewels in Holland to
provide soldiers, and rode from King's Norton to Stratford
at the head of thirty companies of horse, 3,000 foot soldiers,
and 150 baggage wagons, and lodged at Shakespeare's New

---

* About this time the Great Meadow was given the name of the Camp
ground, because they army encamped there for the night.
† A George Lucy entered in the Burial Register for Charlecote in 1646 was a
son of the second Sir Thomas and scholar of Gray's Inn in 1609. According to
Burke he died in France. He is not to be confused with the George who died
for the King.

Place. Westward from Charlecote's turret windows could be seen the glinting of her marching army. The King rode over from Oxford and the pair were united at Kineton with much joy, the little 'Generalissima', in a great plumed hat like a soldier's, happy in the belief that she was bringing her husband reinforcements to win the war. (Her portrait hangs above the library fireplace at Charlecote, a rose in her hand; the painting was a favourite of the King's, who gave it to one of her body-women after he had sent her back to France and safety. It did not come to Charlecote till long after the reverberations of the vexed, uneasy years had died away.)

Spencer went with the King to Oxford, for, according to Anthony à Wood, he took his degree as Doctor of Medicine there in the November of that year, 1642. The three-year sojourn of the Court at Oxford turned the University into a combination of arsenal and sophisticated resort. Most of the undergraduates were sent away, but many joined the garrison and helped the Court ladies to enjoy their enforced *villeggiatura*.

There is at Charlecote, in good preservation, a pass issued to Richard Lucy, as Member of Parliament for the town of Warwick, by the Parliamentary general, Sir William Waller: 'To all officers and soldiers to whomsoever it may come', directing that the bearer is to be allowed free unquestioned access to the town of Warwick 'on his necessary occasions'.

Coming from London, Richard could bring the Charlecote household news of the way the war was going. Unhappy and divided households were common all over England. A sort of stricture had fallen on the county, as may be seen in the reports of the Warwickshire Quarter Sessions. For three years the Sessions were suspended. Two elderly Justices, Sir Thomas Holt and John Lisle, made a brave attempt to uphold the dignity of their office, arriving as usual at the Shire Hall at Warwick for the Michaelmas Session of 1642, but their voices were drowned by the din of 800 Parliament soldiers under Lord Rochfort, who entered the town soon after them, and when they adjourned to the Swan they found it swarming with soldiers and were obliged to retire hurriedly. Sir Thomas Holt was over seventy and had been a JP for

Warwickshire for seventeen years. By 1644 new Justices of
Parliamentary sympathies had been commissioned, Richard
Lucy among them, but Quarter Sessions were not held again
till 1645. Many of the Justices had no strong political feelings,
but most cared about their work, which went quietly on,
even though the Sessions were suspended, the poor or
impotent dependants of soldiers, serving, wounded, or
killed, being added to the liabilities that every community
carried.

There was much minor skirmishing in Warwickshire
through 1645 and the year following. Later the fighting
veered north and east. By order of Parliament, one arch of
Clopton Bridge at Stratford was broken down in order to
cut communications between Oxford and the west. At
Hampton Lucy, across the river from Charlecote, a volume
of baptismal registers begins with the words: 'the note of
those yt. were bapt. 1646 was torne by the souldiers'.
Caesar's Tower and the outer walls of Kenilworth were
destroyed—the castle had withstood too many sieges. Lady
Spencer's house at Wormleighton was burnt.

Charlecote might have shared its fate but for Richard's
position as MP for the county town, and the fact that,
probably by his advice, Spencer compounded with Parliament for his estates. How much he paid is not known.
Fortunately, they had influential connexions, the rather
remote kinship with Fiennes (now Saye) of Broughton
Castle, and the more recent connexion with the Northamptonshire Knightleys. The third Sir Thomas's sister, Bridget,
who had married Sir Richard Knightley of Fawsley, the
friend of Pym and Hampden, had had no children and had
lost her husband in 1639.* The division of the times preyed
on her mind and she lost her reason. The property went
away to a cousin, a young man of twenty-two who had
married John Hampden's daughter. He and Richard Lucy
must have been very nearly of an age and had studied the

---

* By an inquest taken at Daventry 27 March 1640, it was found that she
(Bridget, his wife) was a lunatic enjoying lucid intervals, and that her next heir
was her brother, Sir Thomas Lucy.

law at Gray's Inn together. The Knightleys had always been stirring and militant Puritans. From a printing press at Fawsley had been secretly issued the 'Martin Marprelate' tracts aimed at the Protestant bishops of Elizabeth's reign. The Knightley of that day suffered heavy fines for being an over-zealous Puritan. He had married Mary Fermor of Easton Neston, niece by marriage to William Lucy, so the kinship between Lucys and Knightleys went back four generations.

In the State Papers Domestic for 29 August 1648 the following appears: 'We are informed that there are near 200 horse listed in your county against the Parliament by Sir Joseph Wagstaffe, the which are now lying about Mr Spencer Lucie's house. We desire you to inquire into this business and to secure all persons, horses and arms so listed [enlisted] and to apprehend Sir Joseph Wagstaffe if he be found in your county.' Wagstaffe was that interesting anomaly, a Parliament man turned Royalist; more often it was the other way about. The incident had no sequel, apparently; he was later involved in the abortive rising under Penruddock in Wiltshire in March 1655.

In 1648, while Alice Spencer lay dying in the Queen's Chamber where Queen Elizabeth had slept, the stableyard was full of activity and every stall occupied. All over the park were knots of men and grazing horses. The gatehouse arch was filled in with hurdles, the cobbles of the court sprouted grass, while soldiers lounged, spitting and smoking, at the back door. Alice died that August, and her body, with Spencer and a few old servants as sole mourners, was carried along the avenue of half-grown trees that the first Sir Thomas had planted. Spencer's death, a year after his mother's, closes the melancholy chapter.

Robert inherited and moved in from Sutton, but it seems that Richard came to live at Charlecote at the same time. From Justice of the Peace he became High Sheriff in 1647, and Member for the County the year following.

The last of Sir Thomas's daughters, Alice, had married a neighbour, William Underhill, the squire of Idlicote. She left to Charlecote a portrait of her scowling husband in dark

armour with a cravat of Venice point; he was knighted at the
Restoration. He had served under Spencer Compton in the
war and received recognition for it. But he was a quarrel-
some fellow and nearly lost his family property through
wounding a Justice in a quarrel. He and Alice had two sons
called Hercules and Compton. Their grandson, Samuel
Underhill, sold Idlicote, from which the first Sir Thomas
Lucy had hunted out Catholic recusants.*

Through these unhappy times there were only sober,
childless people living at Charlecote. Half the windows were
kept shuttered, no cheerful noise and activity filled the stable
yard; smoke rose from but a dozen of its forty-two hearths.
The grand lavish days when all and sundry were welcome at
the master of Charlecote's table were of the past. The table
itself, hewn from one great tree, across which Joyce Lucy
had quarrelled with her son-in-law, was little used. There
was very little entertaining now, unless the Fawsley or
Claverdon kinsfolk came, or Sir Simon Archer, that good
man and scholar, or Clement Throckmorton from Hasely,
or Sir Stephen Hales from Snitterfield, John Hales's
grandson.

In many families the harassments and strictures of the war
years bred up a strong, self-reliant generation, determined
that never in their lives would they again be hungry and
afraid, or have to truckle to masters they despised. But it
cannot be said that the religious or political convictions of
the Lucys vividly coloured their lives. With long, sandy curls
falling over a collar of transparent lawn, Richard is portrayed
toying with his gloves and an open book. The globe beside
him and an antique bust on a shelf show that, like his father,
he had intellectual interests; perhaps they were a consolation
to him. He had a number of sickly children by Elizabeth, the
daughter of a Puritan squire, John Urrey, of Thorley in the
Isle of Wight. Behind him are engraved the words, DEUS

---

* Samuel bequeathed in 1762 to his cousin, George Lucy of Charlecote, 'all
my family pictures if he will accept of them'. Alice Lucy took away with her
when she married the half-length Jansen portraits of the third Sir Thomas and
Alice Spencer. These came back to Charlecote at the end of the eighteenth
century through another Underhill marriage.

NOBIS HAEC OTIA FECIT, that have the melancholy finality of an epitaph.

He was again Member for Warwickshire in 1648. The Scots had been heavily defeated at Preston by Cromwell, prisoners were pouring into London, and a sub-committee of the House had to be hurriedly formed to deal with them. Those who had taken arms for the King under duress were to be released on oath never to fight again against England; the rest were shipped across to Virginia and the West Indian islands. The defeat of Preston was the end of the King's party; all Royalists knew it in their hearts.

All through that autumn the terms of surrender were presented and parried; the King played for time and argued skilfully, as always oblivious of his extreme danger. This fencing with words but delayed the inevitable end, though Charles in his isolation of spirit seemed unable to perceive it. Even blundering Rupert, who had offended soldiers of greater reputation than himself by his Germanic tactlessness and impulsiveness, had begged his uncle to finish the war and come to terms with the Army, now the uppermost power in the land. To Carisbrooke, to which Charles was taken, messengers went with terms from the Army's commanders, terms that a man less hopelessly divorced from reality than Charles was would have accepted. But the King imagined he could wear out his enemies by playing them off against each other, the Army against the Parliament and the Scots against both, until at last in the first week of a particularly inclement December he was taken forcibly from the Isle of Wight and conveyed to a melancholy block-house at Hurst in Hampshire, overlooking the bleak Solent—but no bleaker than the thoughts that must have crowded in on him.

It was urged by some that the King's latest proposals should be considered, or at least reviewed. The Commons saw with dismay the prospect of military dictatorship following on the heels of regicide. To many of them the high-handedness of the seizure of the King's person without Parliament's knowledge, and the relentless speed at which events were being pushed on, were a threat to the future of English liberty.

Fairfax entered London on 2 December with his soldiers and made Whitehall his headquarters. It was a Saturday, and no business was done that day or the next. But on the Monday the House began to debate the King's answers, and continued all through the night and the day following. Nerved by anger at the unwelcome presence of an occupying army in London, which, though silent and orderly, was to be felt everywhere, Parliament voted that the King's concessions, inadequate as they were, were yet a possible foundation for the settlement of the kingdom. On this the House adjourned. Next morning, when it reassembled, Colonel Pride with a regiment of musketeers had surrounded St Stephen's Hall. From a list given him of the Members, more than a hundred—all those who had voted to continue negotiations with the King—were prevented from entering the House, and turned back, but about forty broke through, Richard Lucy among them, with his kinsmen, Richard Knightley and Nathaniel Fiennes. Force but not violence was used; the forty recalcitrant Members were sent to an underground tavern below the old Exchequer Chamber, known as Hell.

The scared remnant, or 'rump', who were allowed to take their seats at once tried to have their friends released, but the officers in charge ignored their protests. An extremely uncomfortable night was passed by the prisoners, with only benches to sleep on. On the 7th they were taken from Hell Tavern to cool their anger in an icy corridor of Whitehall, but Fairfax refused to see them. He was only acting under orders. They were no responsibility of his.

After nearly two weeks of discomfort and uncertainty, the forty Members were released, giving their parole not to attempt to return to the House. A pamphlet was later published containing the story—Richard Lucy contributed to it with the rest—protesting that all the transactions of the puppet Government were void from the date of the purge.*

---

* *A True and Full Relation.*

Christmas passed, one of the coldest in living memory, and the days wore on to 30 January, when a murmuring crowd pressed against the ranks of pikemen posted round the scaffold, and sent up a deep groan of revulsion as the royal head fell.

Richard returned to Charlecote after his rough handling and is not heard of again for four years. He does not appear to have attended the Quarter Sessions after this.

The Rump, or remnant, of Parliament that remained after Pride's Purge obediently passed resolutions to the effect that government by a king or a single person was unnecessary, burdensome, and dangerous. In the year that saw Charles I beheaded, the Commonwealth was proclaimed, but the improvised Constitution had no roots either in tradition or in the confidence of the people.

Cromwell, after his subjugation of Ireland, took over the command of the war in Scotland from Fairfax. At Dunbar in 1650 the Scots were broken. The young Prince Charles was crowned King of Great Britain and Ireland at Scone on New Year's Day, 1651, and marched into England in the August of that year, Cromwell pursuing. With such a general in the field against him, the prince was not looked on as a serious menace by the Government at Westminster, whose attention was bent on its own internal dissensions. He was not a serious menace; from Worcester, where his army turned to engage Cromwell's and was heavily defeated, he fled and cut off his long hair and rubbed soot into his cheeks, thinking disguise no disgrace. Roughly dressed, he mingled with servants, but over and over again his great height and swarthiness were half-recognized, and his friends had to hurry him on. It was thought that it might be possible to charter a ship from Bristol to take him to France, to his mother. A young lady of the Staffordshire family of Lane of King's Bentley, of whom we shall hear more later, whose brother had been a Colonel in Charles's army, rode pillion behind the King, whom she addressed as William Jackson, and by her courage and common sense she steered the little party between panic and over-confidence. They came by way of Bromsgrove, where the King's horse cast a shoe, through the outskirts of Arden to Snitterfield, where they took to a muddy lane diving between brambly banks, to avoid a party of soldiers rumoured to be out on the Stratford road. King's Lane, as it has ever since been known, crossed the further boundary of the parish of Hampton Lucy.

After many alarms and changes of plan, young Charles was got out of England. The country in its gratitude voted Cromwell a large income and royal Hampton Court for his country house. Had he pressed for it, he could have been King.

The Rump Parliament was made up mainly of lawyers who battened on the ruined Royalist society with the broking of confiscated estates and pardons. It was recognized that representation must be cast in a new mould. A Bill framed by the Rump Parliament for an entirely reformed House of Commons with arbitrary powers, moved Cromwell to take action. He hurried down to St Stephen's and stood before the Members, his hat pulled down over his brow to show his contempt of them. He roundly accused them of corruption, of obstruction, of fraud and profiteering, and, finally, called soldiers into the Chamber to drive them out. The draft of the new Bill was lying on the table; he crumpled it up and saw the place emptied before having the doors locked. After dark someone came and scribbled on the doors the words: 'This House to be let unfurnished.'

For the second time Parliament had been mocked by violence, instead of being allowed to meander to its logical end. Cromwell's remedy was a Parliament of nominees, men chosen as being of proved integrity by the independent churches of the realm. Among the 139 Members picked by the Council of State was Richard Lucy.

In June 1653 the mandate came that he had been waiting for, while living quietly at Charlecote; it is still in the same condition in which it arrived (as if, once read, it was quickly put aside in a safe place, like something inflammable): 'Forasmuch as upon the dissolution of the late Parliament it became necessary that the peace, safety, and good government of this Common-wealth should be provided for: and in order thereunto, diverse persons fearing God and of approved fidelity and honesty, are by myself with the advice of my Council of Officers, nominated, to whom the great charge and trust of so weighty affairs is to be committed. . . .' The dread associations with the name of Cromwell had not been softened by the events that had followed the execution of Charles. Like a muffled drum-beat, it rolls on: 'I, Oliver Cromwell, Capt. General and Commander in Chief of all the Armies and Forces raised and to be raised within this Common-wealth, do hereby summon and require you, Richard Lucy Esq. (being one of the persons nominated) personally to be and appear at the Council Chamber . . . and hereof you are not to fail. Given under my hand and seal, the sixth day of June, 1653. O. Cromwell.'

So much had happened since Pride's Purge that the indignity of it was almost forgotten; still no doubt it was with a certain uneasiness and stiffness that Richard resumed his place in St Stephen's as a member of the Barebones Parliament (called after one of its members, who bore that unfortunate name of ridicule). The other Knights of the Shire who sat for Warwick were Thomas Willoughby, Sir Richard Temple, Bt, and the regicide Colonel Purefoy of Cawcot, whom the Warwickshire Bench knew as an active Parliament man—he was later one of Cromwell's Council of State.

There had been too many sharp-practising lawyers in the Rump Parliament; but the 139 Members of the 'Little' Parliament replaced legal training with theory, and played havoc with established laws. Cromwell now found himself more troubled with a parliament of fools than of knaves. But for the sake of the Constitution, some rags of prestige must be allowed to clothe it, there could not be a repetition of the dissolution of the Rump. In a few weeks the present House had romped through more reforms than the sober Long Parliament would have attempted in a year. As a landowner, Richard Lucy heard with alarm that tithes and Church patronage were to be abolished. Disestablishment was carried by a majority of two, against loud protests. The moderates, like himself, cast about for some means of avoiding political shipwreck.

Eighty of them, more than half the House, met on the

morning of 12 December at an earlier hour than that at which Parliament was accustomed to assemble. Quietly the Speaker led them out into the street, and citizens going about their morning chores were mildly surprised to see the grave, black-suited gentlemen pass up Whitehall to place their resignations in the Lord President's hands. The fanatic minority arrived at the usual hour to find the Chamber empty, and were dispersed by a small body of soldiers.

Richard stayed in London that winter and must have seen the Lord Protector ride unsmiling to the Guildhall and receive the sword at Temple Bar, watched by a curiously silent and apathetic crowd.

In his father's day the great officers of State had lived and entertained in splendid houses in Whitehall and along the river; the King lived in his palaces, and society fell into the natural, easy pattern of an accepted hierarchy. Now the great ones of the Commonwealth lived awkwardly in the palaces, in which their wives never felt really at ease. There was no society in the old sense. Richard's cousin by marriage, daughter-in-law of the baronet,★ was intimate with the ladies of the Commonwealth and could be amusing about their quarrels over precedence.

It is not known if Richard was reappointed an MP in the general redistribution of seats. His uncle, Sir Richard, sat as MP for Hertfordshire in 1656. Robert was married by now to Margaret Spencer,† whom he had been courting for five years, and a daughter—Bridget—was born in 1656. The Richard Lucys moved to Sutton, where they remained till Robert's sudden death four years later.‡

Robert's widow and her little girl stayed on at Charlecote. The Richard Lucys had lost two sons (both called after their father) and a daughter. The two remaining children, Thomas

---

★ Sir Richard Lucy, who married Elizabeth, daughter of Sir Henry Cocks and widow of Sir Robert Oxenbridge. Their son was called Kingsmill after his grandmother, Constance Lucy's, family, and inherited part of the Hampshire properties. He married Theophila, daughter of the 8th Lord Berkeley.
† Of Ufton, Warwick.
‡ Richard was back on the Bench in 1658, in virtue of his having succeeded to Charlecote.

and Constance, and their cousin Bridget woke the echoes of Richard's childhood, when there had been twelve of them to fill up the big table, with as many dogs scrapping underneath it, and a couple of hawks drowsing by the hearth as well. The only rules of that happy home had been the simple rules of behaviour—no shooting with catapults indoors, courtesy to guests, silence in the presence of elders. Books were not to be taken out of their shelves without permission, but were readily shown and explained by their father and pored over for hours by Spencer, who was interested in medicine, and Richard, who read greedily everthing that came his way.

At their father's death the library had become his. He must sometimes have fingered the *Orbis Terrarum* with regret. Life, which had seemed to be opening out with such promise when he first sat on the Bench with his father and was returned to Parliament with him, had gone grey. His mother's death had been hastened by Spencer's estrangement. Thomas and George lay in unnamed graves. Now that Robert was gone, Richard's horizon had narrowed down to that of a country landlord revolving round the Quarter Sessions. At Oxford and at the Inns his contemporaries had talked lightly of seeking political and religious freedom across the Atlantic in Raleigh's colonies of Virginia and New England. There was a serious project for the building of a town in New England to be called Saybrook, jointly financed by Lord Saye and Lord Brooke, which should be not only an investment, but a retreat from the winter of their present discontents.* But Richard believed then that he had a future in politics at home. No one thought the war would last six months; when it had dragged on for six years, he knew in his heart that mild traditionalists like himself were wanted only to fill the back benches of a subservient House of Commons. He turned back to his books.

Into this sober atmosphere there blew occasionally a

---

* Richard's brief will, in which he disposes to his only beloved son, Thomas, all of which he dies possessed in this country and in his Majesties Dominions 'wheresoever they lie', makes one think that he did take shares in one of the companies of merchant adventurers who were colonizing America in his youth.

reviving wind in the person of William Lucy, the Rector of Burghclere in Hampshire. After Oxford, where he took a BA degree at Trinity, he went for a year to Lincoln's Inn, at about the same time that his brother Thomas was settling down to squiredom in Warwickshire. Anthony à Wood thought he threw up the law from 'a desire of a sedate and academical life'. More likely he perceived that at the University there would be opportunities for the sort of polemical wrangling he most enjoyed. He nearly lost his chance of a Bachelorship of Divinity at Cambridge by a sermon he preached at Commencement in praise of the Dutch theologian, Arminius, so much favoured by Archbishop Laud. Arminianism, which aimed at a return to modified ritual as against the stripping by the extreme Dissenters of all the graces from the practice of religion, was the fashion among the educated younger clergy (William Lucy was twenty-eight and held the Kingsmill family livings of Highclere and Burghclere). Candles were coming back, and vestments, and even images of the saints, and the simple and fanatically minded saw it as the beginning of a return to Popish practices.

The King's intervention secured him his BD, and Sir Thomas from Warwickshire had to support it with a stately note to the University authorities pointing out that his brother, being descended from an ancient family of barons, came within the limits of a University Statute by which privy councillors, bishops, nobles, and their sons had the right to be admitted at once to a doctor's degree. It was stretching the truth rather far, but in the Lucy armorial roll the descent of the Charlecote line from the baronial house of Lucy of Cockermouth was plainly set out. King James had liked Sir Thomas and was friendly to Brother William, proposing him for a chaplaincy to the Duke of Buckingham and half-promising to get him made Master of his old college, Trinity, Oxford.*

---

* This went, however, to that astute opportunist, the Reverend Robert Harris, Vicar of Hanwell, who had preached the third Sir Thomas's funeral sermon.

During the Civil War years William had, as he says of himself, little leisure to steal from 'domestique troubles'. (He had ten children in all, and through him was founded the branch of the Lucys who established themselves in Somerset and Devon. Like his brother Thomas, he was a patriarch. After his generation there are no more such ancestors.) The uneasy years went by, bringing division into families and setting friends apart. William was a firm Royalist; during the years when he had been obliged to live quietly at Burghclere he had never concealed his loyalty. He wrote later of himself in a letter to Archbishop Sheldon: '. . . for my tenderness of that great cause wherein I have been both active and passive to my ability, I have so regarded it that I have given no office . . . to any who hath not actively or passively had an interest in it, nor any tenant that made me know his doing or suffering for it, hath paid me above five years' purchase for a lease of 21 years. . . .' (This was after his adherence had been rewarded with the See of St David's, whose cathedral was roofless.) During the enforced passivity of the years at Burghclere he occupied himself with writing a rambling treatise on 'The nature of a minister', dedicated 'to my ever most dear and now only brother, Francis Lucy', in the dedication of which he speaks with sadness of the times when 'there was a rebellion against virtue itself, and men's friendship was extirpate, root and branch: for the communication of friends scattered about the Kingdom was broken by the intercepting, yea, the betraying of letters, to the writer's prejudice. . . .'

With his habit of outspokenness, it is surprising that the Rector of Highclere kept his livings as long as he did; the hardships endured by the clergy during the Interregnum were pitiful, and William, a warm friend, stretched every penny as far as it would go to help his needy and persecuted brethren, and when his own means failed appealed, not in vain, to his nephew, Richard.

His pride was his library; but that was eventually taken (some of the books found their way to Charlecote) and the sequestration of his livings followed. There must have been for the William Lucys four anxious years. His father had left him some rents in Gloucestershire, part of Dorothea Arnold's dowry, so his family did not starve or go in rags, as many of the families of the sequestered clergy did. He had spirit left to confute the errors of 'Mr Hobbes his Leviathan' in a pamphlet published under the name of 'William Pike, Christophilus', a pun on the family coat of arms. It must have been with some relief that his nephew at Charlecote heard the news of the King's gracious intention to bestow a bishopric on his Uncle William. St David's was a long way off; there could be in the future very little coming and going between Abergwili, where the Bishop's palace was, and Charlecote. Yet the older generation had a gusto and a zest for a quarrel that had been bred out of Richard's wearier generation. The Bishop of St David's spent the remainder of his life at Brecon, where he restored the College. The snug, tight society of a county town suited Madam Lucy, born Martha Angell of Crowhurst in Sussex, and her daughters, who married Brecon worthies. The Bishop's descendants dissociated themselves from the Warwickshire line. The portraits of the Bishop and his wife, which their daughter-in-law left to Mr Vaughan of Trebarried, have disappeared. There came back to Charlecote only a small covered cup of silver gilt engraved with the Royal arms and those of Lucy, with the words, CAROL. IIND. REX. WIL. LUCY, EPIS. MENEVEN.* 1663. D.D.—the not too extravagant expression of a King's gratitude.

After Cromwell assumed the title of Lord Protector, a killing frost fell on England, draining the colour out of life. Sunday became a day of punishments. Any Sunday gathering, other than for the purpose of ordained prayer, was frowned on. Even to walk to the next parish to hear a sermon preached showed levity.

Charlecote church had always been more like a barn than a church; the little wooden bell tower was not added till the end of the seventeenth century, when it was given a painted

* Meneven was the ancient name of St David's.

ceiling as well.* At the time of the Interregnum it was
crudely whitewashed and a lock was put on the door to keep
out the village hens which wandered in from time to time.
In the chancel, where the hollows in the worn pavement
held water all through the winter, stood the three splendid
Lucy tombs, dimly visible by the little light that struggled in
through cobwebs. By order of Archbishop Laud, the Communion table had been placed at the east end of all churches,
where no one could place their hats or lean their elbows on
it.

After the service children walked sedately home beside
their parents, afraid to dart aside to snatch flowers from the
hedgerow. Cold meat was the Sunday fare, since a smoking
kitchen chimney might point to sinful plenty. Doors were
shut, the village street stood empty in the tempting Sabbath
noonday sunshine. Only the stump of the maypole
remained. Worse still, every man righteously informed about
his neighbours. William Tompson, an ale-house keeper in
Charlecote, was in trouble before the Bench for selling ale
without a licence to do so. The Bench was very busy just
then with the suppression of ale-houses, where men's
tongues could be dangerously unloosed, and which could
be, and often were, used as rendezvous by malcontents.

Richard's name appears more and more seldom among the
names of the active Justices.† Several times he was himself
presented by indignant neighbours for failing to repair flood-
gates which had become choked with osiers, and letting the
bridge over the Thelesford brook fall into decay. There was
now a highway to Warwick through Charlecote, but it
seems to have been nobody's business to keep it serviceable.
There was a long wrangle over Barford Bridge, which had
been broken down in the war to prevent the passage of
troops, until the county took over the responsibility for
mending it. The people of Hampton Lucy flatly refused to

---

* An entry in the Churchwarden's accounts for Charlecote for 1673 says:
'Paid for six yards and a quarter of silk and fringe for the cloth and for tassels
for the pulpit 15s 6d.'
† The Michaelmas Sessions of 1665 were, anyway, suspended on account of
the plague.

repair their footbridge over the Avon, which was always under water in the winter.

In 1660 Richard must have been a deputy-lieutenant, for he signed a warrant by which the arms of the late regicide, his fellow MP, Colonel Purefoy, were delivered to the Warwick armoury. The last recorded action of his life is the swearing-in at Michaelmas, 1670, of a new high-constable for the Hundred of Kington, the parties concerned obligingly coming 'to the house of Richard Lucy, esquire, situate in Charlecote between the hours of one and two o'clock in the afternoon' and the business was put through in the presence of two other JPs.

If Richard failed to attend the Quarter Sessions, it may have been because some infirmity took hold of him in his later years, though he was hardly into middle age. Now that much of the work of the ecclesiastical courts had fallen on the Bench, indictments were chiefly for dissent (non-conformists being most suspect as anti-monarchist), for disparagement of the Book of Common Prayer, failure to bring children to be baptized, profanation of the Sabbath, and so on, while the problem of unemployment appeared insoluble, the unemployable being moved on from parish to parish.

Richard's last appearance on the Bench was in the seventies. In 1675 he prosecuted some Hampton men for poaching two of his perch and a pike to the value of elevenpence. As the fish are described as being of the goods and chattels of Richard Lucy, Esq., they must have been lifted from the artificial fish-ponds in the Park. A session in the stocks would usually have been considered sufficient deterrent for such a small theft, but, like his father and his grandfather before him, the Squire of Charlecote could not forgive trespass. John Bottom, a poor labourer, was discharged, but John Dickens, a miller, and Robert Mason and John Stichbury, shoemakers, confessed to the crime, and were sentenced to be stripped from the waist upwards and to be openly whipped through the village of Hampton Lucy till their bodies were bloody.

Richard died at fifty-six, and for the last year of his life devoted himself to the pleasure of adding to his library. He had many of his uncle the Bishop's books in sober dark calf bindings, the eloquent sermons of Isaac Barrow, the *Animadversions* of Robert South, Rector of Islip in Oxfordshire, and others, and he added to them Archbishop Tillotson's *Rule of Faith*.

He added to his father's medical books that Spencer had liked to pore over, Wirzing's *General Practice of Physic*, Bartholin's *Anatomy*, and Venner's *Via recta ad vitam longam*. He bought, too, Casaubon's translation of Marcus Aurelius, and the first edition of Dugdale's great work on the families of Warwickshire which had brought the historian to Charlecote to study the parchment roll of the Lucy descent.

His sister-in-law, Robert's widow, had perceived that if she stayed buried at Charlecote the only hope of a marriage for the child Bridget would be with a county Justice, such as her cousin Constance had been matched with (the son of her father's lifelong friend, Robert Burgoyne of Wroxhall). Robert Lucy had been left Sutton outside the entail, and as he made no will it passed to his daughter. Richard had further settled £2,000 on the girl and given Robert's widow an annuity for herself of £800—she lived for fifty years after her first husband's death, on into the eighteenth century. Taking herself off to London with Bridget, she sought out the Kingsmill Lucy cousins, and in that milieu brought off a marriage for her daughter with a Catholic peer of a fairly recent creation, Thomas South, Lord Molyneux, whose father had been outlawed by Parliament for supporting the King.* More remarkable still, she achieved a brilliant second marriage for herself with another Catholic Royalist peer, Thomas, Lord Arundel of Wardour. (It is remarkable that in one generation two Lucy wives remarried Catholics.)

That year of 1677 saw the end of two generations of Lucy men; the Bishop died in October, and news of the death at barely fifty, of the youngest of the third Sir Thomas's sons, Fulke (too young to have been included in Cornelius Jansen's picture), who had married a Cheshire lady, been made a

---

* Bridget's great-grandson conformed to the established Church and was created Earl of Sefton.

knight and disappeared as completely from the Charlecote scene as if he had emigrated to the New World, had come earlier in the autumn.

It was now seven years since the afternoon in May when the little seaport of Dover had been shaken by cannon fire, and cheering crowds had pressed to the water's very edge to see their King come home again. He had knelt on the sand, the King who had blacked his face in order to ride unrecognized through Warwickshire, and given thanks for deliverance from exile. England was unaffectedly glad to see him; smiling faces met him at every turn. He permitted himself to remark with gentle irony that he wondered that he had delayed returning for so long, seeing he had so many loving friends. All seemed set fair for the new reign.

All over the world where English merchant adventurers had set foot and prospered, the Dutch had followed. The fierce commercial rivalry between the two countries now flared into hostility; the hearts of all men under forty leaped up at the prospect.

Charles II's new Navy was to take the brunt of the war. Mr Pepys heard the Duchess of Albemarle (Monck's wife) cry 'mightily out against the having of gentleman Captains with feathers and ribands, and wished the King would send her husband to sea with the old plain sea Captains, that he served with formerly, that would make their ships swim with blood, though they could not make legs [bow] as Captains now-a-days can'. These were the leathery men who had served under Blake in the first Dutch wars.

There were many idle and frivolous young men about the Court who wangled themselves commissions. In June 1667 Pepys writes again: 'The news is confirmed that the Dutch are off Harwich, but had done nothing last night. The King hath sent down my Lord of Oxford to raise the countries there. . . .' Later he speaks of Lord Berkeley, 'who is going down to Harwich also to look after the militia there: and there is also the Duke of Monmouth, and with him a great many young Hectors, the Lord Chesterfield, my Lord

Mandeville and others: but to little purpose, I fear, but to debauch the country-women thereabouts'.

Among the young men thus commissioned was Thomas, Richard's son, aged twenty-five. Through the influence of Lord Berkeley, whose sister, Theophila, it will be remembered, had married his cousin, Kingsmill Lucy, he was procured a captaincy under Aubrey de Vere, Lord Oxford.

He was at Harwich with the troops that guarded the coast from surprise invasion during Albemarle's and Prince Rupert's victorious four-day action against the Dutch at sea in July 1666.

In June of the year following, when Mr Pepys was sending his wife out of London and burying his gold in the garden on hearing that Dutch ships were coming up the Thames, Captain Thomas was with his troop of horse at Woolwich, where merchantmen were being scuttled in order to make the river unnavigable. The panic that spread through London died down. By July peace had been made, but the army was not immediately disbanded. Captain Thomas had himself painted by Kneller at about this time as large as life, booted and spurred, in a long, buff-coloured coat sashed with scarlet, with a fine lace cravat and ruffles. He looks out of the canvas with composure, holding his hat with a deep border of dark fur in one hand, his gloves and riding whip in the other. Beside him a black page holds his charger, while his troop is to be seen in the distance. The portrait is in the idiom of contemporary portraiture, but it marks a new epoch in Lucys. The military bearing, the black page, the air of command—here is worldliness made manifest. To partner it there is Kneller's companion piece of Captain Thomas's wife. Men, it is said, get the wives they deserve. Thomas's wife was a beauty, the daughter of a Berkshire gentleman, Robert Wheatley of Bracknell. She chose to be painted (looking very undressed indeed beside Alice Spencer in her close cartwheel ruff and Richard's wife Elizabeth in her modest lace tucker) in a loose gown of blue fringed with gold, a lily in the helpless hands that look as if they had never done any useful work, in an idealized garden by a cascade.

Captain Thomas came in to Charlecote in 1677 and lived only five years to enjoy it, being then in his late thirties, but during that time lived vigorously. He appears to have had a house in London, where his wife resided and where their one child, Elizabeth, was born. Charlecote was by now rather shabby; the number of hearths had diminished from forty-two to thirty-seven. Captain Thomas planned to plant vegetables where Alice Spencer had made box-bordered paths and alleys of pleached fruit-trees, and take in land on the north side of the court to make a formal water-garden according to the French and Dutch ideas now fashionable.

There should have been water to spare—in a wet February springs bubbled up everywhere out of the uneven, hillocky ground overgrown with thorn bushes that had been the first Sir Thomas's coney warren. There must have been some laughter from his fellow Justices at the Easter Quarter Sessions of 1682 when Captain Lucy was presented for stopping the current of the Avon at the two main arches of Barford bridge to make his water-gardens down at Charlecote. True, it was on Sherbourne land, his own property, but the stoppage flooded the grazing fields on the Barford side and people complained. It is not known if Captain Lucy promised amendment. His handsome appearance and military dignity (he was in command of a troop of the King's Household Guards, a small standing army that the King kept for his personal protection) had already given him more prestige in the county than his father, Richard, had known.

Thomas was a member of the Tory Cavalier Parliament that sat for eighteen years. He was MP first for Yarmouth in the Isle of Wight (where he had property from his mother) and in the years 1678 and 79 and in 81 was Member for Warwick. He sat in the Parliament that met at Oxford and split on the question of the succession to the throne. He lodged in Christ Church, where the King was housed, saw the ancient walls lit nightly by bonfires with which undergraduates demonstrated their loyalty to the Crown, and was present with the rest of the Commons in the packed room in the Schools (generally devoted to the passionless pursuit of geometry) when the King coolly overset his critics, and averted the danger of a second civil war by dissolving Parliament.

Charlecote had seen the last of the Puritan Lucys in Richard. The Government of the country at his death was a Government of young men, sons of the Protestant squire-archy, the Tories of a later date, who united to protect their way of life by presenting a front against Nonconformity. Thomas, though, was not of the type of magistrate who enjoyed throwing harmless people, whose consciences would not let them conform to the established Prayer Book, into gaol. He had nothing of his great-grandfather, the first Sir Thomas, in him. He sat dutifully on the Bench, accepted the Recordership of Stratford and dined affiably with the burgesses. He carried the borough's assurances of loyalty to the King in person on the occasion of the discovery of the Rye House Plot, and received of them in return the grant of two leaseholds in Stratford for an old servant.

The place was entailed in the male line. So far Katherine had given her husband only one daughter,* and had no intention of being shut up in the country to breed. She had her own waiting women and footmen and a black page to hand her morning chocolate. She was fond of cards and frequented the Duchess of Portsmouth's set at Hampton Court. She was a very passable imitation of the real thing, and eight months after her husband's death she made a dazzling marriage with Lady Castlemaine's son, who had been born in a Fellow's room at Merton College one summer while the King and Queen were at Oxford.

The old gable-ended hall was hardly the setting for a lady of fashion. Elizabeth, Mrs Lucy, lived on there and enter-tained the cousins—the Underhills from Idlicote, the Spencers from Yarnton, the Kingsmill Lucys, the Knightleys and Broughtons; but it was no longer a family home. If Captain Thomas had lived longer, he might have made alterations to

* This child, Elizabeth, was made a ward in Chancery. An Act of Charles II's reign granted fathers free disposal of the custody of children during minority. She was married while very young to Clement Throckmorton of Haseley, a Protestant branch of the Throckmortons of Coughton. She had one child, a daughter Lucy, who married a Bromley of Baginton.

the fabric, or pulled it all down and built a pretty, ornate puzzle-box in the prevailing style. He contented himself with laying out the north side of the house in neat geometrical parterres separated by gravelled paths. Water was deflected from the fish-ponds to fill two large rectangular brick pools in which it was proposed to domesticate carp.

In the account book there are two significant entries: 'June 1684. Pd. to your Honor in the Parlour 4 guinnies, the same to your man, Thomas Clarke, for your use and by your orders, 20 guinnies'—and in August of the same year: 'Pd. To your man Tho. Clarke by your orders after going to Sir Justinian Isham's £20.' These were considerable sums of money, and it seems probable that Captain Thomas was a bold but unlucky card-player. It was the vice of the age. His Spencer, now Sunderland, cousin at Althorp, whose father had been created an Earl and had fallen by Richard's side in the King's cause at Newbury, was, besides being an agile diplomatist, a frantic gambler.* The Cavalier activities of his Spencer kin had kept Thomas's father, Richard, away from Althorp and Wormleighton. Captain Thomas had no such scruples; he early acquired a taste for gambling which his wife encouraged, and moving on the rim of the Sunderland orbit was able to gratify it.

Sir Justinian had not long succeeded his brother at Lamport in Northamptonshire. The Lamport agent, Gilbert Clarke, felt it necessary to admonish his master: '. . . they say you do not game, that's the chief cut-throat, and I hope you will have a care to live virtuous in other things for God's sake as well as your own. . . .'

It seems probable that Captain Thomas visited Lamport to view the three artificial lakes there and learn something about their management. Improvements to these had recently been carried out by Sir Justinian and they had been stocked with breeding carp. If the visit ended with cards in the parlour for higher stakes than was prudent, it would

* Macaulay says of this Robert Spencer, Earl of Sunderland: 'The passion for play raged in him without measure and had not been tamed by ruinous losses . . . his ill-luck at the hazard table was such that his estates were daily becoming more and more encumbered.'

be only common courtesy on the part of a host toward a guest who could conceive of no other way of spending an evening. On this occasion it was not Sir Justinian who was the loser.

Another recurring payment—'to my lady going to Astrop; to Mr Hopton to take lodgings at Astrop by your order'— shows that they visited the popular Restoration spa in the little village of Astrop near the Northamptonshire border of Oxfordshire, where a well, revered since the Middle Ages as a holy well, was found to be a chalybeate spring. Celia Fiennes saw it on her travels, but thought it dirty. It was a favourite resort of dons from Oxford for the cure of asthma, and the Lucys, the Ishams, and the Knightleys met there and listened to music or promenaded in the gravel walks between high box hedges, and in the evening met for cards or dancing.

As if he had all time before him, as if in fact he lived in hopes of having a son, Captain Thomas planned brick gazebos for his new formal garden, and a boathouse; and turfed the court between the projecting wings of the house which before had been cobbled; the greenness contrasted pleasantly with the mellowing bricks.

The agent's accounts record the wages paid for this work in the new gardens:

Given to 6 men that brought gravill to the garden with
    their teams. .... 6s.
Pd. to Robert Ward for 26 days work round about the
    water course and wood works. .... 17s. 4d.
Pd. to Thomas Thompson for 10 days and a half of
    changing the pool in the garden. .... 10s., etc.

A strawberry house and an orangery were constructed. One John Ward was paid 8s. 4d. for '4 apricock trees and 2 oringes'. Perch and tench were not the only fish eaten at Charlecote; there is an entry for '3 pair of ffish called Souls 3s. 6d.' and 'Pd. for a taill of sammon 3s.' A recurring entry, 'to the chimnay man for hearth money £1. 17s.', shows that Captain Thomas did nothing to enlarge the house.

James Howell, the author of *Howelliana*, describes the house of a country gentleman★ of about this time:

. . . I never saw yet such an orderly punctual attendance of Servants, nor a great House so neatly kept; here one shall see no dog, nor a cat, nor cage, to cause any nastiness within the body of the House. The Kitchen and Gutters and other offices of noise and drudgery are at the fag-end; there's a Back-gate for the Beggars and the meaner sort of swains to come in at; the stables butt upon the Park, which for a cheerful rising Ground, for Groves and Browsings for the Deer, for rivulets of water, may compare with any for its highness in the whole land . . . for Ponds, for stately large walks, green and gravelly, for orchards and choice Fruits of all sorts, there are few like in England.

It might have been a description of Charlecote in every detail, except for the Groves, which were still wanting, and the deer of which there were as yet few, if any.

About this time the parchment roll of arms was lost. In 1619, at the time of the Herald's visitation to Warwickshire,† it must have been produced and after that is no more heard of. Thomas and Katherine were the children of their world, where a plausible tongue and a sharp eye to the main chance were more useful than ancestors; all in all, rather a seedy world.

Captain Thomas is buried at Charlecote, where he died suddenly of smallpox one morning in November 1684.‡ His will, made as soon as he sickened, begins hopefully: 'As my dear wife is now with child . . .' If the child were to be a son, all the estate would be his, it being entailed in the male line. Katherine was to have all the household gear from Charlecote, including the jewellery, for her lifetime, and to be guardian to the coming child, but if she did not educate him in the Protestant religion his guardianship should pass to trustees. The unborn son is to be taught in 'the Grammar

---

★ Lord Savage's house at Long Melford, Suffolk. *Howelliana*: ed. Jacobs.
† For the purpose of looking into the credentials of those who claimed the right to bear arms.
‡ Sir Edward Turner, writing to his son-in-law, Sir Justinian Isham, on 24 November, says: 'Captain Lucy died lately of the smallpox. His troop is given to one, Captain Adderly.'

Schools and Universities of this Realm or in the Study of the
Laws of this Realm'. The child died at birth, and Katherine,
with the household gear and Alice Spencer's pearls, vanishes
from the Charlecote scene.*

Captain Thomas's plan for new gardens had been only half-
realized, leaving heaps of gravel and bricks lying about on the
raw earth and the new fish-pond slowly filling up with weed.

The second and third Sir Thomas Lucys had had long
families of vigorous, intellectual, combative children. The
short successions that followed drained the stock of vitality,
diminishing family characteristics, as short successions are
apt to do. Of all the third Sir Thomas's children only Fulke,
the youngest, who had settled in Cheshire, became the father
of eight sons, three of whom now succeeded each other at
Charlecote.

Of the many beam and plaster houses individual to Cheshire,
Bramhall—built by a sixteenth-century Sir William Davenport—was, with its startling ornament of black and white
quatrefoils, its tall striped chimneys and outside gallery, one
of the most impressive. The ramifications of the Davenport
family spread a close network all over east Cheshire by the
end of the seventeenth century. The township of Henbury in
the parish of Prestbury had been Davenport property for
three hundred years. A lesser house than beautiful Bramhall,
more a grange than a gentleman's seat, sheltered the Daven-
ports of Henbury and was called Goyt Hall. In 1640 the last
Davenport of Goyt Hall died, leaving a sole child, Isabel,
directing in his will that she should be married to her cousin
John Davenport, in order that the name might never be
dissociated from the place.

The girl, however, thought otherwise. What freak of
chance brought Isabel Davenport of Henbury and Fulke,
youngest son of Sir Thomas Lucy of Charlecote, together, is

* After his master's death, the agent continued to send large sums of money
to his mistress in London. He alludes to her once only after her remarriage as
'the dutchess', and after that the payments stop. She was buried in the Duke of
Albemarle's vault in Westminster Abbey, where her husband, who was created
Duke of Northumberland and who survived her, was laid beside her.

now beyond discovering. He cannot have been twenty or
she more than sixteen when they were married in 1656.
Fulke settled down in Cheshire as master of Goyt Hall and
lord of Henbury, was knighted, and represented his adopted
shire in Parliament. He gave Lucy family names to his many
children, George and Spencer in memory of his dead
brothers, Alice in memory of his mother. But family piety
stopped there, and Sir Fulke of Henbury never saw Charlecote again.

Davenport, his eldest, was an officer in his cousin
Thomas's troop of horse. He found himself at the age of
twenty-four master of a large estate in Cheshire, heir to a
Warwickshire property he had never seen, and custodian of
his fourteen-year-old cousin, Elizabeth Throckmorton, till
she should attain sufficient age for her husband to claim her
and her dowry of £10,000. The Court of Chancery allowed
him £60 to keep a household in London for her. She was to
have masters for dancing, music, reading, writing, and the
French language, and £22 'for pocket money and other little
diversions'. The Lord Chancellor further stipulated that 'a
woman of fashion as a governess and companion' be provided. Her guardian found it hard to make ends meet:

'Mrs Throckmorton having constantly the use of Mr
Lucy's coach for her visits, airings, and other business, Mr
Lucy finds himself obliged to keep more than a pair of horses
in town, for which he craves a reasonable allowance.' She
needed three horses in all 'to ride out for her health.'*

Davenport's bachelor establishment at Charlecote was
frugal, as the agent's accounts show. He looked forward to a
soldier's life and had no intention of marrying. In his long,

---

* Mr Lucy's estimate of his young cousin's needs 'in order to appear clean
and decent' was adequate, but not lavish. Four pairs of silk stockings and four
of thread, two pairs of stays at £2 a pair, a number of petticoats, quilted,
flannel, and hooped, holland aprons for everyday wear and cambric ones for
best, four dozen gloves, and nine handkerchiefs (no shoes), are listed. The
most expensive necessity was a 'best laced head and ruffles' and a handkerchief
to match, costing £30. While the workmanship that went into the stitching on
of yards and yards of fine Valenciennes, and all the quilting, tucking, and
ruffling, cost next to nothing, stuff was expensive: 18s. a yard for silk for a
best mantua that took eleven yards; 10s. a yard for damask for a petticoat.

careful will, he makes provision for his widowed mother and leaves legacies to his sisters, Alice, Katherine, Isabella, Mary, and Bridget. The Duchess of Northumberland must be compounded with—had he been less of a confirmed bachelor he might have tried to induce her to return the pearls—and the manor house of Henbury sold to pay off Captain Thomas's debts. To Captain Adderley, who succeeded Captain Thomas as his commanding officer, to Lieutenant Richard Leigh, Cornet Chetwynd, and Captain Coningsby of his troop he leaves money to buy rings. Among the family papers are a number of bills for his clothes: coats of ash-colour and sad-coloured cloth lined with flowered silk, dimity and taffeta drawers trimmed with lace, nineteen dozen of silver buttons for one suit, eleven dozen of gold and silver buttons for another. His footmen wore *feuille-morte* liveries laced with silver; muted colours were the mode.

By the summer of 1690 his regiment was under orders to sail for Ireland. One brotherly letter survives, written by him from Chester just before embarkation, to his young brother and heir-presumptive, George, who was studying the law in Cheapside with a Mr Baker, an attorney, and to whom he has sent money:

. . . what ever you receive you must account for, and as I am and shall be forward in hazarding myself for ye recovery of ye estate, so at ye same time I hope you'l be as frugal in disbursements as 'tis possible to imagine; as to parting with your master 'tis not a thing which I am judge of; for my part I should rather choose to get as much knowledge as I could of my profession, though I had some angry looks and words, which import nothing.

After four chaotic years, James II had been firmly escorted out of the kingdom which he was quite unfitted to rule. The nearest point of disaffection where he could hope to find support was Ireland. He set up a seedy court in Dublin and established a ramshackle Parliament that issued bad money. James's Dutch son-in-law, William, had no hold on the affection of the English, but his stiff uprightness won him their respect. He crossed to Ireland in June 1690, and laid siege to the town of Limerick, where young Davenport Lucy was killed by a stray cannon-ball only two months after his regiment landed, and Charlecote passed to George, the would-be lawyer.*

Davenport could not turn out—indeed, he did not attempt to do so—his Uncle Richard's widow from Charlecote. She died in London in May 1690, three months before he, himself, was killed: the agent took his expenses out of the Charlecote funds in order to spend sixteen days in London arranging for her body to be taken back to the Isle of Wight, the home she had left forty years earlier.

George did not take immediate possession, having thrown up the law and followed his brother to Ireland, where he joined Marlborough—his having a Spencer grandmother was no doubt a recommendation.

While Davenport was outside Limerick, George was at the Boyne. It is probable that he was later with Edward Russell (Lord Orford) at the Battle of La Hogue in the May of 1692, since he commissioned an artist unknown to paint the spirited sea-piece of a sea-battle between the English and the French which still hangs at Charlecote, its bravery of blazing ships and glassy waves hardly dimmed by time.

He was, however, resident in Warwickshire by 1696, for he was appointed Colonel of a troop of militia with powers 'to set out and furnish an account of the horse and arms of every Papist, or reported Papist, in the County'.†

The following year he married a lady called Mary Bohun. The Bohuns were in trade. They were Coventry tradesmen, and had refined their name from Bown. Mary's great-grandfather, Ralph Bown, was a cap-maker of Coventry, an ancient trade, one of Coventry's earliest. Many of her relations were Mayors and Sheriffs of their ancient city. Among the Lucy family papers there is a memorandum by Mary's father, John Bohun of Finham, in which he sets forth his family's claim to bear arms. He remembered his father

* Three other brothers, a Thomas, a Robert, and a Spencer, who came in between them, had all died, from what cause we cannot know. There remained a William and a Fulke of the Cheshire lot.
† Under an Act of this year, obliging Catholics to contribute toward the furnishing and upkeep of the Militia.

telling him that an ancestor of theirs had been an officer of Sherwood Forest and had left to his descendants a bugle or horn tipped with silver, hanging from a green silk twist. A great-uncle, he says, came 'very near to suffering Martyrdom in the cause of religion in Queen Mary's time but [was] delivered by her death'. 'Dr Philemon Holland would say to my cousin Abraham Bown of London when a boy—"I knew your great-grandfather; he was a wise Senator"—being ready to weep when he spake of him.'

They were fierce Protestants, and all the sons were called by Bible names—Abraham, Isaac, Samuel, Daniel. Most of them were attorneys-at-law in London, but John, the father of Mary, was of the line that had invested in property in and about Coventry. She and George were married at Stoneleigh in April 1697.

In the previous century it had not been thought undesirable for the daughters of landed gentry to marry out of their class. Maria, William Lucy's daughter, who married Christopher Hales of Meriden, was marrying into a family two generations removed from the yeoman. Her mother, Anne Fermor of Easton Neston, was the daughter of a merchant of the Staple of Calais—though this was the aristocracy of trade. It was by then beginning to be recognized that women were entitled, within limits, to shape their own lives, and the manners and traditions of the hall were carried to the grange. This had a levelling effect—women have always been powerful levellers, generally for the good of society. But the same latitude has never been extended to men, and his Knightley, Throckmorton, and Berkeley kin thought it a pity that George Lucy should have allied himself with the grand-daughter of a Coventry hatter.

The century which had begun with the third Sir Thomas studying at Lincoln's Inn in the London of Shakespeare and Ben Jonson, passed through the uneasy years of the Interregnum, and seen Lucy sons estranged from their parents and brother divided from brother, ended with Colonel George and his Mary pacing the gravel paths of their new Dutch garden. In the centre of the court in front of the house a large marble basin had been sunk for fish for the Master's table.

This convenient arrangement lasted till the beginning of the nineteenth century. On the north side of the court was a high wall on which grew peaches and grapes; beyond that an unshaded lawn, later used as a bowling green. Beyond that again was—or would be—a pleasance with a maze, as yet only knee-high. From the gatehouse arch a double avenue of stripling elms led to the village. Everything was ruled off in straight lines, edged with balustrading punctuated by box trees in tubs, cut to grow alternately round and pointed, like toy trees.

The gazebo at the end of the double canal (which was so cold that swans could not be persuaded to stay on it) was a charming octagonal red-brick building with stone dressings, topped with a cupola and a flag; it had a fireplace and windows, and could be fished from in all weathers and used as a garden house on sunny spring days.

On the river side two boat-houses were built just below Mrs Lucy's new flower garden. A view of the west prospect of Charlecote, painted in about 1695,* shows a busy, contented riparian life going on, men mowing and scything in the Camp ground, a boatload of people about to disembark, other boats moored to the bank, cows calmly grazing. In the foreground there is a picnic party of ladies in fan-shaped lace head-dresses and gentlemen with dogs and horses. In the distance the houses of the village present almost identically the appearance they do today. Over it all lies the mellow sunlight, turning the Elizabethan bricks to golden-orange, of a century of longer, brighter summers.

The marriage of George and Mary Bohun was childless. Four years after Mary died (in 1708), George took her young cousin, Jane Bohun, who much resembled her, as his second wife. He could not live alone. He rented a house in Bolton Street, a leafy lane off Piccadilly, that he might attend the gaming tables and his wife show off her silks in the Park. The portrait that Dahl painted of him has the air of prosperity that a high colour, a confident regard, and a profuse full-bottomed wig impart, and would be recognizable anywhere,

---

* Attributed in the absence of any proof to John Stevens.

in any country, as the portrait of an English gentleman, a
Colonel of Militia, with a country house of fading brick set
about with neat lawns.

In the Charlecote account book already quoted from there is
a record of a sum paid in July 1685 to Edward Hunt, a
stableman, for new breeches and boots to enable him to ride
one of the Militia horses 'when Monmouth was uppe'.

All through the summer of 1685, when Charlecote was
masterless after Captain Thomas's sudden death, Monmouth
was gathering the support in the south-west which he
squandered in one bloody night on the wastes of Sedgemoor.
Warwickshire called out the Militia—Captain Thomas
should have been alive to ride with them to the mustering in
his beaver hat and his buff coat and point lace ruffles. The
fear of another outbreak of civil war died down. But in the
first decade of the new century Protestant Warwickshire
turned to watch with alarm a new danger reddening the
skies. James had tried to Catholicize England. William, the
interloper, strove wearily but indomitably to bring religious
tolerance to his adopted country and steady the rocking
balance of power.

On James's death in exile at St-Germain, his son was
proclaimed Pretender to the English Throne by the French
King. At Charlecote in 1708 the church bells were rung all
day, so that the ale consumed by the ringers cost 7s., when
news came of the defeat by Admiral Byng of a French fleet
going to the Pretender's support in the Firth of Forth. The
same ringers were called on again in July of the same year
and given 2s. 6d. for celebrating the capture of Lille by John
Churchill. The Whig majority in power that financed the
war, sought to control and limit the power of the Crown. It
stood for the new England of traders and bankers. The
opposition or Tory Party represented the solid ribs of
England, the landed classes with their dependants, whose
ancestors had fought in the Barons' wars, grown rich at the
Dissolution, and become securely entrenched under Elizabeth. When in 1705 George Lucy sought election as a Knight
of the Shire there was decided opposition by a number of

Whig freeholders. These were of the yeoman and tradesman class which had a long history of complaint against the land-owning gentry. He did not secure election—the first Lucy for many generations to fail to do so.

As a soldier, George Lucy was probably Whig in sympathy and, as a landowner, Tory in practice. In July 1715, as a Justice of the Peace, he examined two men who gave information upon oath of riots in and about the town of Birmingham directed against Dissenters and their places of worship. Dr Sacheverell, the eloquent mouthpiece of the High Church party, had visited Birmingham six years earlier and stirred up a large multitude to gut a meeting-house with fire. There had been periodic outbreaks ever since, but this latest was serious, several persons having been killed and two meeting-houses attacked. It was beyond the ability of the Constabulary of Birmingham to deal with the rioters.

The Justices moved with what appears to be intentional deliberateness (Dissenters were a nuisance from all points of view), and on the day that the upper meeting-house was fired and many people hurt (Sunday 17 July), the High Sheriff roused himself from his Sabbath apathy to send a circular letter to the JPs, bidding them meet him at the White Lion in Stratford on the day following. Accordingly, on the Monday the Justices assembled, and warrants were sent to the Chief Constables of the various hundreds, authorizing them to apprehend the rioters. The militia and the Sheriff's posse were called out, grooms and house servants were crammed into coats and boots that did not fit them, and mounted. The turn-out presented by the Militia was shocking to the orderly soul of Colonel Lucy. The men were of the meanest sort, 'a mercenary Rabble'. Hampton Lucy was bound to contribute one footman to the Sheriff's posse, for four days' service; the word *nil* occurs under the heading 'new muskets' and 'new sword-belts'. The footman had to go as he was, straight from the harvest-field, armed with a reaping hook, as his forebears had answered the call to arms for Crécy.

By the following Friday (22 July) nothing at all had been done. On Saturday a letter was sent 'by an Express' to the

High Sheriff of Staffordshire, pointing out that as the riots had begun on the Staffordshire side of the county he must do his part in rounding up rioters.

It was decided to make an entry into the city of Birmingham on the 26th. The problem was what to do with the Militia in the interim. On Sunday the footmen became unmanageable: 'The Foot that composed part of the Sheriff's posse upon ye muster at Warwick, amounted to upwards of 400 men; whilst ye High Sheriff and gentlemen were endeavouring to form them into Companys and make Officers over them, the said Foot began to be tumultuous and mutinous, making demands of exorbitant allowances. . . .'

The more substantial freeholders and householders, some in sympathy with the rioters, having absented themselves from the posse, it was found impracticable to make the remnant into a serviceable force in so short a time. It was decided to disband the Foot 'and tho' they were somewhat tumultuous, yet they were dispersed with Proclamations, without coming to Severities'.

Meanwhile, the letter to the High Sheriff of Staffordshire had miscarried, he being away from home, and the now disbanded posse had become a greater menace than the rioters, many being still in the possession of the arms that had been issued to them. A new posse was hurriedly formed with warrants to disarm the members of the old posse.

Finally on Tuesday, 16 July, as arranged, the High Sheriff and about sixty horsemen entered Birmingham 'without any manner of opposition or Noise of ye faction'. It was admirably timed. The criminals, forewarned, had fled or concealed themselves; in the end only two were apprehended and brought to justice.*

The figures of Justice Shallow, of Dogberry, and Constable Elbow thread in and out of the story of the flustered Justices and the unmanageable posse. George Lucy, disgusted by the public disgrace of his militia, drew up an expedient for regulating it, commenting on the apathy of the public

* *The Journal of the Birmingham Riots.* Lucy MSS.

toward its defences, and proposing more pay for the Constables. In a letter from His Royal Highness the Prince
Guardian of the Kingdom, George, by the Grace of God,
signed by Walpole and Torrington, the pay is graciously
conceded.*

George Lucy was not overburdened with family feeling. He
had two brothers left, William, the Rector of Tolland in
Somerset, and Fulke, as yet unmarried. Alice, the eldest
daughter of Sir Fulke Lucy and Isabella Davenport, had been
married off to a curate called Hammond,† the son of a
Shropshire parson, and had died in her thirty-seventh year,
leaving a large family. Sir Fulke had invested his son-in-law
with the livings of Gawsworth in Cheshire and Syresham in
Northamptonshire, and settled a modest income on his
daughter. Colonel George at Charlecote did not think it
incumbent on him to make the long journey to Cheshire to
visit a brother-in-law with whom he had little in common,
or to invite his sister's children to stay at Charlecote. He and
Jane were themselves childless.

Jane's dowry was derived from the rent of Spitalfields
Market in London. Her father, George Bohun of Newhouse,
had bought up the rents of the Market from the family of
Balch, who first established it on a derelict site where before
the Dissolution there had been a hospital. When after the
revocation by Louis XIV of the Edict of Nantes, all French
Protestants were outlawed from France, and French craftsmen fled to any country that would shelter them, the
Government of England gave a grant to the Huguenot silk-
weavers. In the fields round the market they built their two-
storey wooden houses and set up their looms. A French
church was built for the weavers, which brought Jane in a

---

* The final comment on the rising is supplied in a letter from William Eden
to Lord Townhend, 25 August 1715: 'Since the arrival of the King's Messengers all things have been very quiet. The eyes of many of His Majesty's poor
misled subjects begin to be opened since the grand incendiary, Dr Sacheverell,
is removed from among us.'
† According to east Cheshire records, a Mr Hammond succeeded to the
incumbency of Chelford in the parish of Prestbury in 1716. The Hammonds,
though a Shropshire family, had been settled for some time in Cheshire.

ground rent of £30, the ground rent of Spitalfields Square being over £800 in 1709.

Jane Lucy's elegant silks, the beetle's-wing satin, the cinnamon plush, and the velvet stripe were the work of her tenants, whose hands had to be rubbed continually in lard and fine sugar to keep them smooth enough to handle the raw silk. The weavers grew pot-herbs, bred pigeons, sang French chansonettes and lived an idyllic life with a Columbarian Society, a Floricultural Society, and a Society for Shakespeare readings, hard by the site of the old Curtain Theatre and near the church where the Burbages were buried.

With this steady source of income added to the revenue of his Warwickshire properties, George Lucy should have been a very rich man, but he, too, liked a gamble, and in the year before he died ventured over £3,000 in the South Sea Company and lost it all.

Jane Bohun had made a more ambitious marriage than her sisters, and in Dahl's portrait of her she has the pleased, conscious air of the one who is the beauty of her family. She was twenty-five years younger than her husband. She did not find Charlecote much to her taste. It was thought to be *démodé* to live in a crumbling old hall, its rooms lined with wormy wainscoting, every window-pane creaking and complaining when the wind blew.

Colonel George set about carrying on Captain Thomas's improvements. The artificial ponds were stocked with carp and the great basin in the court with trout. He had one Joel Lobb carve him two whinstone pillars to carry statues, and bought from Edward Hurst, of Hyde Park Corner, a leaden shepherd and shepherdess to stand on them.* Till the nineteenth century there was a lead statue of Diana with a buck and a bow and a crescent moon guarding the entrance to the lime avenue. Of the three mulberry trees he planted in the north garden two are alive, twisted and shapeless, but still bearing fruit.

He was proud of the house's antiquity and its associations,

* Now in the court.

and too prudent, or perhaps too indolent, to pull it down to suit the fashion or to please his silly young wife. He held his hand from demolishing the great bay window in the hall where the family coat of arms hung like jewels on a background of tinted glass. He spared the minstrel's gallery, though it was out of date: nobody wanted to listen to harps and fiddles nowadays; keyboard instuments were the mode. He installed in it an organ on which Jane could show off her musical accomplishment. The airs of George Frideric Handel, much admired for his opera, *Rinaldo*, and now living and composing in England, sounded remarkably well in the Great Hall, empty of any furniture but the long dining table, which was too cumbrous to remove.

In the painting of the west aspect of Charlecote there is another gabled wing on the river side that had disappeared by the time the 1722 edition of Dugdale, which contains a print of Charlecote, was published. Here in Colonel George's day was a parlour, a study, bedrooms, and servants' attics, where now there is a gravelled terrace and part of the 1836 library block. Panelling of walnut, cedar, and mulberry woods was ousting the old square wainscoting. Jane must have a new staircase wide enough not to crush her panniers, and the old worn stair, slippery as glass, that led to the bedrooms in the north wing, was replaced, and the walls lined with large fielded panels in oak. The same Joel Lobb who carved whinstone pillars for the pleasance was commissioned to carve four Corinthian capitals and 50 feet of medallion cornice for this staircase. Over it was a painted ceiling, with Fame trumpeting the triumph of Virtue in the style of Verrio.*

In Jane's sitting-room—the room in which Katherine Wheatley had held her card parties—there were narrow looking-glasses with borders of gilt and coloured glass set into panels above the fireplace, and between the windows, trifles of silver and lacquer on fragile tables, and blue and white china bowls filled with dried rose leaves in the window embrasures. The sparse, old-fashioned furniture, the tasselled

* Removed to the south wing in 1836.

crimson chairs and stiff settles of the third Sir Thomas's day, and the stump-work settees and stools of Richard Lucy's, were banished to the empty gallery where the Aston children used to learn their lessons. No one nowadays ran a loving hand over the gold-tooled calf bindings in the study.

George Lucy paid a master-builder in Warwick to take out the old creaking mullions on the river front and put in long sash windows with flat stone borders, and to make a double window on the north side to flood the elegant new staircase with light and let in the westering sun to fade it to the brown of a moth's wing. The improvements were graceful and not out of place; the builder's name was Francis Smith.

George had himself and Jane painted by Dahl, a Swedish painter much in vogue at the time, who had already taken his likeness and Mary's in the early days of their marriage. The second portrait does not flatter him. His hair, worn *au naturel*, is grey, and the handsome, fleshy face has sagged. The confidence of youth has broadened into complacency.

The lure of the gaming tables or the dullness of the neighbourhood drove George and Jane back to Bolton Street, Piccadilly. The heir-presumptive, William, the Somerset-shire parson, was more often at Charlecote than its owner; two rooms were kept for his convenience, while in the rest of the silent house the shutters were kept closed. Charlecote Old Hall had begun its long sleep which, with short inter-missions of wakefulness only, saw the eighteenth century out.

CHAPTER 6

A Man of His Period

> But what have I to do (who am so happy to have a good old
> House) but to make it decent, and to content myself with [it], as
> it is already designed?
> George Lucy to Mrs Hayes. Bath, 1765.

In a letter written in 1721 to his sister's husband, the
Reverend John Hammond of Gawsworth in Cheshire, Dr
William Lucy announced his decision to exchange his excellent Somersetshire living of Tolland (with glebe lands worth
£50 per annum) for that of Bishop's Hampton* at his
brother's pressing request. As an uncle he was anxious to
find a good living for his sister's son, young Jack Hammond,
who had been rather wild at Oxford and had distressed his
father by running into debt. The boy was in a fair way to
make amends for his folly. The Rector of Tolland was
persuaded that a fling at Oxford was a sure indication of a
vocation for the Church, and, having pacified the authorities
and paid off the Oxford tradesmen, took the young man as
his curate. In July 1721 he was writing to his brother-in-law:

> *Charlecote, July 21st, 1721*
> Give me leave to congratulate ye upon your son Jack's success in
> the Rectory of Tolland, which he now holds by my Resignation:
> by virtue of which he was Instituted into that Living and Inducted
> by myself. . . . As soon as I had secured your Son in the Living
> and Resign'd, I came to look after my own Interest here in
> Warwicks; I have therefore to this End taken Institution into the
> Living of Hampton Lucy. It will bring me nearer to my Relations.
> I cannot say that it will be much to my advantage, having so good

---

* A peculiar or special jurisdiction allowed it the advowsons and incomes of
the neighbouring parishes of Wasperton and Alveston.

an Interest in my good Lord Bishop of Bath and Wells who has lately given me a Prebend of good value, there being a Demesne Manor, and Land belonging to it. So I shall continue a Free-Holder in Somersets. after having quitted my other interests in it.

In Captain Thomas's lifetime Hampton* had been held by a cousin, Dr Harvey Broughton (of the Staffordshire family, descended from the third Sir Thomas's daughter, Bridget, the child with the bow in Cornelius Jansen's picture). After Dr Broughton's death in March 1721 the Rev. William wrote to his brother-in-law: 'The Parsonage House at Hampton Lucy not Habitable. Mrs Broughton will allow nothing but what ye Law will oblige her to for Dilapidations. To which she shall speedily submit: *Curat lex*, etc. Since I wrote this I understand Mrs B. will compound.'

It appeared likely that Colonel George would have no children now; there was, however, no reason to suppose that he would not live to a mellow, port-drinking old age. He and Jane were at Charlecote less and less; the second Mrs George Lucy did not care for the country.

Though regretting Somerset, his Prebendal stall at Wells and his rich acres in the Vale of Taunton, Dr William set vigorously about improving Hampton Lucy. Workmen had just begun to demolish the old Parsonage house in the hot August of 1721, when the news came that Colonel George had collapsed and died very suddenly in London. Immediately William took up his pen to acquaint his brother-in-law in Cheshire with the situation:

'He has left no Will, so I'm intitled to his Personal and Real Estate, paying his Debts and discharging all Incumbrances. I have only time to tell you that I humbly beg your acceptance of a suite of Mourning. I would likewise desire the favour of you to acquaint my Brother Foulke how affairs are left, that he may not give himself or me any unnecessary trouble.' (Of the eight sons of Sir Fulke Lucy of Henbury

---

* It is impossible to discover exactly when the name was changed to Hampton Lucy. It continues to appear on deeds and wills as Hampton Bishop or Bishop's Hampton. William Lucy held also the advowson of Preston Bagot, property of the Spencers of Claverdon and Sherbourne.

there remained now only two, himself and this younger brother, Fulke.)

In earlier letters Dr William had often sighed over the uselessness of attempting to redeem this detrimental. In 1699: '. . . all our relations on this side the Avon are in perfect health, my brother Fulke is going to increase ye number. I can't commend his prudence or admire his choice.'* He later adopted Fulke's sons in order to remove them from what he considered pernicious parental influence, and arranged for their education to be supervised by his brother-in-law, the Rector of Gawsworth.

This brother-in-law also disappointed him.

I'm sorry [William wrote in the September of 1721 after Colonel George's death] that my Brother Foulk Lucy's children have occasioned you so much trouble. But I hope you can't resent anything from me on this Account, since I was no ways Instrumental in it. I shall endeavour to ease you for ye future of what seems at present so disagreeable to you. And to this end I should be glad if they could be boarded in Macclesfield, and there go to school for a year or two till they are big enough to be removed to a better. As to the Account you gave me of what was due to you from my Brother, I shall, I hope, take care that Justice shall be done to you with all convenient speed. Especially since you have been the first that has been so particular with me on this Occasion, almost as soon as my Brother was laid in his Grave. But I shall overlook this. . . . I have lately had a Dun from one Harrison in Yorkshire on F. Lucy's account. The debt he pretends due is near £300. If it is not too much trouble you may acquaint F. L. from me that I have now no hope of his reforming. He is an Idle, Thoughtless, Extravagant Person. He must live with more Care and Thought if he expects any favour from me.

Colonel George's widow also sank in his estimation:

Mrs Lucy, not content with her Exorbitant Jointure, claims a share in Spittle Fields, tho' £3500 in Money and a 3rd Part or Portion of

---

* His choice was a Miss Elizabeth Mason. In the Charlecote Library there is a copy of Horace Walpole's *Anecdotes of Painting*, inscribed: 'the gift of the Author, Oct. 7th, 1780'. It was given to his friend, William Mason, the grandson of Elizabeth Mason's brother, William.

Lands left to her by her Father, Bohun, was the Express Consideration for it. . . . I presume she will force me to a Chancery-Suit which will neither, I hope, be to her Honour, or Advantage. A most Worthless Wretch!

A year later he was writing again to Gawsworth:

. . . I now am startled (as I have had just reason) at my Brother's Conduct. I have paid many long and large summs for him since his Death, and I'm afraid there are some yet behind undiscovered. I will do justice to everybody as fast as I can; and I hope in a little time, I shall make my affairs more easy. . . .

The remainder of the Henbury estate had come to him, and in order to cope with Fulk's creditors and Colonel George's debts it was found necessary to sell it. He was as full of family feeling as Colonel George had been lacking in it. 'I am endeavouring to get some place for Davenport that may be a decent subsistence for him,' he wrote to the brother-in-law in Cheshire about his second son, who had had a legal training. 'I design to take him with me into the Country: I suppose my neighbouring gentry in Warwicks. will put me into the Commission of the Peace. Whenever I am, I will take my Nephew for Clerk until something better offers. I will do what I can for him, being now a regular sober man.' To his brother Fulke who keeps sending requests for money he says he will send no more, since there is 'no conduct, no management'.

He intended to install his youngest nephew, George Hammond, who appears to have held a curacy in Northamptonshire, as Curate at Hampton as soon as the new Parsonage House should be completed: 'He deserves all favours and Countenance from his Relations and best Friends. He slaves for a decent Competency.*

* The system of pluralism, by which the well-to-do clergy accumulated livings which they seldom or never visited, bred lively disrespect for the Church. The greedy pluralist and the wretched curate, paid a pittance to do the work, were the butt of the satirists. For the curate there were only kicks, the scrapings of the dishes, the cold corner out of reach of the fire, the trudge home to his cottage on foot after dinner at the Hall. He must not hold opinions, but with an obsequious smile agree with everyone. He must endure

The new master of Charlecote rode across the park every morning to see how the building of the Rectory was progressing. It was the work of the same Warwickshire firm of builders, the brothers Smith, Francis, and William, who had improved the Hall in Colonel George's day. Hampton village was built of red brick from the brickfields that had supplied the first Sir Thomas's needs. Hampton Rectory was to be of brick with stone quoins, a square house topped with a balustrade, with two rows of tall windows across its broad face and a round canopy over the front door. Dr William looked on his handiwork and was satisfied that he had raised for himself at least one enduring memorial. He would lie in the vault of old Hampton Church with no florid marble monument above him to trumpet his liberality, but a worthy Rectory on the one hand and a school on the other (which he proposed to endow with scholarships) to pay their silent tribute to a man who had put the dignity of his cloth and his respect for learning before personal vanity.

The Chancery suit with George's widow had begun. 'Mrs Lucy has lately (I thank her for Nothing), disclaimed any Right to those Lands'—the ground rents of Spitalfields. She claimed instead the income of the Charlecote lands settled on her by George Lucy, which amounted to £800 a year. She was on the way to a second husband, the Hon. Robert Moore, and was determined to have every penny owing to her from Charlecote under the terms of her marriage settlement.

At about this time Dr William was painted by Richardson seated in his elbow chair in the billowing robes of a Doctor of Divinity, one gloved hand grasping a crested cane—a man of many chins with small eyes that look out of the canvas with a hard, intelligent stare.* He had done well for Charlecote. Colonel George's debts were nearly all paid, the

---

the rudeness of servants better paid than himself, and in spite of hunger not seem over-eager for what was offered at the table. Two generations back he would have been expected to leave the table before the pudding. He was 'the first and purest pauper of the village', in Sydney Smith's phrase.

* He also had a duplicate done to hang in the Rectory.

sons of his favourite sister, Alice Hammond, were well placed. George Hammond was about to contract a most suitable marriage with the daughter of Underhill of Idlicote. Her grandmother had been the third Sir Thomas's youngest daughter, and the young couple were thus first cousins at one remove.*

It was quite out of the question that brother Fulke, a heavy drinker and gambler, should inherit. Dr William told Mr Hammond in August 1723: 'I shall write Foulke a letter to assure him that if he takes his children from School so frequently, he shall take 'em entirely to himself. I never was so decently maintained at School as they are.'

The orderly progress of Lucys from Oxford and the Inns of Court to a seat on the Warwickshire Bench and thence to standing room in the House of Commons was threatened by vacancy. The noon-day glitter of Warwickshire cornfields fresh from a passing storm, or bloomy stretches of parkland under skies of rolling cloud, should have been the setting for another family picture; the old gabled Hall would have looked well in the distance with a thunder-cloud coming up behind it. Only a robust dynasty was lacking.

Dr William's wife, Frances,† twenty years younger than himself, had not been able to bear him a living child. When he made his will he had evidently not altogether abandoned the hope that he might yet have a son. He was fond of his Hammond nephews, but disliked the idea of succession through the female line. All the descendants of the third Sir Thomas were named in order of strict priority. After the sons of the improvident Fulke, it was to go to the line of Sir Berkeley Lucy, the Baronet, on whom the Kingsmill estates in Hampshire had devolved, or, that line failing, to the descendants of the Bishop's eldest son, now settled at Castle Cary in Somerset. His Hammond nephews would only succeed when every male holder of the name of Lucy in the

* Jack Hammond, the eldest, who had been his uncle's curate at Tolland after leaving Oxford and succeeded him as Rector there, had married Sarah Morley, the daughter of a Somersetshire gentleman, John Morley of North Petherton. Their first son, whom they called Lucy Hammond, was born at Tolland.
† Daughter of Henry Balguy of Derwent, Derbyshire.

direct line had been eliminated; but even such an unlikely eventuality was provided for.

Looking back over his sixty years, Dr William's Oxford days appeared to him as the happiest of his life. He left two thousand pounds to found four yearly scholarships to Magdalen Hall, his old college, for boys from Hampton Lucy Grammar School—near relations of the Lucy family to receive preference, or a boy from his old home of Kilton, near Tolland in Somerset.

The west wing that contained the parlour and study was pulled down between 1720 and 1722. In Dr William's accounts small sums are recorded to Mr Smith, master builder of Warwick (as late as 1737 his widow was still paying off Smith's account).* Workmen from Stratford were also employed by Dr William on the Rectory at Hampton, and the retiling, thatching, and glazing of the old houses in Charlecote. Workmen are great carriers of tales, and one of the glaziers, an elderly Stratford man who bore the name of William Shakespeare Hart, was the grandson of the poet's sister, Joan, and remembered as a boy hearing first-hand accounts of the poaching affair. When the actor Betterton had come down to Stratford twelve or thirteen years earlier, asking for any information about the man Shakespeare, the poet's great-nephew and namesake had been able to tell him tales gleaned from the memories of old people living in the villages of Snitterfield, Alveston and Charlecote, to which his profession of glazier and carpenter took him. He did a lot of work for Dr William, glazing Nason's house in the village (a descendant of the Nason who appears in the first Sir Thomas's wage book) and later received £20 for repairs to the Summer House in the Garden, which had glass on all its six sides.

By now Rowe's Preface to the *Works* had been published. Stratford, though mildly proud of its successful son, was not yet prepared to go to the lengths of forging links with his

---

* Surviving letters to his clients show that Smith usually claimed remuneration at the rate of one shilling in the pound for journeys, supervising the work, surveying and measuring. Colvin: *Dictionary of British Architects*.

early days. Charlecote villagers knew the Harts—they were
humble people working for their living, not like the Quynys
and the Barnards, descendants of Shakespeare's daughter,
and lived in the tenement in Henley Street where their
grandmother and her brothers had been born. It was a
tumbledown place and no great advertisement for Shakespeare Hart, who could turn his hand to any sort of repair
work if he had a mind to.

Dr William's accounts are sprightly: quite a lot is spent on
wine and lost at the races, he resents having to pay Fry, the
painter, an exacting, impudent fellow, but enjoys treating
his friends at the Bowling Green, and importing fiddlers
from Derbyshire to amuse his guests. His last letter to his
Hammond brother-in-law in Cheshire is dated August 1723.
He died in London of smallpox in the February of the next
year. The wrought-iron gates surmounted by his initials
which Thomas Paris had made for him had just been
delivered and set up in the court when the eight principal
rooms were draped with black and the escutcheon hung out
on the porch.★

William Lucy's widow meant to spare no expense, though
she wrangled with the undertaker over his accounts for two
years. The cortège took three days to reach Charlecote
church, where the body was to lie for a night before being

★ A lament by an unknown hand for the death of Dr William Lucy, DD,
pictures the arrival of the good doctor in the realms of bliss in elegant iambics:

> Ye Souls! who oft upon his lips have hung,
> And catch'd the dropping Manna from his Tongue,
> From vice by his persuasive Doctrine gain'd,
> By his instructive Life to Glory train'd
> Say with what Joys your grateful Hearts o'erflow'd
> When the dear Man installed in Bliss ye viewed.

The Bishop of St David's is described greeting his nephew:

> Behold! a Prelate of the Lucy's Race
> Impatient flyes to thy belov'd Embrace. . . .

Consolation for his loss is to be found in the thought of his benefactions to
young scholars, 'within old Wainfletes walls'. It brings to the mind's eye the
monument that William Lucy ought to have had, all built up to a splendid
apotheosis, with Virtue and Charity flanked by trumpeting cherubs bearing
the recumbent doctor in a full wig and a marble toga to heights of bliss.

taken on to Hampton Lucy to be laid in the vault there. It had rested at Woodstock, where the landlord received a mourning hat-band, and at a farmhouse on Edgehill, where the farmer was given a pair of fine black leather gloves. As he died of smallpox he was buried in sheep's wool. The large double elm coffin was enclosed in lead and placed in a case 'set off in the best manner' with gilt nails and gilt handles. The six sable hearse-horses, housed in black velvet, carrying seventeen plumes of black feathers between them, drew a velvet-covered hearse stuck round with pasteboard shields on staves painted with the family arms. The arms were again painted on buckram escutcheons verged with silver, and on paper ones for distribution in the villages through which the procession passed.

Twelve yellow flambeaux for journeying after dark cost six shillings. All the house and outdoor servants at Charlecote, as well as the mourners who accompanied the hearse, were put into mourning cloaks, and fifty-two guineas were spent on mourning-rings alone. All in all the funeral of William Lucy cost nearly two hundred pounds.

Very different was brother Fulke's shabby interment four years later. Black hat-bands, scarves and shammy gloves were reluctantly conceded to the bearers and the officiating clergyman, but there was to be no gathering in the house, no draperies of black, no hatchment on the porch. 'The company to meet the corpse at Welsborne, to have a glass of wine there, and come directly to Charlecote Church . . . Master Lucy desires Charlecote Church may be put in mourning.'*

His sister-in-law, Frances Lucy, exasperated but striving to be charitable, had written to Gawsworth in August 1728: 'The unhappy gentleman has brought himself into fresh trouble on a very idle occasion, the story is too long to tell you but he is put into the Crown Office, and I fear will find

---

* There is a memorandum book of 1724 recording Fulke's purchases of the best red port and many quarts of Malaga wine or 'the mountain'. In the margin Fulke has scrawled 'Mdm. my poor wife, was seiz'd with the Convulsion Thursday morning——' She was given to 'Hysterick Fitts' (and, it is to be feared, to drink), and predeceased him.

it difficult to get out again.' Two years later she was writing again about Brother Lucy's effects, which consisted of 'Old Cloathes and some few Household Goods, all in the possession of Persons he had Boarded and was indebted to, more (as they said) than the value of the things in their custody, and they absolutely refused to deliver them up . . .'

Jane Bohun had died in childbirth and her second husband meant to recover her share of the rents of Spitalfields, which she had made over to George Lucy in return for an income from the Charlecote estate. The defendant, Frances Lucy, denies that the complainant has any right to these rents, and states that she has employed Mr Davenport Hammond of Doctor's Commons to collect them for her, but that he has been much obstructed by the complainant's forbidding the tenants to pay. To Cousin Hammond she wrote: 'The remainder of Henbury Estate is now ordered to be sold as also Spittle Fields, tho' there is above £4000 of the Family's Money lies dead in Mr Popham's* [the agent] and the Tenant's Hands, which I'm sure would answer all present Demands, might it be dispos'd of accordingly. These are great Hardships which I'm heartily grieved at but can't help.'

A noonday quiet now falls on Charlecote. The twelve-year-old heir and his brother proceeded, as their uncle had intended they should, to Westminster School, and thence to Oxford. It was understood that during the years of young Thomas's minority his uncle's widow would remain at Charlecote. Nothing is known about this Thomas, the son of Fulke (*no conduct, no management*), who was the youngest son of Sir Fulke of Henbury, who was the youngest son of the third Sir Thomas, except that he was subject to epileptic fits and was never able to take his place in the world as an adult.

The noisy babble of personalities all trying to make themselves felt—Dr William the pluralist, Colonel George who fought under Churchill, Richard with the divided allegiance, Spencer, who followed the King, turbulent William of St David's, back to the last ancestor of the Jansen

* Richard Popham, Dr William's steward, was buried in old Hampton Lucy church in 1730.

portrait—falls silent, and the country sounds are heard again, the ploughing, reaping, and threshing that had been going on peacefully since Domesday.

A Court Baron was held under Richard Dighton the Steward for the manors of Hampton Lucy, or Bishop's Hampton, and Charlecote in November 1737, at which jurors were sworn in upon oath and presented offenders in precisely the same manner that their forebears had done under Fulke de Lucie. The wording had not changed. As always the chief indictments were for allowing water-courses and drains to become blocked with leaves and mud, for allowing chimneys and bridges to become ruinous so that they were a danger to the neighbours, and for permitting horses, cows, sheep, and pigs to wander unyoked and unringed (the penalty for each horse being 6d., for each cow and hog 4d., for each sheep 2d.). The Lord of the Manor was reminded that he must do his share of work to the highways, four days in each month, on pain of forfeit.

James Fish, a Warwick district surveyor,* made a survey of the properties of Charlecote and Hampton, Hatton with Fulbrook, and Hunscot, in 1736, with a map in which the house with its water gardens, the park with its avenues, the blue ribbon of the river, the farms and leasows, the mills and mill hams, the orchards, brickfields, hopyards and spinneys, in all nearly 4,000 acres, each meadow with its neat edging of trees, is still fresh as when it was painted.

Before Captain Thomas's death Fish had sold much timber off the Charlecote estate to furnish him with ready money; and after it to pay the wages of the workmen employed on the improvements to the gardens. Colonel George had planted stiff walks of elm and lime, and made an orchard where the fruit trees were ranged in battle formation. Between them these two Lucys changed the character of Tudor Charlecote, swept away what was left of the old

---

* This James Fish of Warwick had in his possession the ancient inventory of the lands and chattels of the Trinitarian priory of Thelesford which Dugdale saw, with the names of its priors. A few torn pages of the copy his clerk made of it have survived, but the register itself most regrettably perished.

warren and opened up spaces of grassland, into which, some time in the early eighteenth century, deer were introduced.

The face of Warwickshire was changing; Drayton and Camden would have lamented the total disappearance of Arden, and the encroachment on the old Wealden of coal-mines. Where there were rivers and canals to convey the coal from the mine it could be bought cheaply; in the Charlecote account book an entry under 1687, for Davenport's expenses during one of his short visits, mentions '2 hundred of coalls' as costing 1s. 10d., much less than the cost of the malt required for a month's brewing or the price of three War-wickshire cheeses. In Dr William's day the price of coal was 10s. a ton. In the Felden the open fields were by now almost all enclosed; that it was so in Charlecote is seen clearly in the map of 1736, but the days when closure had roused angry protest were over. It was for the most part placidly accepted as inevitable. There was still some strip cultivation in Hampton, but most of the old corn-producing land was now laid down to pasture.

Charlecote Old Hall, low by the sedgy river, the gilt weather-vanes at its four corners catching the sunlight, kept its Elizabethan character. To the elms of Old Town, spared by the hand of the improver, rooks returned yearly to rebuild their township in the rocking branches; in May the cuckoo's early, unflawed note went echoing up and down the river reaches. The place slept; taste and progress had not yet seriously threatened it.

When his elder brother Thomas died in 1744, George, the younger son of Fulke Lucy's two sons, was thirty. The only allusions to the childhood of these two boys, aside from their Uncle William's concern for their education, is in a red account book belonging to Fulke Lucy, where the entries 'Oct. 31st 1724 pd. for Tom Lucy's new wigg—5/- (he being eighteen years old); Nov. 13th, given to Tom Lucy and Geo. 1/-; Dec. 10, Given at ye School at Meadely when they Broke up 10/-', and to a servant, Jenny Naylor, 'given her as a p'sent for her Care of Georgy's Leg—5/-', occur between payments for oysters and old brandy.

Drawing a handsome allowance from the Charlecote estate, George was able to live extremely well at Oxford, to which he went up in about 1729, aged fifteen, with fond cautions from his Aunt Lucy about avoiding bad company. The gentleman commoners at the University were expected to dress with ceremony for three o'clock dinner in Hall, with silk stockings and curled hair. George wore his own brown hair long and lightly powdered. He was boyishly handsome, with a round face and blue eyes. He naturally took his horses to Oxford, and passed the time by hunting three days a week in the winter with local packs and in summer by riding out to Wytham and Otmoor, as his ancestor, the third Sir Thomas, had done, boated to Godstow and up the broad reaches of the Thames, or attended cock-fights on Port Meadow. Gibbon was writing in the 1750s that the conversation of undergraduates stagnated in a round of college business, Tory politics, personal anecdotes, and private scandal. The tuition was careless, the tutors being often as deep drinkers as their pupils. College discipline was slack; Matins and Vespers could be evaded for the small fine of 2*d.* a time; for getting into college after the gates closed, a bribe of 3*d.* sufficed. The poor scholars who cleaned the boots of gentleman commoners often wrote their essays for them.

George's college, Balliol, had a reputation for high Toryism and riotous living. The awarding of degrees was so perfunctory that the young gentlemen fitted it in between all-night drinking parties and a visit to the barber. After having breakfast with the Master and listening to a dissertation on the Thirty-nine Articles over the cold side of beef and boiled eggs, the candidate presented his chosen examiner with a gold piece, having dined him well the night before. The *viva* was a formality and an applicant holding sound Tory views was in no danger of being refused his BA.

George Lucy, after five happy, riotous years, left Oxford with his servants and horses and a BA degree in about the year 1734. He lived for a time in Lichfield, where he studied the law in an attorney's office, and from there removed to Charlecote, where his elder brother was mentally unfit to carry out his obligations.

Dr William's widow—harassed-looking Frances, painted in pale blue much too young for her—spent the last years of her life in her native Derbyshire, and was buried by Dr William's side in the vault of Hampton Lucy Church the year before her elder nephew died.

All the older generation of Lucys was gone now; of near kin there were only the Hammond cousins: Jack, the Rector of Tolland, was the father of a long family by his wife, Sarah Morley (her appealing portrait with a white pet dog is at Charlecote). Their eldest son had gone to Corpus Christi, Oxford, and become a don there but had succumbed to smallpox very young. The next boy, John, was only eleven when his first cousin at one remove, George, succeeded to Charlecote.

At Hampton Lucy the Rector, George Hammond, who had married Alice Underhill, was childless. Davenport was practising in London as a lawyer and there is no record of his having married. The younger Molyneux, Broughton, Burgoyne, Throckmorton, and Underhill cousins were delighted to welcome a new régime at Charlecote. The place had been practically shut up for twenty years. Lord Molyneux (whose grandmother had been Robert Lucy's daughter) sent his congratulations and a present of wine. He would like to see his kinsman blessed with a wife (there had been three childless generations at Charlecote) and could recommend a most agreeable good-natured young lady, a connexion of his own, Lord Cardigan's sister. He begged to be allowed to have a copy taken of the Sea Battle in the Mediterranean, and of its companion piece of the Battle of the Boyne. If the same hand that copied for him the Cornelius Jansen family picture could carry out the commission, he would be greatly obliged, the family piece at Woolton being much admired. (He would appreciate a hundredweight of the best Warwickshire cheese to be sent by the Warrington carrier.)

George Lucy talked a great deal about marrying, but had no real intention of doing so. He had no brothers' debts to pay off, and was in enjoyment of an income of about three thousand a year. He was passionately interested in his health; young as he was, port-drinking at Oxford had brought on gouty tendencies. His candid, fresh face and his ingenuous letters are disarming. His natural kindness of heart went with a simple shrewdness. He feared boredom and the curtailing of his freedom. He loved his dogs, enjoyed fine clothes, and playing *cicisbeo* to pretty women without becoming too much involved, drank too much for his own good, but more surely impaired his constitution by the appalling experimental medicines which he was always eager to try. He was full of curiosity: he dragged his gouty leg to the edge of Vesuvius that he might look into the crater, visited Lisbon to see for himself the havoc of the earthquake, bumped all over Europe in an unsprung chariot, danced at Garrick's Jubilee, and to the very end had an appetite for a whole tench boiled in ale and dressed with lemon and rosemary.

George revered, as well he might, his Uncle William's memory. That good man, an ardent student of form in horses, had often been displeased by the tendency of humans to run contrary to expectations, as when his brother-in-law, the Cheshire parson, to whom he had sent presents of tobacco and whose sons he had hauled out of debt, was the first to dun him for money owed by his deceased brother. It was perhaps as well that good, irascible William did not live . to see his nephew and heirs grow up.

Each generation binds burdens on the back of the next. His uncle's bequest to Hampton Lucy Free School of four scholarships to Magdalen Hall had not yet been put into effect. The Hampton schoolmaster, Griffiths, writing in February 1746, points out that the recipients of the scholarship will waste it in idle mischief if they are required to spend more time at the University than the statute requires— that is, nine terms in three years:

. . . if your undergraduates are obliged to be resident during the long vacation and the two Winter months, December and January, when no business is done, no Governor perhaps in the House, no servants to attend—no provision to be got in the kitchen, no drink in the cellar (which I know has been the case) but everything brought from the shop, what can we hope for from raw and thoughtless young fellows, but, that having no companions in their own House, they will range about in quest of idle ones, will lounge about having no employment, indulge themselves in every vice without check or discipline, become a scandal to their society and the University, as well as a grief to their friends and relations.

In the schoolmaster's opinion, any promising scholar would be better off with a county curacy.

The money for the scholarships had ceased with the rents of Spitalfields. George, anxious to carry out the spirit of his uncle's bequest, presented Hampton School with two exhibitions to Hertford, Oxford, which had just obtained a charter giving it college status and was in need of endowments. Though no scholar himself, he had the age's reverence for scholarship. It shocked him to find his Uncle William's books tumbled about all anyhow in an attic at Charlecote. The Doctor had died before he was able to convert another room into a study, to replace the one in the west wing which had been demolished.

The water-gardens were found to be very expensive to keep up; the brickwork was constantly in need of repair. George had one of the canals filled in and made into a shrubbery. The year after he succeeded, the 'front Cupillo in the Great Garden' was rebuilt (this was the summer-house described by a later generation as a frightful Grecian building, and replaced in 1857 with the present orangery).

The new master of Charlecote was very careful of his health. The ten-foot, six-leaved screen that Colonel George had bought from John Rowland in 1720 painted in the Chinese manner and backed with gold leather, protected him from draughts when he dined alone in Jane Bohun's parlour.*

We begin to be aware that Charlecote had its domestic problems. Cooks could be dirty, thriftless, and lazy, menservants diced, exceeded their weekly beer allowance, and

---

* Mar. 8 1720: For painting the outside of a ten foot six leave skreen
    upon Cloth   £5. 0. 0.
For a skreen frame   £1. 0. 0.
For fold leather welting   18s. 0.
For gilt nails and making the skreen up   16s. 0.
For cleaning and varnishing the leather and a new painting the
    colours   10s. 0.
For brass hinges   5s. 0.

sneaked off to watch cock-throwing in Hampton. George was pestered by his friends to marry and indeed it began to look as if he would have no alternative in the interests of domestic peace. In a state of indecision he rode over to Snitterfield to ask the advice of his good neighbour and warm friend, Lady Coventry.

The last descendant of the Hales family having died childless, Snitterfield had been sold to Thomas Coventry, who succeeded as fifth Lord Coventry and was advanced to an earldom by William III. His daughter-in-law Lady Anne Coventry was much loved in the neighbourhood of Snitterfield and Charlecote. She had had a sad life; her husband, the second Earl, predeceased her and her only son died at Eton in his ninth year.

She had rebuilt the Hall in the late seventeenth-century style, and the old friendly connexion between Charlecote and Snitterfield, that went back to Tudor times, had been renewed. She did not think it was necessary for Mr Lucy to take so irrevocable a step as marrying to solve his servant problems. She knew of an excellent widow with grown-up sons who would be glad of a home. The recommendation was endorsed by the Balguys, in Derbyshire, Frances Lucy's relations. Thus it was that Philippa Hayes came to live at Charlecote in 1744 and the place settled down to tranquillity under her long benign rule. Mrs Hayes's Memorandum Book, written in brown ink with a good many blots and smudges, tranfixes for us the sleepy, uneventful years that slipped by, each one so like another, until from being a woman in vigorous middle age she had become old, and the last entries are in a shaky almost illegible hand.

New servants were engaged for the new squire at the local hiring fairs:

Oct. the 10th (1744)	Elizabeth Mercer came to be Dairy Maid to Mr Lucy.
Oct. the 16th	May Elson came to be Cook to Mr Lucy.
Oct. the 18th	Bridget Hall came to be House Maid to Mr Lucy.
Oct. the 16th (1745)	Elizabeth Washbrook came to be Dairy Maid to Mr Lucy.

Jan. the 20th (1747)	James Mounford came to be Park Keeper and Game Keeper to Mr Lucy [the Park had been newly paled and stocked with deer].
May the 31st	John Austen came to be Groom to Mr Lucy.
June the 25th	Elizabeth Webster came to be Cook to Mr Lucy in place of May Elson.

Writing to Mrs Hayes from London, to which he had fled from domestic politics, George says: 'I'm not at all surprised at my favourite's [May Elson's] conduct, because I always apprehended the first man that asked would be Master of her person, to say no more. I would have you act in what manner you think fit; her behaviour has been such that I think not the least regard ought to be had for her . . . [but] consider with yourself whether at present you can do without one . . . for as to a London Cook, I don't like my entertainments so well as to be at such an Expense.'

The Jacobite menace had passed; London was hysterically gay. At the Ridotta the press of people was so great that George wrote: 'I never knew the rooms so hot. I was the same as if I had just come out of a Bagnio.' He was mortified at not being able to attend the Ridotta, having had a bad run at whist and not feeling able to afford a new suit of black (the Court being in mourning). He had just bought himself an expensive suit from Hunt the tailor in Paternoster Row, of white satin embroidered 'with silver wyar spangles, pearl and bullion, both sides through, and finished with cross rosette spangles, the new Cumberland pattern.' The waist-coat was of 'richest blew Florence satin' which also lined the cuffs. Fine clothes were, and remained, one of the keenest pleasures of his life.

In May 1747 he wrote to Mrs Hayes at Charlecote:

I am just going to light up my windows for a Sea Victory obtained over the French by your friend Anson.* The news is, that they

* Defeat of the French fleet off Cape Finisterre, 1747. Lord Anson, with whom he was acquainted, rendered George some service in connexion with the voyage to Portugal.

upon a cruise met with the merchant fleet under Convoy of five French men-of-war, took the five men-of-war and several merchant ships, and were in pursuit of the rest. This news came by express, and may be depended upon for truth. I have heard nothing of your Hoop; but if it comes you may depend upon its being taken care of.

Hogarth was pinning the follies of London to his canvas like rather damaged butterflies in a show-case. Hoops provided much mirth, since gentlemen were bound to wear swords and the crush at smart entertainments was terrific. In an earlier letter George had written that at the Ridotta 'you now and then see something to divert you; one man stabs his sword into a lady's petticoat, another loses his bag to his wig, and the lady's hoop now and then shows a handsome leg. Such are the joys of this blessed place.' He enjoyed it all, the drums, the crushes, the late-night visits to the Ridotta, the mornings in the Bagnio in Jermyn Street, the rides to Richmond, the fireworks at Vauxhall, which was too crowded with the commonalty for his taste, the apt mimicries of Mr Foote at the French Opera House in the Haymarket. At Charlecote Mrs Hayes sat down at her pearwood escritoire and made out commissions for him to execute in London; tea, Bohea and the finest green from Thos. Twinings & Son at the Golden Lion in Devereux Court near the Temple, powdered loaf sugar, the best all-nut chocolate, Jordan almonds, French barley, Jamaican pepper, cinnamon, pistachio nuts, coffee beans, hartshorn (a restorative made from powdered horn), white starch, French brandy, paper for lining shelves, and so on. In her Memorandum Book there are pages and pages devoted to 'Fowls from the Tenants' and 'Fish taken out of the Old Canal', which formed the simple diet of the country household. Blankets were bought from Witney in Oxfordshire, coarse linen was bought at the back door from travelling hucksters. For pantry and kitchen use, and for the tenants' dinners, huckaback was considered good enough; the footmen and kitchen maids were hard on knife-cloths and dishclouts; but for Mr Lucy's table only damask was used, and smooth flax sheets were kept for his bed and for his use when travelling.

Tulipomania had come to Charlecote in Colonel George's day, when the stiff parterres had been planted with the flowers Dutch King William loved. During the uneasy years Marvell had written sadly of happier times before the Interregnum:

> When gardens only had their towers
> And all the garrisons were flowers . . .
> Tulips, in several colours barred
> Were then the Switzers of our 'guard'. . . .

The favoured varieties, feathered with indigo and rose or flamed with orange and sulphur, fetched fantastic prices. Mrs Hayes's son John at Zurendonck, an obscure corner of Brabant, where his regiment was awaiting marching orders (the Peace of Aix-la-Chapelle had just been concluded), wrote to her:

'As to what you mentioned about Mr Sherwood's tulip roots, I had sent to a gentleman at the Hague for a dozen different sorts before I received your letter, but he sent me word that he could not get any that answered to the description I gave him, for less than four ducats, that is near two guineas sterling apiece. . . .' Mr Sherwood was George Hammond's curate and did the work of Charlecote, Alveston, and Wasperton, and eventually became Rector at Hampton Lucy. He lodged at Charlecote to bear Mrs Hayes company when Mr Lucy went to take the waters at Cheltenham. He was a passionate gardener, and the ladies of Bath with whom George Lucy played quadrille for a shilling a fish gave Mr Lucy flower seeds to send him. He planted the cedar in the Rectory garden that is still there.

Blue-and-white china for the house was bought at the local fairs. In 1752 'One very large China Dish with a blue ground and Landscapes upon it, one very large China Dish flower'd with Red and Green, 2 large flat China Basons for Soop, coulered China, one Red and Gold 2 Quart Punch Bowl upon a white ground, 2 pair of China Images, white, a pair of blue China Parrotts, a pair of white China Cocks.' All the china used 'for common' was blue-and-white, and chocolate was drunk from flowered blue-and-white cups and poured from a chocolate-pot of the same pattern, some of which is still in use.

George Lucy sent Mrs Hayes a dozen bottles of Cheltenham water and all the little Charlecote community was dosed with it. Her letters to him, in a rambling but readable hand, are all about the movements of the neighbours; after illnesses and death, journeys were of the first interest. Mrs Dewes of Wellesbourne plans to visit Cheltenham and can be entrusted with a letter or a parcel; Miss Mordaunt of Walton is in London for the season and has promised to buy Mrs Hayes a fan as cheap and genteel a one as can be found. She sends the third volume of *Peregrine Pickle*, and a *Hymn to the Nymph of Bristol Spring*, with a volume of *Gil Blas*, and *is* pleased to find that Mrs Hayes is 'commenced a great Book-worm'.

Rumours of courtships, weather, and the state of the roads fill Mrs Hayes's letters to her employer. She is indignant that ladies going to the Stratford assembly complain they hardly dare attempt the road by Mr Lucy's park, it is kept so ill. Weather-bound travellers stay the night at Charlecote (the upstairs bedchambers are infested with rats; they are only fit for bachelors). A dog goes mad and bites a keeper. Many of their friends are being inoculated for smallpox. Every day Mrs Hayes goes out visiting or is visited.

July the 7th 1753.

The Day you left us we made a visit to Hampton. . . . Rector gone to Warwick to regale at the Swan with a choice collection of friends, Holyoake, Wigley, Jerry Hopkinson, and little Cornwell the Tailor, upon a turbot and a roasted fawn, which he did not seem to like. He came home just as we came away, really soberer than one would imagine. [After the lean years of his first curacy, George Hammond had taken rather too kindly to a life of ease.]

The weekly letter to Cheltenham begs George to buy paper: 'I wish you would furnish yourself with a stock of paper at Cheltenham. I think I have heard it is a famous place for that commodity and you have none of any sort left. . . .'

He was deeply interested in his own health and full of concern for Mrs Hayes's colds and Mr Sherwood's nervous fever. She writes in July 1753 to tell him that she has put herself in the Doctor's hands for a strong dose of Physick: '. . . never poor Devil sure was so sick in the world. I lay for above an hour quite insensible and they did not know whether I had life in me or not, but the old proverb was on my side and your humble friend is in Statu Quo today, but never will I venture upon Calomel again in such quantities. . . .'

From Cheltenham George Lucy moved to Bath, which he found crowded and dirty. Smallpox was raging in the poorer quarters, but it did not occur to him to risk inoculation for himself.

When not in pursuit of health, the Master of Charlecote dined his neighbours in the Great Hall, of which the wain-scoting had been 'new varnish't'. Round the long table assembled those whose forebears had dined at it in the days of the third Sir Thomas before the blight of the Interregnum had fallen on Charlecote.

George had his own conception of public duty, though there is no reference to attendances on the Bench. The park then lay all on the north side of the house. Its southern boundary ran from Hunt's Mill at the far corner of the village, along the Wellesbourne Brook, variously known as the Dene Stream or, more poetically, as the River Hele, and ended at the old Slaughter Ground behind the stables. The Stratford road turned sharply right at Hunt's Mill and, following the boundary of the park, crossed the brook at a footbridge called the Slaughter Bridge, in full view of the house, and, skirting the lime avenue, took its way through two enclosed fields, the Hither and the Further Town Grounds, into a bridle lane that led to Hunscot.

The old right of way through the ford below the house had fallen into disuse, for in autumn and winter the river was often impassable. It had been used in the past by carts wishing to cross the Great Meadow to Snitterfield and in the Civil War by soldiers. The rumbling traffic on the road so close to the house was a nuisance. In an earlier letter to

George Lucy at Cheltenham, Mrs Hayes had remarked: 'Squire Chester and his Lady passed by the Stable Gates on their way to Knowl but did not doe us the favour to send in, which was rather overlooking us. . . .'

At the Quarter Sessions at Warwick in October 1754 the High Sheriff held an inquisition on Mr Lucy's complaint of this inconvenience. A jury (including George's Oxford friends, Sir Harry Parke and Matthew Wise, of the Priory, Warwick) sat on the matter. The suggested new road was to be a continuation of the road through the village, crossing the Wellesbourne Brook and looping in a piece of land known as the Wellesbourne enclosures. George was to promise to erect a good and substantial stone bridge over the old ford, and to put the road into good repair, and always to keep it so.

Mr Venour, the parson of Wellesbourne, whose property was thus infringed, in high indignation contested the Sheriff's writ of *Ad Quod Dampnum* and took the matter to the Court of Chancery, where a decree was given in Mr Lucy's favour.

The road now runs round the perimeter of the park, for George eventually bought up the Wellesbourne enclosures after Mr Venour's death and added them to the park.

A young curate called John Dobson, a connexion of Sir Charles Mordaunt of Walton, Charlecote's near neighbour, now became George's secretary-companion. Together they went to Scarborough to see what the waters would do for George's gout. He had found 'little of wit or scandal stirring here', though the company was good: 'We have the honourable Mr Greville with Lady Betty Germaine and many Baronets.' (It was to this northern spa that Elizabeth had sent Burghley to repair his 'old crazed body'.) George returned to London to more late whist parties, went down to Charlecote to give dinners for Warwick and Stratford Races, at which he acted as Steward, and from there to Buxton, Cheltenham, and Bath, in search of health and gaiety.

To Cheltenham Mrs Hayes sent news of the neighbourhood in July 1749:

The Dean [of Down] and Mrs Delaney* are at Welsborne, and Mr and Mrs Dewes brought them here yesterday to see the House; for it can't be a visit as I had not been there to call. They spent their whole time walking about, only the old Lady gave us an anthem upon the Harpsichord, she really plays and sings uncomparably, but as to her extraordinary qualities I had not penetration enough to find them out, for she is a strange disagreeable woman. . . . Mr Dighton insists upon my telling you that he would have you look out for a Wife at Cheltenham for do all he can, there is no hopes for you at Clopton.

To divert him because he liked her to make mild, unmalicious fun of his friends' foibles, Mrs Hayes wrote to describe the visit of some neighbours who had stayed two hours:

the reason why I mention all this is to tell you what had like to have been The Melancholy consequence to Mr Sherwood, who was so much fatigued with doing the Honours of the House that he was sure he should have a violent fever, and was most excessively low-spirited and reduced to water gruell and Broth, by the help of which and two quiet days without seeing any Body, he seems to be tolerably recovered.

She did not, however, take her employer's symptoms lightly:

I am sorry [she writes] to hear there is so little Company at Cheltenham; methinks I would have it flourish for I must have a

---

* Mrs Delaney, the friend of Swift, wrote to her niece, Mary Dewes at Wellesbourne '. . . the Duchess has just shown me a sea-caterpillar she has in spirits, which was found at Buxton that is beautiful. . . . If Mr Lucy had the eyes of a virtuoso he might pick up such a thing for one?' At Wellesbourne Mr John Dewes had just built himself a pretty red-brick mansion, and Mrs Delaney had made two shell-work chimney pieces for it. Shell work was the rage. The parson of Snitterfield, Richard Jago, wrote an ode to Lady Coventry on viewing her fine chimney piece of shell work:

> *Shells in your hand the Parian rock defy*
> *Or agate, or Egyptian porphyry—*
> *More glossy they, their veins of brighter dye.*
> *See! where your rising pyramids aspire—*
> *Your guests, surpris'd, the shining pile admire.*

In 1758 Mrs Delaney was writing to her niece Mary Dewes: 'I am glad Mr Lucy is so well; I wish he would bring some shells from Naples; there are very pretty ones there, though none extremely rare.'

regard to it as it hath been of service to you. I should be glad to hear what Dr Tomlinson says to you, and whether he is content with you useing the Waters only, or if you still go on the Medicines, how you sleep, and if you get strength and many other particulars which I am afraid you will think too tedious to relate, especially if you have mustered up a set for the Black Table, where I wish you good success. . . .

After dull Cheltenham, he found Bath diverting.*

At the time of the death of Frederick, Prince of Wales, he wrote:

People here are extremely busy equipping themselves with Mourning which is to appear on Sunday next, mine will only be a Raven Grey Frock, Black Silk Waistcoat, Black Trousers. Our Ladies here are rather plain, the prettiest women in the place, in my opinion, are the two Miss Comptons, daughters of the Consul; we are related but not acquainted.

The last of the descendants of Sir Richard the Baronet, who had inherited the Kingsmill estates from his mother, Constance, wife of the second Sir Thomas, was Sir Berkeley Lucy, now living in London and of a great age. His only surviving child, Mary, had married Charles Compton, Consul at Lisbon, younger son of the fourth Lord Northampton, who had by her these two daughters and a son, who became the seventh Earl.

George soon made himself known to his pretty cousins and received an invitation to visit them at Lisbon, which appealed irresistibly to him. A bad attack of rheumatic fever, from which his recovery was slow, prevented him from accepting it. He became increasingly nervous about his health; it made him more than ever unwilling to undertake matrimony. Mrs Hayes wrote urging him: 'Why don't you strike up to the great Fortune, you who profess to love money so much?' (He was a hopeful but persistent loser at

---

* The visit of George III to Cheltenham in 1781 drew the attention of the *beau monde* to the rustic Cotswold market town. But not for another thirty years did the metamorphosis begin that turned Cheltenham into a town of creamy elegance, a smaller, leafier Bath.

all games of chance.) George found it safer to admire married
ladies, writing from Bath in November 1753:

I dined yesterday with Knightley, his lady I am in love with for
her sweetness of temper and affability, not to say anything of her
person which I think very agreeable. . . . The Knightleys and a
few more of my intimate friends leave the first full Moon, so I
shall be left alone; be that as it will I come here for my health and
if I can but obtain that I shall be very thankful; I met my dear
Fanny by Mr West's Park as I came here, how happy I should have
been to have been nursed by her, my cure would have been so
quick that I should have eat some Minced Pie at Charlecote at
Xmas, but I hope it is it will not be a great while before I see you.
Pray hath John try'd the New Hunter? How doth she shine?

Mrs Hayes replied with news of his herd of deer:

. . . I thought the best expedient was to consult Richardson [the
keeper] what fees was usually given for fawns, his answer was half
a Guinea a Brace, and as they would have you appear in a very
generous light, a Guinea over, besides contingent expenses. Lord
Brooke gave 3 for his fawns from Brettby, yours I find doe not
come from thence but from Sir Robt. Burdett's Park at Foremark. . . . Your servants returned safe last night with the Fawns.
They have only brought 3 Brace, 3 Males and 5 Females, 7 of them
very hearty strong Fawns, the other Pert, but had not been drop't
above 3 Days. . . . James thinks they will be much the couler of
Old Unicorn. . . . James teazes me to Death to ask you to let him
kill a Buck and bring to you as they are now in high order and
won't be so long. I was the more unwilling to deliver this Message
as you might possibly think I wanted some Venison myself, but so
far from it I declare none shall be Eat at home by me when you are
not there.

Having won his suit in Chancery about the road by Hunt's
Mill and the ford over the Wellesbourne Brook, George sent
for David Hiorn or Hiron of Warwick to build him a bridge.
The Hiorn brothers were builders and stone-masons; they
came from Oxfordshire, and it is thought learnt their trade
under the Smith brothers, to whose Warwick business they
succeeded.

Writing to George Lucy in March 1755, David Hiorn
explains that the side of the bridge toward the ford is

designed 'as plain as may be, the front toward the Park is a little decorated, the ornament in which will not be attended with any great Expence more than if plain, the Balisters are only ½ round, and the wall at the back of them solid to the roadside, we have kept it as low as I believe in a flood it will admitt of. If the Lake is opened and the banks sloaped as the line shows, I think it will have an agreeable Effect from the park side.'

Agreeable the effect certainly is, and has the happy knack of all eighteenth-century building of enhancing the contours of landscape so that the brook and the grass slopes on either side are drawn together by the gentle arch of the bridge. This was not accident; it came of a deep feeling for landscape that even commercial architects like the Hiorn brothers possessed.*

In March 1755 Mrs Hayes wrote: 'Pray have you either Sun or Moon at Bath, they doe not think proper to make their appearance here.' She gives him news of his dogs; he had five spaniels, Spruce, Rover, Daphne, Flora and Spring. 'You have had a great increase of yr. Dogs. Daph. brought forth 9, but they were all destroyed but one, which to be revenged she buried herself. Flora produced 6, of which 2 only were saved and she took it into her head to carry one of these about in her mouth till she had killed it. (When Spruce was dying George wrote sadly from Italy: 'if my poor Spruce is not dead before this reaches you, I should think if you gave her a little laudanum on a piece of Butter it would make her exit the least painful.')

George found that bobbing in the dirty water of the hot baths in a stiff yellow calico gown, in company with ladies of uncertain age similarly dressed, palled when the novelty of it wore off and he found the treatment improved neither his gout nor his rheumatism. His attack of rheumatic fever, which had partially paralysed his hands, had made him dread the damp of winter. In 1755 he decided to visit Portugal, at

---

* David Hiorn built Foremark Hall in Derbyshire for Sir Robert Burdett. Jointly the brothers were responsible for a number of churches in the Midlands, and for the construction of Sanderson Miller's design of the Shire Hall, Warwick.

the invitation of his cousin, the Consul, with young Mr Dobson, and there they stayed till the following June.

Mr Dobson, who made a living, as far as one can see, as a travelling companion-cum-secretary, wrote delightedly to Mrs Hayes about his patron's improvement:

To-morrow morning we change the scene and remove from Lisbon to the Baths of the Caldas situated in one of the pleasantest Parts of Portugal; Mr Lucy intends to bathe and drink the waters alternately; our stay there will probably be regulated by success; tho' I believe it can hardly fall short of six weeks. . . . I am unable to add anything to my former accounts of Mr Lucy's good state of Health, for indeed his Hands are at present the only Invalids.

Miss Mordaunt of Walton had written despondently to Mrs Hayes: 'One thing I think probable that Mr Lucy, who dare not venture upon an English woman, will bring a Portuguese lady with him; you know he is a great admirer of fine teeth, which they are famous for, and Mr Dobson says they have fine eyes. . . .' But George was not looking for a wife in Portugal. He visited the scene of the Lisbon earthquake and collected curious coloured stones to brighten Lady Anne's shell-work grotto instead.

The lasting memorial of his Portuguese tour was a black-and-white Portugal merino ram and several ewes, which travelled by sea and arrived thin and terrified at Charlecote, but settled down placidly on Warwickshire grass, where their descendants browse to this day.

George would not have been a man of his period if after this taste of travel he had not succumbed to the fashionable fever. In October they were off again, this time to Italy. In a stout vellum-bound notebook, Mr Dobson wrote down his impressions of the tour. He was single-mindedly bent on self-improvement. They had formed their ideas of Venice from the paintings of Canaletto, and were disappointed with the actuality. Mr Dobson, who writes distantly of himself and his patron in the third person, observes that 'indeed at a Distance [Venice] appeared like the Venus of Cities, rising out of the Sea in wonderful Beauty; they were no sooner within her Streets but many lovely Ideas vanish'd; for the ordinary Houses are of Brick covered with kind of Plaister which the Damps arising from the Water moisten and destroy; once or twice they perceived a Smell upon the Canal almost as offensive as the Billage Water of a Ship'. He was fond of boring facts, such as 'Thirty thousand Jews inhabit this astonishing City' and 'Five hundred Oxen are slaughtered every week for publick Use'. They soon left Venice and had a miserably tedious journey by water, were unimpressed by Bologna and crossed the Rubicon without noticing it. Alarmed by the thought of malaria, they did not linger in Rome, but hurried on to Naples, where the sulphur in the air was said to be health-giving. Lodgings were taken out at Grumo, and Mr Dobson was delighted with Herculaneum, where he saw an ancient kettle which reminded him of one in the kitchen at Walton.

George Lucy confessed in a letter to Mrs Hayes that time spent 'to use the polite phrase in hunting Virtu' was rather wasted on him, 'as I had the misfortune not to look into an old brick wall as far as others'. He had successfully evaded education at Oxford, and formed his aesthetic judgements spontaneously, and often very happily. His descriptions are not loaded with classical references, as Mr Dobson's are. He is more interested in the fact that at Puteoli they have peas ripe in the natural ground in December. Clothes are his chief preoccupation; Naples is most sociable—'people here dress much and I have been obliged to daub myself all over Silver, accompanied with a Sword and a Bag Wig'. He rides out in the morning in his one-horse chaise and in the afternoon in the chariot (both accompanied him from Charlecote). He begs Mrs Hayes to have a box made and to send out to him the best embroidered suit, the light-coloured suit of uniformity laced with gold, the white Dresden waistcoat with the two pairs of velvet breeches, the one red, the other black, and half a dozen more shirts with the Dresden ruffles tacked to them ('the Lace'd ones I don't care to venture these dangerous times').

Mr Dobson has a good deal to say about the inclemency of the celebrated climate of Naples. 'In a sharp Tramontana the Fountains have been adorn'd with hanging Icicles; and

Snow has fallen in the Streets.' During their residence out at Grumo 'they gave themselves little Concern about Virtù; Mr Lucy employ'd his Mornings in riding or bathing in the Sebelthus; and when he walk'd he studied Agriculture'. Mr Dobson went up the slopes of Vesuvius on a donkey and Mr Lucy in a carrying chair on the backs of eight men.* Mr Lucy confessed to Mrs Hayes how greatly he admired an Italian lady married to an Englishman: 'you will excuse me if I am a little lavish in the praise if this Lady, for to tell you the truth I think she is one of the handsomest women I ever saw, even Lady Coventry would be in danger of being eclipsed by her.' But he was longing to be at home again. 'You never mention anything about my poor dumb animals in your letters, nor what improvements are made about my House.' He sends his best compliments to dear Lady Anne Coventry. 'I have written to Mr John Mordaunt to beg he will advertise the Races at Stratford and also act the part of Steward, so that if I do remain here, the young Ladies will not want a Cicisbeo.'

His fine clothes never reached him; the ship in which they had been sent was boarded by Moorish pirates and the box carried off to Algiers.

Mr Dobson wrote to the Rev. M. Hammond at Hampton Lucy in October 1757:

A very sprightly Lady of my Acquaintance has given it under her own Hand that no Body opens a Letter from abroad, without expecting something clever in it. This is a mortyfying circumstance to us poor Travellers who find themselves depriv'd in an Instant of that great Privilege of being dull, which is the inherent Birthright of the scribbling Fraternity. Not having any particular Propensity to be *clever*, I am determined to play the *learned* part; and, I hope the Treasures of classical Antiquity which I shall lay before you will excuse me from attempting to be ingenious *alla moderna*. I thought in the first place to discourse upon a Roman Ruin which I visited three Days ago, but for fear of doing Injustice to the Brick and Mortar of those wise and happy Architects of Atella, I shall only observe that I saw an old Arch, and touched an old Wall,

* He brought back an enormous slab of cooled lava to Charlecote as a souvenir of this expedition.

with a Pleasure much more easily imagined than described. Have
you tasted any Fig-Peckers at Hampton? Delicate Birds as small as
Larks, and covered with the most exquisite Fat. In Italy they call
them Beccafichi; they feed upon Figs and Grapes. [Then a mis-
quotation from Martial.] But O! my good Friend what would you
not give for a Glass of Falernian Wine! . . . Virgil extoll'd the wine
of Rhoetia, but at the same time, gave the Preference to this
Falernian Vine;—
  —*eloquo te Carmine dicam Rhoetica? nec cellis ideo contende Falernis.*
I shall conclude with assuring you that over an excellent Bottle of
Hampton Claret, Traveller Dobson will say anti-classically—
minimum Falernis Incidet Unis (sic). We are just come in from a
disagreeable walk of two Miles in the Dark and some Rain; our
Chariot run up against one Bank and genteelly threw us upon the
other; we have, thank God! received no manner of Injury and are
in excellent Spirits.

George longed for a Charlecote pheasant and found the
Beccafichi no substitute. He had come to Italy for his health,
and to this end had allowed himself to be half-frozen in the
Tramontana and choked with sulphur fumes on Vesuvius,
but he could not endure to be away from Charlecote for
another summer.

In March 1758 they left Naples for Rome, *en route* for
home. The weather was kind and the city at its loveliest.
George resigned himself; 'we have now been ten days, and
after the 3 first which I took to rest myself, we entered upon
the study of Virtù; we spend at least 4 hours in the morning
in this business—all the week long we are in a hurry (except
Sunday which is always allotted to me as a day of rest).
Agreeable to your orders I have shewn my face and person
to the celebrated Pompeo Battoni, to take the likeness
thereof.'

The fashionable painter demanded a great many sittings—
the picture could not be completed in less than four weeks.
Mr Dobson, busily filling up his notebook with observations
on *virtù* was delighted at the respite. Once in Rome, George
determined to enjoy it. He entertained and was agreeably
entertained in return. In the Battoni portrait he looks fresh-
coloured and younger than his forty-eight years, though

already inclining to stoutness, in the suit of blue velvet laced with gold. There is no languor or ill-health apparent in his looks. Charles Lucy, a poor relation living in Rome who got a precarious living by copying old Masters, called on him. He had written asking for commissions in the past, and George, glad to employ him, set him to work copying various subjects (chosen by Mr Dobson as being suitable for hanging in the bedrooms at Charlecote—a Virgin with a Cupid, a Satyr with a Cupid, Tobit and the Angel, the Daughter of Herodias). Pleased with the idea of italianizing Charlecote, George ordered a set of twenty views in tempera of Italian scenes and ancient buildings for the parlour, and two large *verd antique* tables mounted with brass rims.

He made the acquaintance of Robert Mylne,* later to be the architect of Blackfriars Bridge, the brilliant young son of an Edinburgh surveyor who had just won the coveted prize of the Concours of the Rome Academy. Mylne drew for him a number of copies of Raphael's heads and Piranesi's views to lie on the *verd antique* tables at Charlecote and delight the young ladies of Walton and the neighbourhood. He bought also some marble busts, copies of the antique, which had charmed him, and for Mrs Hayes a bouquet of feather flowers under glass, indistinguishable from reality.

He could not enjoy Rome with an undivided mind because of the war between France and Germany, which he feared might hinder his return to Charlecote. He wrote cheerfully to Mrs Hayes in April 1758:

We heard last night that there had been an engagement between the Prussian and Hanoverian forces, under the command of the Prince of Brunswick, and the French, and that the latter had five thousand killed upon the spot, as many taken prisoners, and all their baggage taken. If this news be true, it will greatly facilitate our journey homewards.

They arrived at Florence in the first week of May, but had no time for its incomparable beauties, apart from one ecstatic

---

* Among the family papers there is a recipe for a 'Wash for colouring Brick fronts, endorsed Mr Mylne'. It was never used, but it makes one wonder if he did not intend asking Mylne to give Charlecote an up-to-date façade.

exhausting morning in the Grand Duke's gallery. Sir Horace Mann, the English envoy, invited them to his weekly conversazione, and they dined with the Comptons, who were also on their way back to England. The talk among the English visitors was all of the difficulty of getting a pass through the French lines. After much harassing indecision, George decided to cross the Alps into Switzerland and make through Bavaria for the Rhine, and thus reach Holland.

Though his rheumatism was much improved and he could use his hands and walk without a stick, draughts gave him neuralgic pains in the head, heights made him giddy, and he became so stiff in the joints after an hour or two in a jolting coach that he had to be lifted out of it; yet he intrepidly undertook the return journey by roads that were precipitous and often partly washed away by floods.

Mr Dobson, notebook on knee, wrote it all down; his enjoyment was undiminished, in spite of the 'Buggs which make intolerable Depredations upon English Bodies'.

The journey up the Rhine by boat against a head wind was necessarily slow. George was in dread all the time, knowing that Cologne, their destination, was garrisoned by the French, but they were not molested and got at last to The Hague, where he was able to draw breath again, and even to write to Mrs Hayes about the flatness of Holland and the large size of its cattle. 'Should be obliged to you if you would have my bed altered', he wrote—the lumpy bug-ridden beds in foreign inns had made him long for his own—'and instead of the feather bed order another mattress; and instead of the cords of the bedstead, lay some flat boards the breadth of the bedstead, no matter what sort, provided they are clean and free from insects.'

The news of Sir Berkeley Lucy's death at the age of eighty-seven had reached them in Rome. The male line of Richard Lucy who was the second son of the second Sir Thomas ends here, for Sir Berkeley's only son had died young. The line of the Castle Cary Lucys, descendants of the Bishop's eldest son, had apparently by now petered out, though descendants of the younger sons of this branch are heard of in Devonshire in 1789 and at Ledbury in 1785. But there was no cause for perturbation; the master of Charlecote was still in his forties; he would marry any day now.

One of his pleasanter duties on coming home was to ride over to Snitterfield House and pay his respects to Lady Anne Coventry. The old lady received him in the square parlour filled with her shell work. He confided to her that he had had such a glut of *virtù* that it was a pleasure to return to his old-fashioned hall, but at the same time the place struck him as being in need of improvement. The idea of improving Charlecote remained at the back of his mind for a whole year, during which he picked up the threads he had dropped nearly two years earlier. Bath drew him back, for he had missed the gaming tables more than he liked to admit.

Mrs Delaney thought Bath ideal; 'all the entertainments of the place are in a small compass, and you are at your liberty to partake of them or let them alone just as it suits your humour'. The organized idling of the day made an evening at the tables even more attractive. In the mornings it was polite to ask first for a friend's health; the evenings resounded to the cry, 'What are trumps?' Physicians did not discourage the distraction of gambling, seeing their patients more nearly ready to die of ennui than of illness.

George wrote to Mrs Hayes in February 1760: 'The very first I have played in the public rooms was last night for half crowns with Mrs Wise and some other persons who I was Unacquainted with, they beat me, but not to hurt; 'tis stupid enough but better than doing Nothing. I'm often pressed to the Gold Table, being told how some of the Performers are inferior to me in play, but the weather has been so bad that the Gudgeon don't bite, and I believe I shall leave them to prey on each other.'

A young painter, almost unknown, had come to settle in Bath since George Lucy's last visit there, and was beginning to be talked of. He was a quick worker and could produce a very tolerable likeness from a few sittings, not like Signor Battoni who had had to be flattered and cajoled into undertaking a commission at all. Mrs Delaney wrote rather disparagingly: 'This morning went with Lady Westmorland

to see Mr Gainsborough's pictures—the man that painted
Mr Wise and Mr Lucy—and they may well be called what
Mr Webb unjustly says of Reubens—they are splendid
impositions.' George wrote to Charlecote that he had been
'sitting for his Phiz' in the artist's painting chamber. 'I was
with Mr Gainsborough on Monday last, from two of the
Clock till four, by which I lost my dinner; whether I looked
the better or the worse for it, I know not. . . . The dress is
to be entirely altered, a blue cloth coat with a little gold
embroidery, which the painter thinks will give it a little
more life. . . .'

Neither patron nor painter was quite pleased with the
finished portrait, though George wrote to Mrs Hayes in
March of the same year (1760): 'My picture, I am told, is so
like that people who are Unacquainted with me challenges it
for a person they have seen in the rooms, dressed in such a
habit; but after all this, don't set your heart upon it lest upon
the view you should be disappointed.'

The artist provided a frame and the portrait, a head and
shoulders, was hung in the drawing-room, which was rather
dark and did not show it off to advantage. The free and
brilliant emphasis of Gainsborough's late style had not yet
developed—the execution of George Lucy's head is tight and
in effect dull. Another likeness, which was most probably
turned over to a pupil to finish, was taken for the Rector of
Hampton to hang in his study.*

Mrs Hayes saw him return to Bath with regret; she feared
he found Charlecote dull in spite of her care for his comfort.
The Italian pictures had arrived by canal from Pickford's
wharf in London. Carved and gilt wood stands were made
for the *verd antique* slabs. A pair of large gilt mirrors of
Chinese design from Chippendale's workshop were ordered
and hung in the big north bedroom where George Lucy
slept, but seldom were their protective holland bags
removed. The housemaid, Bridget Hall, who had come to
work under Mrs Hayes fourteen years ago, had to be given
notice. She had been drinking heavily for some time and the

---

* The receipt for the painting is among the Lucy papers; it cost eight guineas.

fact could no longer be ignored. Lady Chedworth of Stowell in Gloucestershire, to whom Bridget applied for a situation, wrote to Mrs Hayes for a reference:

Madam,

I beg the character of Bridget Hall, your housemaid—she says she can distill, get up fine linen and work well with her needle—a valuable servant by the account she gives of herself.

Now, Madam, do me the favour to answer these queries. Whether Bridget is strictly honest and may be trusted alone in a fine house of goods. Whether she drinks, her nose and face being very red, or whether it is a humour. Whether she is very good-natured and will bear a fault. Whether she is healthy and strong and cleanly, and keeps the house so. And I must intreat to know the reason you parted with her. I intreat you, Madam, not to veil any of her faults, and you may depend on my keeping it a secret if you desire it. I hope you will pardon the freedom, but it is a great charge to take care of my house, which obliges me to press for her true character. . . . I beg your answer by the return of the post—it will be vastly obliging. Pray how long did she serve you? How many years?

Mrs Hayes feared that this domestic upheaval had driven the master of Charlecote from home. He was drawn back, however, in the summer of 1760 on his appointment as High Sheriff and by a new and absorbing interest. In the September of 1757, while he and Mr Dobson were at Naples, David Hiorn had completed the bridge that carried the new road from Charlecote to Stratford, over the Wellesbourne Brook. The buildings of Hunt's Mill that had stood since Domesday were demolished, and a walled kitchen garden built on the other side of the road, with a fine disregard for convenience (it was a walk of half a mile from the kitchen door). The brook at this point, fed by the mill-stream, formed a pond and with the banks sloped, as Hiorn had suggested, made a pretty piece of ornamental water, reflecting the swans who preferred it to the Avon (they were ringed on one foot and had one wing pinioned to ensure that they did not desert). George, coming to his property with a fresh eye after the Italian tour, was delighted with the effect. He saw now that Captain Thomas's water-gardens were outmoded as well as

being troublesome to maintain. They did not complement
the old house,★ which had originally risen out of a thickly
wooded landscape, but overweighted it all one side, with a
formality that did not suit the rustic brickwork: the park
with its radial avenues had nothing to offer the eye.

Lady Anne at Snitterfield had long ago suggested he
should employ Lancelot Brown, the landscape gardener. Her
husband's cousin, the sixth Earl, who had married Miss
Gunning, had been faced with just such a problem on his
Worcestershire property of Croome. Indeed, it had been a
far more daunting proposition than Charlecote, lying as it
did low on marshy ground between the Avon and the
Severn. Lord Coventry had decided in the end to sweep
away the sagging Jacobean house with its courtyard and
gatehouse, and build something worthier. The man who had
conceived and carried out the ambitious plan of draining the
park by underground culverts and forming an artificial
stretch of water in which the rebuilt house would stand
reflected, was nicknamed Capability. He had been associated
with William Kent over the remodelling of Stowe for Lord
Cobham, and more recently had worked wonders at Warwick, where the Castle was situated between the river and
the growing town. By extending the castle lawns down to
the river's edge and piling up screens of greenery behind it,
he had made it into the most romantic pattern of ancientry
in England. Horace Walpole found it enchanting: '. . . one
sees what the prevalence of taste does; little Brook who
would have chuckled to have been born in an age of clipt
hedges and cockle-shell avenues, has submitted to let his
garden and park be natural', he wrote in 1751.

Brown was much in demand, but not spoilt by success, or
above undertaking quite small and insignificant assignments.
While staying with Lord Warwick, he had ridden over to
advise on the opening out of the Wellesbourne Brook to give
the same effect in miniature as the artificial water at Croome.

★ It will be remembered that Foxe wrote of Charlecote in 1545: '. . . you
know the lie of that house, how it is deserted on every side, shut off by hills
and thickets from almost all light. . . .'

In Mrs Hayes' Memorandum Book there is the entry: '1757. Sept. the 29th. Mr Brown began to make alterations upon Wellsborn Brook, under the direction of Horsbrough', who must have been one of Hiorn's workmen.

In April 1761 George wrote:

Mr Brown was here [in Bath] on Sunday last and staid until Tuesday, when he called upon me, not upon business as he said, but to enquire after my health, and told me he should not be at Charlecote till May, which I suppose will be June at soonest. I did not well know how to construe this visit; I told him the time was elapsed for a second payment which he said was no matter as he did not want [lack] money, but upon my offering him a £100 note he pulled out his pocket book and carried it off with him.

In May 1760 an agreement of five articles was entered into between George Lucy and Lancelot Brown.*

Article I
To widen the river Avon, and lay its banks properly, giving them a natural and easy level; corresponding with the ground on each side the river.

Brown had been successful with Moor Park in Hertford-shire, the seat of that Lord Anson for whose victory over the French at Finisterre George had lit a candle in the window of his London lodgings. Like Charlecote, Moor Park lay low, and lost much of its impressiveness by not dominating its surroundings. Brown flattened the ground all round it and in the middle distance raised what Walpole called 'so many artificial molehills' crowned with plantations. He repeated this plan at Charlecote. His contemporaries were ready to accuse him of vandalism for sweeping away so many fine, straight avenues of well-grown trees and dotting stiff, fenced-in clumps about instead. They could not visualize, as he could, a day when the clumps, thinned out, would become groups of two or three noble trees placed with an

---

* The original has been lost, but it is quoted in Mary Elizabeth Lucy's journals. Though she was often careless, there is no reason to suppose she did not record the substance of it.

artist's precision, leading the eye on to dreamy distances of
fallow and woodland.

The avenue from the gatehouse to the road was thinned,
and the line of elms leading to the churchyard renewed. The
lime avenue planted by the first Sir Thomas was now in its
prime and was preserved.* Sentiment and taste struggled
for mastery with George and in the end economy dictated
the limit of the improvements, which cost only £525.

Article 2
*To sink the fosse quite round the meadow, of a proper width, to make it a
sufficient fence against the deer, and of a proper depth to hide the pales
from the terrace. . . .*

This was modified in favour of *Article 3*:

*To fill up all the ponds on the north front of the house, to alter the slopes,
and give the whole a natural, easy, and corresponding level with the house
on every side.*

The neatly ruled gravel walks, the brick canals, and all the
formal layout of the late seventeenth century were swept
away, and Nature came back into her own.

The Great Meadow sunset-wards across the river was
levelled flat, and semicircular clumps of trees were planted in
the middle distance to lead the eye toward the gently wooded
slope of Welcombe on the horizon. George liked to think of
himself as a farmer; the Great Meadow had always been
arable land, and arable it remained. The lowering of the river
bank on that side made it more liable to flooding and less
productive, till by the end of the century it had gone back to
fallow.

Capability's signature on Charlecote is in the concealed
damming of the sluggish Wellesbourne Brook so that it
tumbles in a noisy cascade into the Avon, and the conversion
of Captain Thomas's formal parterres and bowling green
into a raised garden divided from the park by a ha-ha, which
makes the browsing deer appear to tiptoe on the very edge

---

* The same thing happened at Ashridge, where there was an ancient avenue
of limes which Brown spared.

of the cedar lawn. With endless cheap labour at his command, it was a mere bagatelle to him to build the cedar lawn six feet above the level of the court and carry it on, shaped like the prow of a ship riding high above the green wash of the park. Wherever a dark accent was needed, he planted the Scotch firs he loved—in the Wilderness, and by Hiorn's bridge. The great cedars of Lebanon on the lawn now spread their layers of shade as he meant them to. Just past their prime, his oaks, chestnuts, walnuts, and beeches throw their afternoon shadows on the cropped turf in a way that must make the most indifferent beholder catch his breath with the realization: *here is England*.

The idea of making the Avon serpentine according to the contemporary ideal of beauty was abandoned when it was seen how much more beautiful it was when opened out into great lake-like stretches.

Last of all, Capability agreed to find all the necessary trees, to replant any that might die, and to sow with grass-seed and Dutch clover all the altered ground. The work was begun in May 1760, under the direction of his foreman, Midgeley, who in the year following started work on the improvements to Castle Ashby.*

In the midst of these delightful preoccupations, the Rev. Mr Hammond, who had been in failing health for some time, died at Hampton Lucy, and Mr Sherwood, who had been waiting patiently for the opportunity, succeeded him as Rector.

The flood of 1947 that destroyed so many of the Lucy papers ruined the bulk of George Lucy's letters, but between 1760 and 1765 it is clear he was absent from Charlecote a great deal. He writes from Bath in 1762 about highwaymen who threatened the safety of travellers:

We are in a sad way here, robb'd on all sides. If I go to the Loo Table I lose my Money; if I go out of Town, I stand a good chance

* In the Memorandum Book Mrs Hayes wrote: '1760. May the 3rd, Mr Brown began to make the Ground within the Stable Gates under the direction of Midgeley.' This refers to the hollowing out of the approach to the house on this side, which so artfully gives it the effect of being set on rising ground.

to meet a Collector; it is no longer ago than Thursday last, a Gent. riding out in a Chaise about four in the afternoon with his Serv't was attacked and robb'd between the Upper and Lower Bristol roads . . . and about three miles from this Noble City. If the Magistrates dont take a little more care, it may be well soon if we dont loose our lives as well as our Money; I think one may draw a parallel between what Rome was before the time of Sextus Quintus, and what Bath is since the death of Nash.

The last observation did little to comfort Mrs Hayes. She thought she might revive George's interest in Charlecote if she had some of the best rooms done up. It was really time. He was ready to be interested if it did not involve too much expense. After telling her of the state of his latest cold ('I hope to God my cold is getting better'), he agrees to look for damask for curtains at Petingals. He asks the advice of various ladies; 'the hanging in Festoons they say will certainly darken the rooms. . . . I did before I left Charlecote give orders to have the sashes of the Hall painted which may be done at the same time with the Parlour. . . . I shall submit to Standbridge in painting the Cornish [cornice] of the best room and think the colour should be white to correspond with the rest, but as I pretend to no judgement in these Matters, my only consideration is to take Nothing from, but add as much light as I can to your room.' Standbridge had seen some decoration in Lord Plymouth's house that he thought very fine, but George was firm. He would not have his doors and cornices picked out with silver, which must tarnish in a room where there was not a constant fire kept. His untutored taste was good. '. . . What have I to do (who am so happy to have a good old House) but to make it decent, and to content myself with [it], as it is already designed?'

Between 1763 and 1769 all the old wainscoting was taken out of the principal rooms. He decided on a chaste white marble chimney-piece from Messrs Gilliam Taylor of Piccadilly and Hyde Park Corner for the drawing-room. It was said that Mr Lucy must surely have had matrimony in mind, for the room when finished was feminine in every detail. William Hiorn's estimate for new doors with moulded architraves, for an 'enrich'd cornice', for 'Norway oak sashes and frames made in a light manner and hung compleat and glaz'd with best London brown Glass . . . the finishing colour dead white . . .' came to under two hundred pounds. The elegant white room, showing off the views of Italy, the busts of Brutus and Portia, the branched candlesticks, and Jane Bohun's looking-glasses, was the proper setting for a lady of fashion, and hopes for the future were raised again.

In the dining-room* at the foot of the great staircase the ceiling was raised and a carved stucco cornice run round it. It was lined with shallow fielded panels to match those on the stairs, painted white, and the panels of doors† and the window-frames were carved with ovolo mouldings. A large fire-screen, worked with a bouquet of flowers by Dr William's wife in her widowhood, kept the heat of the fire from the diners' backs. From the windows Capability's new layout opened up a view of the river and the distant prospect of Hampton Lucy.

Lady Anne should have been alive to advise and encourage. She had died very old in the March of 1763 and was buried at Badminton, the home of her childhood. George wrote to Mrs Hayes describing the impressive night funeral, at which he was a pall-bearer:

. . . Mr Phelps and Myself set out for Badminton about twelve of the clock, and arrived there between Three and Four, where we found a decent dinner provided for us, where we sat till near tenn, when the Undertaker came to inform us they were preparing for the Solemnity. Our Scarf and hat bands being put on, we were ordered out one by one, and our place given us. I had the honour of the Right hand at the Head. . . . The processions began soon after tenn, when we walked quite round a very large Court, amidst great numbers of wax flambeaux, in very bad weather. When we came to the church door the plume of feathers with the Pall and Escutcheons (under which she likewise lay in state at Badminton) were taken off and an extreme handsome Coffin appeared, whether covered with Cloth or Velvet I know not, three rows of large gilt Nails went round the Coffin, adorned with Coronets on the Sides,

---

* Now the Tapestry room.
† The sketch for these is among the Lucy papers.

and a large plate on the top with her Name and Age; the ceremony was performed by Mr Jago [the Snitterfield poet-parson] in a very handsome and proper Manner. . . . As I understood Mrs Morrice was there, I desired the Butler to inform her I should be glad to speak with her. When, after a flood of tears, we began to cheer up, talked a little, then parted. . . .'

Mrs Hayes's handwriting in the Memorandum Book has been growing increasingly shaky, as it records 'Woodcocks kill'd at Charlcote', and fish taken out of the pools and from the Great Bason in the Court. In November 1768 there is the entry: 'Mrs Stokes came to be House-Keeper to Mr Lucy.' This was the year that George first had the idea of complementing the stone bridge over the Wellesbourne Brook with a wooden copy that should span the Avon just below the cascade. A Coventry builder called Standbridge supplied an estimate and a drawing, but the structure did not survive a series of bad winters—only the remains of the stone piers show where it once stood.

In 1769 George was again asked to be High Sheriff, and as his soul delighted in showing hospitality and wearing rich clothes, he was happy to accept. He appointed William Hunt, the Town Clerk of Stratford, as his Under-Sheriff.

Garrick's Shakespeare Jubilee took place that year. The date of this rejoicing was arranged to coincide with Stratford Races, of which George was Steward, where a Jubilee Plate, worth fifty guineas, was to be run for. It was unthinkable for a Lucy to miss a day's racing, but Mr Garrick's public breakfast was tactfully timed for nine o'clock in the morning. The guests staying in Stratford had been woken at five with a fusillade of cannon shot, bell-ringing, and songs composed by Mr Garrick. Dr Arne's Oratorio *Judith* was rendered in the church with an orchestra and choruses brought from Drury Lane.

The grand parade of visitors round the town headed by the great Garrick himself took place in a downpour. George's bad leg would in any case have prevented him from joining in it; he drove off to the races, returning for the dancing at night in the wooden Rotunda hurriedly erected on the Bancroft. Rustic Stratford gazed with awe at this building, which had an orchestra capable of holding 100 performers and was lit by a chandelier of 800 candles. Two wagon-loads of fireworks had arrived from London with hundreds of fancy lamps for stringing along the streets and house-fronts.

Next day it was still raining; the Rotunda could only be reached by duckboards. A damp but attentive audience heard Garrick discourse on Shakespeare and joined in the singing of an ode, composed by himself. The only way to ward off chills was to drink turtle soup, hot brandy, and madeira in great quantities. As soon as the rainy dusk came on fireworks were set off. Set-pieces and illuminated transparencies fizzled out in the steady drizzle. But the festival spirit, once aroused, inflamed with Shakespearian ardour and hot toddy, refused to be damped. The midnight masquerade in the Rotunda was hysterically gay. Most of the guests wore dominoes, though a few had answered the challenge to appear in Shakespearian costume. Lord Grosvenor wore an Eastern habit, brought back from the Grand Tour. Mr Boswell appeared as a Corsican Brigand, and tried to recite some verses of his own, but no one would listen. Tradition has it that George Lucy wore the suit of plum-coloured cloth trimmed with silver lace and silver filigree buttons that is still preserved at Charlecote. The dancing did not end till five, and by then the coaches were too deep in mud to be moved and the guests had to walk to their lodgings through the wet dawn.

The deer-stealing legend, which had gone underground since the early part of the seventeenth century, reappeared. It had lain forgotten for over a hundred years, yet had mysteriously remained alive in country memories, which were burnished up for the benefit of the antiquarians who drove out to Charlecote from the Festival at Stratford to gaze with awe on the simple wooden park gates on which the poet was alleged to have hung a rude rhyme lampooning the prosecuting JP. A tumbledown barn on the Fulbrook part of the Lucy estate was pointed out as Shakespeare's Deer Barn, for it was there that the young man was supposed to have stowed his quarry. A tumbledown stile, of which the top bar collapsed, flinging the unwary climber to the ground,

was christened Shakespeare's Stile and became a feature of
the place. The cottagers did good trade in souvenirs, fragments of the poet's cloak, the deer's horns, and so on;
Stratford was already leading the way with wooden boxes
made out of the mulberry tree that had sheltered the poet in
his years of retirement.

Foote, Garrick's rival, was delighted with the fiasco of the
Festival, with the fireworks extinguished as soon as lit and
the gingerbread amphitheatre that tumbled to pieces as soon
as made. It was too easy a target for ridicule. The year
following Garrick replied with restraint to an invitation to
organize another Festival at Stratford, saying that he was
very low after a long illness, and suggesting that the annual
commemoration should take place on Shakespeare's birthday; remembering the mud, he urged that Stratford, as well
as being the happiest, should also be rendered the handsomest town in England: '. . . see your streets be well paved
and kept clean, do something to the delightful meadow,
allure everybody to visit the *Holy-land*, let it be well lighted
and clean underfoot, and let it not be said, for your honour
and I hope for your interest, that the town which gave birth
to the first genius since the Creation is the most dirty,
unseemly, ill-paved, wretched looking place in Britain'.*

A candle had been lit which the rain of that Race Week of
September 1769 nearly extinguished, but which, smouldering on, was to turn into a fixed luminary.

Mrs Hayes had resigned the reins to Mrs Stokes and kept
her own room. It was natural, and in every way suitable,
that young Jack Hammond (he was in fact thirty-six) should
be offered the post of secretary to his cousin at Charlecote,
his father, the Rector of Tolland, being dead and he having a
mother and a sister down in Somerset to support. Jack
Hammond gladly exchanged the prospect of a Somersetshire
curacy for that of eventually succeeding to the livings of
Charlecote and Hampton Lucy, when they should fall
vacant. Mr Blake and Mr Sherwood, the incumbents, were
vigorous as yet, so he put all his youth, good temper, and

* See Ivor Brown and George Fearon, *Amazing Monument*, 1939.

adaptability, at the service of his cousin George, whose poor health was such a source of concern to his many friends.

Mr Hammond would have been less than human if he had not occasionally dwelt on the unlikelihood of his cousin marrying now. George Lucy was fifty-five and had acquired the habit of bachelorhood. He lived an invalid life,* rising late, and going slowly round the estate on horseback. He still dined out, but seldom further afield than Walton (the Mordaunts), Alveston (the Gray Skipwiths), Ettington (the Shirleys), or at the Rectory at Hampton Lucy. When Mrs Hayes died in January 1772, after a prolonged decline, he felt the death of such an old friend keenly. She had left him all her small personal estate and made him her executor: 'I also give to George Lucy, out of the great regard I have for him, my cornelian seal, and desire he will accept my buff tabby to cover his easy chair.' (The large wing elbow chair is still at Charlecote, but the buff tabby is long worn away.) After her funeral in Hampton churchyard, he turned aside to the Rectory to visit his old cousin, Alice Hammond, now bedridden. The late Rector's widow had her own rooms, with pictures and furniture that had come to her from Idlicote, overlooking the Park, for Mr Sherwood, the Rector, was a bachelor, and Smith of Warwick's Rectory was too large for a single man. Well, Jack Hammond would marry one of these days and fill it with children.

The episode of Thomas Lucy of Cobham brings Mr Hammond clearly into focus. Unlike his father, the one who had given rise to so much concern at Oxford and had succeeded his Uncle William as Rector of Tolland, he was not inclined for a scholar's life. There are a number of his father's books in the library at Charlecote, which show the Rector of Tolland to have been a knowledgeable collector, among them the Aldine Cicero of 1560 and the 1555 edition of Olaus Magnus. Jack the younger, of whom we know very

---

* In a letter dated 26 February 1770, a friend recommends some efficacious powders: 'but as you may be fearful, please let any of your servants take a dose first'.

little indeed, was not bookish. The pleasant dawdling round of visits to Bath and Cheltenham, of hunting and fishing and dining the neighbours, was exactly to his taste; he liked his comforts, and was beginning to look forward to a day when in the natural course of events he would step into the shoes of the master of Charlecote.

The appearance at Charlecote in the summer of 1772 of a man calling himself Thomas Lucy, with the grime on him of a headlong ride from Surrey, gave Mr Hammond's complacency a jolt. No contemporary record has survived, but there are letters in existence from the great-grandson of this Thomas, a man of mild antiquarian leanings who desired to trace his ancestry. Writing to an elderly cousin about the tradition that the Lucys of Stratford were a twig of the Charlecote branch, he says: 'The person I want specially to enquire about is my Great Grandfather, Mr Thomas Lucy. I cannot but think that he must have known more about the tradition than my Father remembers . . . otherwise he would not have been likely to have ridden all the way from Surrey to Stratford to put forward a claim for a large landed property.' The cousin, replying, says that his grandfather, Thomas, had bought the mill at Cobham and that an action had been brought against him for fishing. He was defended by the lawyer who was afterwards Lord Erskine, who won the case for him, but the expenses of it were so heavy that he was obliged to sell Cobham Mill. Picking up an imperfect copy of Dugdale, he was attracted by the entry about Charlecote. The cousin goes on: 'My Grandfather said that an advertisement had been inserted somewhere that all of the name of Lucy should apply'—but he thinks that it had appeared much earlier, in 1725, the year after the Rev. William's death. Without saying so, he gives the impression that the claim to Charlecote was a piece of deliberate bluff, suggested by the study of Dugdale's Warwickshire.

'. . . Mr Hammond, who with my Grandfather was a guest at Charlecote, looked very shy upon him, and when asked why said that he understood he intended claiming the property. . . .'

Thomas of Cobham—or more properly of Slinfold,

Sussex—could trace his pedigree back to the early seventeenth century and apparently bore the arms of Lucy, though his father had been a carpenter. Before the Civil War they had owned manors at Slinfold and Shipley in Sussex, but their property being confiscated had sunk from being squires of moderate estate to small yeomen.

George Lucy, who was never discourteous, received the Claimant and entertained him. The now-lost link which the Claimant must have been able to produce, so impressed George that he proposed to settle a sum of money on Thomas in order that he could set himself up with another mill, which was vastly more to the ex-miller's taste.

It has been said that the money was paid to avoid a lawsuit, but Thomas of Cobham, already ruined by litigation, was hardly in a position to bring such a suit against a man of George Lucy's standing. The relationship with the Warwickshire stem, if it existed, never constituted a valid claim to Charlecote. Mr Hammond, however, was badly shaken. One would so like to know what followed, but the Charlecote records are silent.

There are no more letters from George Lucy; he did not again visit Bath. He rained kindnesses on his friends in the form of chines of bacon, venison, and turkeys, but entertained less and less—after Mrs Hayes' death, hardly at all.

William Dobson, John Dobson's brother, who had a country house out at Twickenham, did small money transactions for him, and writes in 1779 about laying out some £400 in the Funds,* and buying Government Lottery tickets. More usefully, he sent down London gossip, for which George was always eager.

The last years draw on. A small study off the Hall was furnished with shelves by Standbridge, who covered the old wainscoting with canvas to take wallpaper, and put in a new ceiling, and a bookcase at one end with a cornice and pediment, like Mr Sherwood's at Hampton Lucy. By this time the library must have been much depleted. The room

---

* The stock of the National Debt; regarded as a means of investing money. Colonel George had lost money in the South Sea Bubble in this way.

looked north, but, being small, was easy to warm. George Lucy and Mr Hammond sat in it every evening. The master of Charlecote took all his exercise in a pony chaise now, and had to be helped up the great staircase to his bed. The draughts of tar and bark water and the mercurial physic so gaily drunk had sapped a constitution naturally healthy. His friend Dobson sent him from Twickenham in 1781 a Receipt for the Palsy and Rheumatism: 'Two Ounces of mustard seed bruis'd, two ounces of seville orange peel, one ounce of horse-raddish, sliced, two ounces of juniper berries bruis'd, and half an ounce of fennel bruis'd. Put all these Ingredients into a muslin bag, and infuse them in three quarts of mountain wine [sherry] for three days, let the Patient drink a wine glass every Morning, either fasting or at 11 o'clock, and 4 hours after Dinner.'

His weakness increased. He would walk with a stick round the rooms he had improved, and admire Battoni's picture, remembering how he had had himself painted holding one hand out toward the beholder to refute the idea that his attack of rheumatic fever had deprived him of the use of it— it had been wearisome to keep the pose through the long sittings which Signor Battoni insisted on. The blue velvet suit had been cut up in the end by Mrs Hayes for cushions.

He made a will in 1783 at the age of sixty-nine; the executors besides his heir, John Hammond, were Mr Sherwood, the Rector of Hampton, and Mr Blake, the Vicar of Charlecote, elderly men now, the companions of the Bath and Cheltenham excursions of his younger days.

There is one arresting clause; 'all my pictures whatsoever and also all my plate and household goods, linen, and all other furniture of my said mansion called Charlecote House . . . are to continue and remain as Heirlooms forever after in Charlecote House, and no future owner of Charlecote is to permit the removal of them save for reasons of decay.'

The legacies reveal the anxious concern for a large circle of humble cousins that governed George's life. A Mr William Henderson of Middlewich, an apothecary, a Mr John Power of Shrewsbury, a mercer, are named, and 'a Mr Lucy, by trade a butcher and a relative of Mr Richard Lucy late of Rotherhithe' was to have £100—possibly another claimant.

It was the end of an epoch. George himself had been the younger son of a younger son, and many times the lineal succession had been threatened, but there had never not been a Lucy to succeed at Charlecote since the first William de Lucie in the twelfth century. It had all been for nothing, the improvements to the park, the cascade and the bridges, the family portraits, the great bason stocked with carp, the library, the Evidence Closet with charters and title deeds going back to the Middle Ages.

There are no pictures of George Lucy in later life, only of the fresh-coloured, hopeful aspect of his youth and early middle age. He fell into a coma in the last week of November 1786, being aged seventy-one.

Mr Hammond, writing modestly to his sister in Somerset, says that 'the weak state he was reduced to, with the many infirmities that attended him, made all art in physick useless, and put a period to the dear good man on Friday the first of December at four o'clock. . . .'

The funeral of the last Lucy of Charlecote was, in Mr Hammond's words, all that was decent and grand; it ought to have been, for it cost over £450. Hundreds of yards of black bombazine and crepe were used, all the village men and women had black cloaks and hose, the postilions were put into black broadcloth trimmed with braid and buttoned with jet. The funeral cortège from the house was joined by a long procession of black mourning coaches and mourners on foot from Stratford and Alveston, which wound down the lime avenue and over the Wellesbourne Brook to pass through the wrought-iron gates, bearing Dr William's monogram, into the court. The sight was an awesome one, and the deer, feeding down close to the house at that time of the year, in terror stampeded into the river. It had been an autumn of storms and the Avon was full; thirty and more were sucked under the waterfall that Capability Brown had made, and drowned. Could he have known of it, nothing would have distressed George more.

CHAPTER 7

The Romantics

> *Captain Fitzchrome:* You will never find a wife for your purpose,
> unless in the daughter of some old-fashioned farmer.
> *Mr Chainmail:* No, I thank you. I must have a lady of gentle
> blood; I shall not marry below my own condition; I am too much
> of a herald; I have too much of the twelfth-century in me for that.
> *Crotchet Castle*: Thomas Love Peacock.

John Hammond began signing himself John Lucy immediately after his patron's death in December 1786. On 9
February of the year following he received the Royal Sign
Manual from George III which authorized it. No doubts
assailed him. He had lived at Charlecote for so long in the
expectation of inheriting it that it had made a Lucy of him:
always Charlecote had been the centre of the solar system
and the Hammonds the revolving planets.

In 1788 John Lucy married a woman twenty-five years
younger than himself. There had been an understanding
between them for a long time. Back in 1765 George Lucy
had employed a London lawyer called Lane to examine the
ancient will of Constance Kingsmill, to whose Hampshire
estates, freed by the death of Sir Berkeley Lucy, he thought
of laying a claim. There was some correspondence on the
subject for a year or two. Nothing came of it but a friendship
between John Hammond and John Lane, whose sister,
Maria, was still in the nursery.

John Lane was descended from the family of Jane Lane.
There had been Lanes in Staffordshire since Henry II, but the
property of King's Bentley, the seventeeth-century house
with crow-step gables from which Colonel Lane and his
sister set out to rescue their king, was sold before 1750.

Maria Lane was the dowerless daughter of the last Lane of

King's Bentley and his wife, Sarah Fowler. John Hammond had begun to pay his addresses to her when she was just turned twenty. When he inherited, Maria was thirty-one. Writing to his sister, Alice Hammond at Tolland, from Lothian's Hotel, Albemarle Street, John Lucy announced his marriage dryly and without unnecessary verbiage; 'Long before this you must have heard, or seen in the Papers, of my being at last married, may the Providence of Heaven cause it to turn out Propitious and Fortunate; it was quite a sudden start, not that I can account [for] why it should have been so, only as we were long before engaged, Maria thought it trifling to wait longer. . . . Our continuance at this large, wild, Bustling, extravagant City will be but short; as we intend leaving it in a few days and return to Charlecote. We came for a new Carriage, a new service of China, both for the Table, Dessert, and Tea; new Plate, with the exchange of some of the very old, bruised, worn-out at Home. . . .'

The silver knives they bought, with the paper-thin blades, are still in use today. In the bachelor household the china had been much abused; Maria was scandalized at the state of the china cupboard. The Reverend John presented his bride with a tea-poy of Buhl with a key to hang on her *châtelaine*. He had their likenesses taken by William Artaud, a popular portrait painter, and the twin oval portraits hung high up in the darkest corner of the Great Hall for over a hundred years. They do not flatter; a port-wine flush suffuses the bridegroom's cheeks. Maria, with her hair dressed up, twirls a sprig of myrtle. They look a homely, unfashionable pair among the arrogant Dahls, the thoughtful Jansens, the worldly Knellers.

It was the new Squire's wish that the Great Hall should be used for dining. The Chinese screen kept off draughts from the fireside. The musicians' gallery had been pronounced unsafe, but the little boys, Georgy and Jack, when they grew old enough to escape from their nurse, liked to creep up there when there was no one about. Mice had eaten into the works of the organ that Colonel George had installed—

when the children pressed a note its hollow buzzing whisper sounded disconcertingly loud.

Outside in the court the great bason was empty. The pipe that fed it had been broken and not renewed. Mr Lucy talked of doing away with it and grassing over the court. The urns that had crowned the pillars of Dr William's gates had been blown down (one moulders still in a forgotten corner of the garden); on the south side ragged grass grew where in the seventeenth century the walled vegetable garden had been. The stables that used to house twenty and more now sheltered only a pair of carriage horses and the Reverend's cob.

Mr Lucy had grown into his bachelor ways and was altogether too fond of convivial evenings at 'The Talbot' in Wellesbourne. Perhaps Maria reminded her husband when occasion arose that, though he had succeeded to a great property and an ancient coat, the arms she bore were quartered by a King's special mandate with the royal lions of England. Her most prized possession was a watch, an orb of gold with upon the cover a portrait of Charles II set in diamonds and on the back a painted sun, moon, and stars. This, and some Lane miniatures by Nicholas Hone, framed in garnets, she kept in her sitting room in George Lucy's kingwood *escritoire* inlaid with flowers and scrolls in tulipwood.*

The year that saw the birth of young George was the year of the French Revolution and the Declaration of the Rights of

---

* In 1850 the watch was stolen from Charlecote by two men, Bradshaw and Evans. They walked out from Birmingham, coolly carrying carpet bags, very early one morning and cut a pane of glass out of the west door. A shepherd seeing the shutters open, gave the alarm. The thieves were over-confident and were taken on their return to Birmingham, but not before many of the objects stolen had been melted down or passed to a receiver. The nautilus shells mounted in silver gilt that came from Fonthill, the gold châtelaine that had belonged to Alice Spencer, and innumerable pretty trifles were never recovered. When Bradshaw returned to England, after serving a sentence of transportation, he wrote to the Mistress of Charlecote hinting that King Charles's watch had been hidden near a railway bridge. She refused to see him or give him money and the watch, if it had escaped the melting-pot, at least did not return to Charlecote. The Lane miniatures were found in fragments in a ditch, having been wrenched from their jewelled settings.

Man. From the calm Augustan certainties of the eighteenth
century which had been enjoyed only by the educated few,
England was passing into a transition state of vague alarms,
outbreaks of disorderliness and a rocking domestic economy.
The dark tide rising in the north was not perceived in rural
Warwickshire, but it was felt through the weakening of the
squire's hold on his dependants, whose sons and daughters
began to prefer employment in the growing factory towns
of Coventry and Birmingham to the year-round drudgery of
the land. In another thirty years or so the sky would start
clouding over for those eighteenth-century landlords who
were preparing to step into a new century with their world
intact about them.

The pattern of life that had been lived elegantly by the
squirearchy was beginning to find crude imitation in 'Cockney cits' boxes', and in farmhouse parlours which must now
be fitted out with pianos and work-tables and other toys of
leisure. Such levelling was bound to have an insidious and,
from the squire's point of view, a demoralizing effect on the
villagery, who would be wanting baths next.

But still, within the boundaries of his squiredom, the
landlord could ride over his own ground secure in a sense of
being self-supporting. Wages were so low that there was
ample sufficiency of labour in every department. The Reverend John Lucy at Charlecote had something in common
with the twelfth-century baron, confident in a commanding
the services of a small but highly trained army of mercenaries. It was possible in that glow to forget the fret of rents
unpaid, the fall in canal stock threatened by the coming of
railways, and the radicalism that was spreading even to the
labouring class.

In the year of his marriage he had appropriated to himself
the Rectorship of Hampton Lucy, Mr Sherwood having at
last died and relinquished it. The Rectory was shut up, and
the Vicar of Wasperton, who also took John Lucy's duties at
Charlecote, lived in the schoolmaster's house beyond the
church. Mr Sherwood had thought to please his old friend
by appointing a young kinsman of Mr Lucy's to be Vicar of
Wasperton and Headmaster of the Free Grammar School at

Hampton Lucy. The Reverend John Morley was a nephew of Sarah, Mrs Hammond, a Somersetshire man and a BA of Oxford. He appeared to have all the qualifications required by the terms of Richard Hill's bequest of 1635—a knowledge of grammar, Hebrew, Greek, Latin and the English tongue.

His outspoken diary, recently brought to light, shows the smouldering of the country's resentment against radicalism.

May 31st 1793
Attended County meeting at Warwick Race Ground. The object being to stop the war. Gratitude bids me forget Mr Lucy's conduct on this occasion as soon as I can. I do forgive it for it proceeds from mere weakness of intellect not from any fault of the heart. Over one hundred patriots sat down to dinner . . .

June 19th
Walked down to Mr Lucy's for the first time since the County Meeting. Mr Cooper of Loxley was in the study. Mr Lucy joined us and we conversed about his eldest son at school. [Georgy was four at the time.] Mr Clifton coming, I walked into the other room to see Mrs Lucy's Grand pianoforte just placed in the new dining room. . . . After dinner Mr Lucy took rather more than his usual quantity of wine, and said to me, referring to the County Meeting: 'If you spared more time with your family, and busied yourself less with the affairs of the nation it would be better for you.' I replied that private interest was not my sole spring of action. He said he would depossess me of H. L. School and Curacy, etc. etc. before all the company. He abused Lord Dormer and said he should never enter his doors again.

Oct. 22nd
Measles are now amongst us. (NB All my 10 have had smallpox) . . .

Dec. 1st
Mr Foster called and informed me of a considerable altercation which happened last night at 'The Talbot' Wellesbourne between Mr Welch of Wasperton and Mr Lucy, which ended in the former turning the latter out of the room, striking him and giving him a black eye [the quarrel was patched up and the parties apologised].

March 8th 1797
Rode to Wasperton and with Captain Fitzherbert's assistance

distributed £10 1. 6½ to the poor. Dined at Mr Lucy's, (and) made proposals to the farmers of Wasperton to compound with Mr Lucy for the Great Tythes and the small.

March 22nd
In spite of all Mr Lucy and I could do not one farmer would compound with me for the small tythes at the price of 1/- per acre.

Easter Tuesday, April 15, 1800
Vestry Meeting at Wasperton, urged the continuance of a mixed flour of equal parts of wheat and Barley for the poor, 6 lbs. for 12d. Coarse bread is now sold by the Baker for rather more than double the price.

April 28th (London)
Bought a small Barrel Organ of Preston, London, for Mr Lucy for the use of Charlecote Church, £10 15., pricked to 10 tunes. A much better one was £20, pricked at 10 Psalm tunes. Bought Harpsichord (Kirkmay) £25, date 1782. Went to St Pauls to hear an admirable discourse from Dr Parr [the 'Spittal' Sermon]. . . .

May . . .
Barrel organ arrived by Judd's wagon, was roughly handled and it cyphered in every note. Took it to pieces and at last left the instrument in complete order.

July 21st
I am urging Mr Lucy to build a new Vicarage for Charlecote and with some difficulty prevailed. Ordered a new treble for Mr Lucy's organ. Bread 2½ lbs. for 1/- eight weeks ago, now sold at 5 lbs. for 1/-.

Sept. 8th
Party of disorderly people paraded before my house and stopped to sing vulgar songs, one o'clock at night, came from Wellesbourne. Mr Bradley came out with a gun. It was a very unseemly and troublesome affair . . . Bought a new Wedgewood Inkstand, 2/6, and ½ quire of blotting paper 5d.

Nov. 9th
A very high flood and I cannot take the Wasperton service. Send John to tell the people.

Nov. 14th
. . . Have begun to limit bread and flour to our family. Mr

Corbet's Fox Hounds thrown off at Hampton Wood. Nanny baked 80 loaves of mixed flour to-day.

Jan. 18th, 1802

My family now consists of 18 people, including 4 servants [Mr Morley had begun to take in private pupils to augment his income and at the same time to neglect his duties as Headmaster of Hampton Lucy school.]

Feb. 26th

Mr Wallington had his fowls stolen from the barn last night, by a man on horseback it would seem. I sent John to Coventry, being market day, to explore the Poulterer's shops, but without success. Mr Lucy called and left £10 1. 6½ for the Wasperton poor.

April 5th

That most desirable event, the signing the definite treaty of Peace, between this country and France. About 50 were present at the dinner at the school.★ . . . The dinner was good and the party all in good humour and good spirits. I left at 11 p.m. when most of the Farmers departed. A few Tradesmen staid until they were drunk and with difficulty were prevailed upon to leave the room about 2 in the morning.

April 6th

The poor labourers were, according to our plan to have dined together to-day on as good a dinner as we could have provided from what victuals and ale were left yesterday . . . Very little of the victuals and Ale could be distributed after all, for part of the Tradesmen who dined yesterday have been eating and drinking all day at Hawkes [sic] and consumed what was left and are drunk, so the poor labourers cannot be supplied.

[But Mr Morley suggested that the women and children should have bread and butter, tea and sugar, and this was gratefully received. The men did not have to go without celebration after all and new victuals were provided.]

Nov. 11th

Rode to 'The Shoulder of Mutton' at the Bridge Port, Stratford,† to a meeting of the [School] Trustees according to notice,

---

★ To which the farmers had contributed 10s, each, to celebrate the Peace of Amiens.
† Now known as 'The Swan's Nest'.

was in the parlour at 11.20 by the clock in the parlour passage, by the parlour door. No appearance of the Trustees. Wrote 4 letters; at about 2 by the clock arrived Mr Wyatt, Mr Lucy, Mr John Higgins, Mr Edward Higgins, Mr Edward Stanley, and Mr York. Dinner came upon the Table, we all sat down. At dinner all was civility and good manners. After dinner common topics were discussed till about 4 o'clock, when Mr Lucy opened the business by saying that the meeting had been called with a view to dismiss me from the School, but that he hoped as things now appeared to be going on better, no more would be thought of it. Observations not worth remembering were made. Mr John Higgins . . . reproached Mr Lucy for not acting like a man of spirit and for not actually having proposed my dismissal, which Mr Lucy positively denied. Both the Mr Higgins then insisted that Mr Lucy [had] first proposed to turn me out and moreover added 'I was the greatest Jacobin in the County'. Mr Lucy again denied, and great warmth arose between him and the Higgins which I restrained with difficulty. . . .

The unpleasantness arose on account of the rebuilding of the old school,* on which Mr Morley said he had expended £70 out of his own money. He had engaged an assistant and taken on new pupils, but it is clear that he himself was much more interested in politics than in teaching. He held Jacobin, or extreme Radical, views, and the trustees had some cause for their annoyance. But as Mr Lucy's cousin he was in no real danger of losing his appointment. John Morley was the friend of Dr Parr, the militant curate of Hatton, near Birmingham, who made himself conspicuous and disliked by his rampant Radicalism. Parr was the shadow of a greater humanitarian, Joseph Priestley, whose house in Birmingham was burnt by rioters on the anniversary of the Fall of the Bastille in 1791. John Morley's head had been turned by intimacy with these great ones, and he had imagined he could impose his Jacobinism on the young minds entrusted to his care.

April 23rd 1809
Considerable flood water, too high to pass on foot up Mill

* The new schoolhouse which he caused to be built is in use to this day.

Meadow, and [as] there was no boat for a horse, gave up very reluctantly the Service at Wasperton and so read Evening Prayers at Hampton Lucy and Catechized the girls.

. . . [Hampton] Bridge broken in the middle. Borrowed Mr Lucy's mare, on my return took mare to Charlecote and waded through the water.

March 2nd 1810

Endeavoured to the best of my power and (Thank God) succeeded in as great degree as I expected, to put a stop to the most wanton, cruel, and cowardly practice of throwing at Cocks [in Hampton Lucy]. Gave a shoulder of mutton to be bowled for.

John Lucy was a natural reactionary, as might have been expected. He wanted no clever, advanced young men to tell him about the sufferings of the working class. He had inherited an obligation and chose to look no further than its limits. A red-faced, thick-set man, he was always ready with his fists. He looked for the same freedom of behaviour in his workpeople, and found it. Rural Charlecote was more democratic at this time than ever again in the nineteenth century. The farmer, the blacksmith, the wheelwright, and the stonemason were the four supports of a community that had not greatly changed since Elizabethan England. The villagers were not breathlessly respectful towards the squire—servility of that sort was to set in later on.

When old John Lucy died in his ninetieth year, sitting in his predecessor's armchair covered with Mrs Hayes's buff tabby, having just eaten a woodcock for his dinner, eighteenth-century Charlecote went with him. He was succeeded by an anxious generation apprehensive of change, seeking for certainties. In his darker moments the landowner of the next generation saw a dismal picture of his coverts plundered, his ricks fired, the youth of the village lured away to the mills. John Lucy would have broken his stick over the head of anyone who had suggested such a thing.

The elder boy George was sent to Harrow and to Christ Church, and John, the younger, to Winchester and Trinity, Cambridge. They were tall, manly boys, good cricketers, fond of country sports, netting sparrows, shooting larks, coursing hares—fond, too, of cock-fighting on the quiet behind the hayricks at the back of the Malt House in Charlecote village. When they came home for the holidays and brought their friends, the old place came to life. The Reverend saw them off to Warwick and Stratford races with fond pride, recalling his own youth, and paid up their losses afterwards.

George was strikingly handsome and looked well in a broad-collared shirt worn carelessly open at the neck. He maintained a natural fastidiousness through the rough-and-tumble of Harrow, and went on to Christ Church. Oxford was no longer lax in its attitude to learning. At Harrow and again at college, George had admired from afar a boy only a year older than himself, already marked for greatness. In George's second year at Christ Church young Robert Peel took the double first which secured him the University seat ten years later. George could not emulate such single-minded industry, not having in his veins the quicksilver of political genius—he had no incentive to do better than a modest BA, which he did not in fact achieve. Like all his forebears, he loved Oxford, and took a skiff out on the Isis and a punt up the Cherwell, rode in cross-country steeplechases, joined a political debating society, and drank as much as was usual, but not more than was good for him.

In one of the Long Vacations he and his brother John travelled on the Continent, and picked up blackened paintings and objects of doubtful *virtù*—the first sign of what was to be the ruling passion of George's life.

Young John took Orders in 1814, and the year following his father resigned the living of Hampton Lucy and installed his second son as Rector. The Rectory, empty since Mr Sherwood's death, was opened up. The old squarson (he had married late in life and was now nearly eighty) was glad to lean back in the family pew and doze through his son's sermons.*

---

* John Hammond Lucy deserves a chapter to himself; his spare, black-frock-coated presence is still felt in Hampton Lucy, which he ruled with stern benevolence for nearly sixty years. See Appendix.

There had not been a Member of Parliament in the family since Captain Thomas. The seats for Warwick and the county being filled, the Reverend conceived the disastrous idea of buying a pocket borough for his eldest son. This was the genteel way to enter public life: Wellington thought it the only sure way of keeping gentlemen in politics. Through his cousins, the Dormers, he heard that a seat might soon be going begging for a purchaser in Cornwall—the rotten borough of Fowey, a Cornish seaport that existed on its shipbuilding and fishing industries, exporting pilchards to southern Europe. The long war with France that closed the Mediterranean ports to British ships, brought great hardship to Fowey. The pilchards lay in decaying heaps on its quays. Fishing, however, was not its only industry. The place had a lively history of smuggling spirits from France, and ships were fitted up as 'privateers' to roam the Channel in search of 'prizes' which, when taken, were escorted into Fowey harbour and their contents auctioned at 'The Rose and Crown'. After 1815, when the people of Plymouth, only thirty miles away, had crowded the Sound to catch a glimpse far off of the small, bowed figure of Napoleon at the quarter rail of HMS *Bellerophon*, the place ceased to have any importance as a fortified seaport.

The dark, enigmatic, slippery Cornishmen who were George's constituents were something quite outside his comprehension. He was not temperamentally fitted for borough-mongering. Moreover, the seat was not a walk-over. On top of the purchase money there was to be the expense of a contested election. It was necessary to buy up as much 'burgage' property in the town as would command a majority of voters. The buyer of burgage property had to cajole his sitting tenants to vote for him. He had the alternative of eviction—but either way the tenant expected a bribe.

The battlemented mansion called 'Place' that dominated the town had been since the fifteenth century the property of the Tory Treffry family. The Whig Rashleighs from nearby Menabilly owned much of the town and guided its politics. In 1816 Joseph Thomas Austen, whose mother was a Treffry heiress (he took the name later), was the owner of Place. He was single-minded in his ambition to advance the fortunes of his native town.

Fowey had had a stormy political history. It sent two Members to Parliament, and the Town Corporation controlled the voting. The Rashleighs who owned the Duchy Manor controlled the Town Corporation, so that the result was always a foregone conclusion.

But by 1816 the Rashleighs were withdrawing from local politics, and one day it became known in Fowey that the Duchy Manor had been sold to a complete stranger for the fantastic sum of £20,000. The stranger was the Reverend John Lucy of Charlecote and never was money more surely poured down a drain.

It was a blow to Austen. The large bulk of correspondence between George Lucy and Joseph Austen was recently rescued from a coal-store on the Treffry estate. It makes depressing reading. George can be said never to have known real peace of mind again, though Austen's initial hostility changed to kindness when they met. The agreement into which the two men entered, by which Austen pledged himself to further George's political ambitions, and George promised to do nothing to infringe the Treffry family's rights in Fowey, suited both, and their friendship lasted till George's early death.

In Warwickshire, slumping farm prices should have alarmed George into prudence, instead of which he took shares in a copper-mine near Fowey and advanced money for its development. Before his father's death it began to be necessary to fell timber in large quantities on the Charlecote estate to meet expenses. But the Reverend was delighted to have a son who could write MP after his name.

George employed a political agent in Fowey, but Austen in fact ran the borough's affairs for him. His fellow member, Lord Valetorte, son of Lord Mount Edgcumbe at Lostwithiel, took no interest in the place. Begging and abusive letters kept George awake at night. His constituents expected him to be always acting on their behalf with the Ministers, and

threatened him when he failed. In 1824 he wrote despondently to Austen that he was obliged to form a very disheart-
ening and gloomy picture of Fowey affairs: 'I have lately
turned over in my mind the whole case dispassionately and I
think we are as far from having a snug quiet Borough as we
were in 1818 . . . in my belief Lord V. has no intention of
sitting any more for F. . . . He never even returned my card
upon him in London this season.' Lord Valetorte stood
down at the next election and was succeeded by a Mr Eden.

Two years later George was writing: 'The more I think of
Parliament the less relish I feel for another return; nothing
would hurt me more than to see Campbell and Baillie (the
Corporation's nominees) *nolens Volens* seated at Fowey, but
I most unaffectedly wish two Gentlemen of our nomination
could be found. I should retire most *Cheerfully*, and I know,
be the Happier man.'

On the face of it George Lucy of Charlecote had been
blessed with all the ingredients that make for happiness—
good looks, a great estate, a respectable fortune, friends,
leisure. Only a wife was needed to complete the picture.

In November 1823 he was writing to Austen from
Charlecote:

My mother feels infinitely obliged to you for your intended
presents of specimens of the Fowey Mines, but they will be of no
great utility to her, tho' she feels equally obliged. She is leaving
Charlecote to live near London in the neighbourhood of her
immediate friends and Relatives, and I have a new Mrs Lucy to
bring here in the beginning of next month, in the person of Miss
Mary Elizabeth Williams, a daughter of Sir John Williams of
Bodlewyddan, Flintshire, and a Cousin of Sir Watkin Williams
Wynne, to which young lady I need hardly add I am going to be
married. . . .

The old squire had died in January, and George immediately set to making some improvements, for his father had
refused to allow so much as a chair to be moved from its
place.* As soon as the pictures were taken down for

---

* The new George Lucy, though an antiquarian at heart, had no respect for
the injunction in his predecessor's will.

rehanging, it was seen how sadly the silk damask on the drawing-room walls had frayed and faded. Rider's view of Charlecote, printed in about 1821, taken from the edge of the cedar lawn, or the Green as it was still called, having been originally intended for a bowling-green, presents a picture on which Time alone has laid hands, an old Squire's gable-ended house of the sort that touched off the imagination of scores of Victorian novelists—crumbling, sagging, coated with antiquity.

Washington Irving had walked out from Stratford in old Mr Lucy's day and found the place apparently deserted (the Lucy parents were away visiting, and Mr George and Mr John were on the Continent):

Whatever may have been the joviality of the old mansion in the days of Shakespeare, it now had an air of stillness and solitude. After prowling about for some time I at length found my way to a lateral portal which was the every day entrance to the mansion. I was courteously received by a worthy old housekeeper, who with the civility and communicativeness of her order, showed me the house. The greater part has undergone alterations and been adapted to modern tastes and modes of living; there is a fine old oaken staircase; and the great hall, that noble feature in an ancient manor house, still retains much of the appearance it must have had in the days of Shakespeare. The ceiling is arched and lofty; at one end is a gallery in which stands an organ. The weapons and trophies of the chase which formerly adorned the hall of the country gentleman, have made way for family portraits. . . .

He was delighted with the armorial glass and identified all over again for himself Sir Thomas Lucy with Justice Shallow. He loved to picture, as Dickens and Scott and Thackeray did, the joys of Olden Tyme—the tree on the hearth sending up showers of sparks, the rosy children, the buxom maidens filling up goblets, the smoking haunch on the groaning board, the haughty servants, the Master with a round belly, the Mistress never parted from her embroidery frame. Over it all lay the rich, dark yellow glaze of the idealized Past. Nash put figures of this sort into the foregrounds of his 'Mansions of England', where they look like early Victorians in ill-fitting fancy dress.

In the first flush of succeeding to his kingdom, George
sent for Benjamin Wyatt to design a worthy addition to the
house that should at the same time not detract from its
ancient character. Wyatt's elevations were elegant. The man
who had just built the new Theatre Royal in Drury Lane
could not resist making Charlecote look like a backdrop to
The Missing Heir, or the Fatal Secret. The suggested improvements were a jumble of a number of other Elizabethan
houses, with chimneys from Blickling, gables from Ingestre,
windows from Hardwicke; rustic Charlecote, as George
perceived in time, could not have supported so much gran-
deur. In any case Wyatt's estimates were far too high.

In 1823, the year of his marriage, George heard that
furniture and objects of *virtù* were to be sold off at the
breaking up of William Beckford's collection at Fonthill in
Wiltshire.

William Beckford, the son of a Lord Mayor of London,
who had travelled about Europe rapt in a fantastic dream of
a world of which he fancied himself the sovereign or caliph,
had given substance to his dreams by building a vast Gothic
Abbey, of which he was self-styled Abbot. The tower of the
structure, the work of James Wyatt, fell one stormy night,
having been hastily thrown together from shoddy materials.
The Abbey was to have been an enduring monument to
Beckford's pure descent from the Plantagenets—the sap that
nourished his family tree, according to himself, was the most
glorious blood in England. Heraldry was his obsession. At
Fonthill coats of arms appeared on stained glass in corridors
innumerable, shedding a dim heraldic blue and a sombre
crimson. When his extravagances had ruined Beckford and
the Fonthill collection was put up for sale in 1822, that part
of Wiltshire was invaded by sightseers, art dealers and
amateur collectors, so that there was not a bed to be had in
any of the inns around. The sale was conducted by Messrs
Christie and Manson. Later, in the year following, another
sale took place, but this time arranged by a shady auctioneer,
who filled the ruined galleries with dubious rubbish. To the
second sale went George Lucy. He became one of the
subscribers to Rutter's book, describing the real and intended

glories of Fonthill. With the rest of the curious, he wandered through the Oratory, the Sanctuary, King Edward's Gallery and Vestibule, the Grand Saloon or Octagon, the Gothic Cabinet, the Vaulted Library, the Chintz Boudoir, the Lancaster State Bedchamber—absorbing the richness of the gilding, the profusion of carving, the carpets of 'extraordinary costliness', the Garter-blue silk damask and watered moreen hangings. George had travelled in Europe and Europe had formed him. It does not seem possible that the gimcrackery of Fonthill could seriously have influenced him. But the fact remains that on that famous occasion he spent upwards of £3,400 on articles of *virtù* that we should think scarcely worth a tenth of that sum. His visit to Fonthill confirmed in him a taste for heraldic glass, for strong colours, and for much gilding.

Mary Elizabeth Williams was born at Bodlewyddan in November 1803, the sixth of Sir John Williams's long family of eight. Her mother had been Miss Williams of Tyfry in Anglesey and an heiress. The story of her life is set down in a number of stout black notebooks, written when she was an old woman, but still in possession of a fabulous memory.

The three youngest children, Mary, William, Ellen, slept in cribs in the big nursery with Nurse in a four poster bed.

Nurse was one of the race of tale-telling Nurses and whenever we were naughty she used to say a Witch would come and take us off through the window—there was a most horrid old woman named Grassy with a fearful front tooth like an elephant's tusk, who used to come and help in the Wash House, and her husband a frightful man called Long Peter, for he was quite a Giant, who used to brew, and [with] these two dreadful people Nurse used to terrify us, by threatening to call them and bid them carry us off. . . . I had a charming Garden of my very own, and a Spade and Rake and a Barrow and Watering Pot, with my name on them, and I never let a weed be seen. I was devoted to Flowers, and was hardly ever without a nosegay. I had an Aviary full of Canaries, and Goldfinches, close to my Garden—it was lined with Moss, and there were little holes in the walls (it was built of Bricks) for the Birds to build in. . . .

The schoolroom hours began at six a.m. in summer and seven in winter, and breakfast at eight consisted only of a bowl of bread and milk. The governess kept pieces of dry bread as an austere refresher in a cupboard, into which the children were shut if they showed the slightest signs of temper. The mice that came after the bread made the dark cupboard a place of dread. The Williams standard of behaviour was high. Children had to curb their growing personalities; sulks, moods, rebellions, were immediately crushed by punishment, with the surprising result that they grew up cheerful, merry and grateful.

Very early Mary showed a talent for music. The celebrated Mrs Thrale, now married to her Italian singing master, Gabriel Piozzi, had built Brynbella just across the valley from Bodlewyddan, and was on terms of warm friendship with the Williams family. Mary picked out her first tune on the harpsichord from Gabriel Piozzi's knee. Mrs Piozzi found the inexhaustible beauty of the Vale of Clwyd, and the friendly unexacting company of her neighbours, balm after the ill-nature of her London circle. Intellectually the Williamses were not in her class, but there was much pleasant *va et vient* between the two villas. Through the telescope on her lawn at Brynbella she could see stout Sir John Williams talking to his gardeners or looking for a watch he had lost. Mary Elizabeth gives a child's view of her:

. . . the celebrated Mrs Piozzi of Brynbella often spent a few days with us, and I can quite see her in my mind's eye. She was a very pretty little old lady always dressed in Black Satin, with a Black Satin Hat turned up, a brown wig of curls, and to my inexperienced eye a beautiful complexion, but Alas! like Jezebel, she painted her face. I wondered why her cheeks were such a lovely Pink, when one Evening when she was gone downstairs to Dinner her Maid met me in the passage and said 'Miss Mary, would you like to come and help me tidy my Mistress' room?' . . . the first thing that attracted my notice was a Hare's foot on her Toilette Table, and taking it up [I] exclaimed, 'What can this be for?' 'Well!' she replied opening a small box of rouge, 'it is to put the rouge on her face with.' 'Oh! that is why she is so pretty,' and I begged the maid to put some on my cheeks—but she would not, and told me

I must not say a word to anybody about the Hare's foot or the Rouge.

To the Williamses music was as important as food—the mornings at Bodlewyddan were occupied by shooting and riding, the evenings devoted to performance of Handel on the organ—even Sir John was a fine performer on the violoncello:

Col. Browne, Mrs Hemans' eldest brother was very musical and was constantly walking over from Bronwylfa to bring us new Music both Vocal and Instrumental, and it was such a pleasure to me for I could read anything at sight. Mrs Hemans and [her sister] Harriett Browne often stayed a few days with us, and we had such concerts. . . . Dear Papa sometimes joined in with his Violincello. Mrs Hemans played simple airs with great taste and feeling on the Harp, but had no execution. I was very fond of her, and I think she was of me, she had the most winning manners, a sweet countenance, a profusion of Auburn Hair, and large brown eyes full of an ever-varying expression, but Alas! an ugly mouth and very bad teeth.

As I grew older I became daily fonder of study and was passionately fond of music, and drawing. . . . Nurse told me one day that Kitty the Housemaid, and John the school room boy, who waited on us and cleaned our shoes, were both so anxious to be able to read and write, so I undertook to teach them whenever I could in my play hours . . . but they were so stupid, it required the patience of Job to get them to know the Alphabet.

She comments on this some sixty years later:

There were no Schools in the days of my youth, as there are now, so very few servants had any sort of education, but Alas! I must say with all the *over schooling* of the present day, the race of *old faithful servants* is fast dying away.

She does not attempt to describe her parents, but Roberts the old butler who ordered them all about as children, but had such respect for Miss Emma (the eldest) that he left her £100, she dwells on with affection. Growing bald, he was obliged to buy a wig:

. . . we all admired it and told him how it became him—he always dressed well, and on state occasions wore lace ruffles, and a lace front to his shirt, and with his powdered wig looked quite the old-fashioned gentleman. Old Nurse, too: on birthdays she dressed in her Silk Gown, Lace ruff, and Cap with a large bow of Blue riband, and used to come in at Desert to give her blessing, and drink to the health of the particular one whose native day we were celebrating.

Not long before she died, after having been forty-five years in the service of the Williams family, old Nurse realized her life's wish, to see a Royal Duke at close quarters, when the Duke of Sussex dined at Bodlewyddan.

. . . Brother said she must put on her best Silk Gown and Lace ruffs etc. and she should come in at Desert, so when the Bell rung for her she appeared, and Brother gave her a glass of wine, and making the lowest curtsey to the Duke, she drunk his health, wishing him all possible good health and happiness. He was charmed with her. . . .

Mary was becoming thoroughly accomplished. Her lovely contralto voice was trained, she made her brother's shirts and her mother's nightcaps. As a young married woman she did exquisite embroidery, which her governess had thought too frivolous for the schoolroom, and covered the chair seats at Charlecote with gros-point in bright Berlin wool, and fauteuils and stools with pale silk petit point.

My dearest Mamma once took me with her to visit two old Ladies, Lady Eleanor Butler and Miss Ponsonby, who lived together in a beautiful cottage at Llangollen, and had no end of pretty things in their drawing room . . . but I remembered what I had been taught 'to look but not touch'. When I was going away the old Ladies said, 'Come, dear little Mary, and give us a kiss, for you have been so *good*, and not meddled with any of our pretty things, so we shall be glad to see you here again, and there's a nice peach for you,' so I was glad, for I had been looking at the Dish of Peaches with a longing eye. These old Ladies looked just like 2 old Men, they were always dressed in dark Cloth Habits with short skirts, high shirt collars, white cravats, and Men's Hats, with their hair cut short, and when they walked out (they never rode on Horse back) they carried a stick to look like a whip, and a beautiful Italian Grey Hound was their constant companion. They were so devoted to each other that they made a vow, *and kept it*, that they would never marry, or be separated, but always live together in their Cottage, never leave it, nor sleep out even for one night. . . .

When Brother came back from the private tutor's it was a delight to go on expeditions with him; the fond understanding between them ended only with his death: '. . . my greatest pleasure was to take my Basket and go with him to gather wild roses in a wood called Peny Gurrig about half a mile off, where we were never allowed to go alone as there were many old Mine Shafts, [for there] used to be Lead found there. I never saw anywhere such beautiful Briar Roses, not only White and Pink but the deepest Rose colour, almost Crimson. . . .'

With such country delights and musical evenings Mary's early teens passed. Loved and happy, she sang like a bird about the place, so preoccupied with her aviary, her harp, her Spanish lessons and her riding, that she did not realize till too late that she had attracted a young man whom Sister Emma would have liked to marry. Mary Elizabeth was by now nearly seventeen, but by her own request still in the schoolroom studying Shakespeare and Corneille, and painting flowers and butterflies on rice-paper. She could not help knowing that she was thought a beauty, and made for her black curls a baby's cap 'of simple Blonde Net with a ruche of tulle round it, and pinn'd a Pink Rose I gathered out of my Garden on one side of it'—this was to enslave handsome David Pennant, with whom all the Williams girls thought themselves in love.

A young man newly ordained, the Rev. John Lucy, a friend of Brother's, came to stay, but was not particularly noticed in the gay crowd of young people who danced country dances, quadrilles, and reels, at the neighbouring country houses. Mary's fate was coming towards her; she was now '*a come out young lady*', and in September 1822, with her three sisters (Ellen was still a schoolroom miss), went to stay with the Heskeths for the Preston Guild, a civic celebration which took place every twenty-one years and lasted a fortnight, with balls and masquerades, races, concerts and a balloon ascent. In the party was a young Mr Wilson Patten, handsome and a heavenly dancer, to whom Mary was attracted at first sight. Her first taste of emancipation combined with first love lent her spirits wings. At the balls she never sat down. She laughed at everything, thought the Countess of Derby (Miss Farren, the actress) most peculiar, '*a Bird of Paradise* and Diamonds on her head and lovely Humming Birds on the body and sleeves of her Dress, given her by Mr Warburton the great traveller'. After a fortnight she and Mr Wilson Patten parted lovers, 'having exchanged hearts but not *betrothed*—he was not of age, and went home to ask his Father's consent to our marriage which he *refused*, and sent him abroad to travel, bidding him forget me. . . .' The young have to yield, but hearts do not accept such parental unreason, and Mary does not seem to have been particularly cast down. That winter was fabulous, there was never another like it: 'Feby 18th [1823], as yet no frost or snow. The garden still enamelled with Flowers, China Roses, Mignonette, Carnations, Gilly Flowers, Violets, and the woods are filled with Primroses and Miggy saw a little girl eating wild strawberries. The Apricot Trees, Peach and Nectarine Trees in blossom. March 15th Hyacinths out, and I gathered 4 double Pink Hollyhocks. . . .'

The elder sister Miggy went to London in March for her first season, and Mary took up miniature painting and consoled herself during the enforced absence of Mr W. P. with a new mare called Rosabelle.

. . . dear Miggy now came home having enjoyed her season in London immensely. She confided to me that she thought she had made a conquest of Mr Lucy of Charlecote, the Rev. John's brother. She had met him several times in London and he had danced with her, and promised to come to Bodlewyddan in the Autumn as John (*our* brother) has invited him. . . . I perfectly well remember Miggy and I standing on the Balcony (out of Mamma's room) and seeing a Carriage with 4 post-horses drive up, and a smart Valet jump off the Box to ring the Bell, open the Car^g door and 3 young men alight, she pointed out to me which was Mr Lucy, and then flew downstairs to welcome him. . . .

It took Mr Lucy only a very short time to find out which of the Williams sisters he preferred. Mary saw her brief glimpse of paradise receding before the solid reality of this suitable *parti*, approved of her parents. Mr Wilson Patten was disconsolately pursuing his travels. She had no choice:

I had been brought up to obey my Parents in everything, and though I dearly loved Papa I had always rather *feared* him, so I felt I dare not disobey him, so went into the Library as he desired me and there found Mr Lucy waiting to ask me to be his wife. I was so agitated that I never remembered what he said, or what I said, all I knew was that he put a beautiful Turquoise Hoop on my finger, and I rushed out of the room, and flew upstairs to my own precious darling Mamma, telling her everything, and wept bitterly. She kissed, and kissed me again and again, and said all she could to comfort me, adding, 'My sweet Mary, *love will come*, when you know all of Mr Lucy's good qualities, &c.', and it *did* come. . . .

For twenty-two years she was as happy as any human being can reasonably expect to be.

In spite of the fact that Mary thought she could not ever love him, George wrote to her in early November from Charlecote:

My dearest Mary, Your letter just received has gratified and delighted me, so full of feeling and tenderness . . . really I do not say too much when I say you are the delight of all circles, and the Idol of your own—indeed I shall never cease to style myself the most fortunate and happiest of mankind. . . . I do so wish for you here, you may imagine after the lapse of a century in which little has been done, how much is required to be done at Charlecote which in time I hope we shall accomplish, your taste and wishes I shall always consult—but I am anxious to make the house a little comfortable for your reception, so have been very busy. . . .

The wedding was to take place on the 2nd [of December]. Dear old Nurse was in despair at the thought of parting with me, for I was her special pet. I used from my childhood to sit and read the Bible (whenever I was able) to her, as she darned our stockings, her favourite and constant employment, and I always made her caps. 'Oh, my dear Miss Mary, what shall I do without you? Who will read God's Holy Word to me? or make my Caps?' 'I will always be your Milliner, dear Nurse, and make you a lot before I am Mrs Lucy,' and I set to work at once and made her 2 dozen and she was delighted.* And now the eventful Tuesday the 2nd of

---

* A miniature of Old Nurse hangs with the other family miniatures in MEL's boudoir at Charlecote today.

Dec. 1823 was come, and though more than 60 years have passed since then, every incident is fresh in my memory. I fancy I see that dear old Nurse with trembling hands, and tears dimming her eyes, dressing me, her own dear child as she often used to call me, in my Bridal robe of snow white silk, which she entreated she might do, and then standing by to watch my new Lady's Maid, Turner, arrange my hair, and the wreath of orange blossoms—with the exquisite Brussels Lace Veil of texture fine as a Spider's Web falling over all my ornaments, the set of Rubies and Diamonds, the gift of him whose bride I was so soon to be.

(The tiny wedding dress, trimmed with vine leaves and bunches of grapes of the same silk, has now the colour and texture of very old paper. It would hardly fit a well-grown child of twelve.)

I can quite hear the clock strike 3, and the carriages are at the Door, and I get into the family coach drawn by Papa's own four beautiful Black Horses with Postillions followed by many more carriages, &c., and we arrive at St Asaph and find the Bishop Luxmoore waiting for us in the old Cathedral. . . .

The bride was Welsh, a creature of feeling and imagination, and the impenetrable strangeness of her future with a man her heart had not chosen induced a fit of nerves.

The solemnization of Matrimony over, I rose from my knees. I fainted away and was taken into the Bishop's pew, my poor husband in an agony looking at his Bride, not knowing what on earth to do, whilst darling Mamma and old Nurse, weeping, were chafing my hands and sprinkling water (hastily fetched from the Palace) over my face: as soon as I recovered, and all was signed and attested in the Vestry, Nurse wrapped me in a large Swan's down tippet which reached to my feet, with my hands in a Muff of Swan's down large enough for a Harlequin to jump through [the fashion of the time] and the Bride's Maids prepared with old satin shoes to throw for good luck.

Swansdown and silk and rubies, for a December drive of twelve miles to her uncle's house! Cerrig Llyddion, lent for the honeymoon, was large and gloomy.

How well I remember the first evening after our *Tête-à-Tête* Dinner. Mr Lucy did not leave the room with me and I sat nearly

a whole hour by myself in the dismal drawing-room, no Piano
even to amuse me, so I read the proper Evening psalms and
Chapters as I had always been in the habit of doing, and when I
put away my Bible and Prayer Book I thought of bye-past times,
how calm, how cloudless my childhood had passed away, like a
long long happy summer holiday! And then again what sorrow
filled my heart when I thought of the parting from my most dear
parents and the home I so loved. . . .

Dear Bodlewyddan! humming with the warm preoccupied
life of a large affectionate family. Far away, only guessed at,
lay Charlecote; all she knew of it was that it was in sad need
of repair. George had warned her that she would not find it
comfortable. With what misgivings George stayed that hour
alone in the dining-room, we can only imagine. This was no
place for a honeymoon; the fainting fit in the Cathedral had
unnerved him.

The next day my husband asked me if I should like to go to
London as this was such a dull place. . . . We arrived in London
late on the Saturday and went to Kirkham's Hotel in Brook St. We
went to St George's, Hanover Sqr., on Sunday. Monday we drove
half over London seeing sights till I was almost bewildered, but
delighted. 10th: we went to Drury Lane, the Play was *Guy
Mainwaring*, most charming. Thursday we went to Errard's and
chose a Harp (the very Harp which my children and now my
Grandchildren play on)* and then to Broadwoods and bought a
Grand Piano. 12th: went shopping and my husband gave me
endless beautiful and useful things—a Fur Cloak, Silks, lovely
Lace, in fact anything I expressed the slightest wish for—a Dressing Box, writing Desk, and Work Box all so handsome in Buhl,
and which I have now. . . .

Thus she recaptures the bubbling mood of the moment,
the freshness of which had never faded. The chilly Cathedral
wedding and the gloom of the honeymoon house were
dispersed by London, its Christmas shop-windows, crowds,
and sights. So vividly interested—her holly red cheeks and
black eyes glowing from the depth of an immense bonnet—
she enchanted her husband, who was not himself possessed

* It still stands in MEL's boudoir.

of much vitality. Her Welsh voice, with the lilting accent that she never lost, would have charmed a bird off a tree. He felt his choice was perfectly justified. 'You are the Mary after my own heart,' he often told her.

He was all anxiety to please her, but more anxious still to take her home. They left London on 15 December, slept at the Posting Inn at Tetsworth and entered Warwickshire in the early twilight of a winter afternoon.

It was dusk when we drove through the Park Gate and there was a Torchlight procession of the Tenantry drawn up by the old Gateway to welcome us and many were on the flat leaden roof with Flambeaux in their hands to cheer and hurrah as we passed underneath. The Church Bells were ringing forth their merry peals, and the House blazed with lights from every window. The Domestics all marshalled in line in the great hall to receive and have a look at their young Mistress; how shy I did feel with all their eyes upon me, and how glad I was to escape upstairs, and how I longed for morning when I might walk all about, and see every hole and corner of my new home. . . .

She goes on to say:

It was very different then to what it is now and the Great Hall did indeed look, as Washington Irving said, 'as it might have done in Shakespeare's time', with its old worn paved floor, its small panes of glass in its large Oriel window, and every window frame creaking and rattling with every gust of wind, and so Cold! Oh, so Cold! no *hot air then as now*. No beautiful garden in the Court, only a few large beds with shrubs and old-fashioned flowers. I soon caused my husband to let me root them all up and I planned the present one. . . .*

From now on the old-fashioned 'Hall' was dropped, and Charlecote Park it became and has remained. On the marriage of George Lucy, Charlecote emerged from its dilapidated retirement and became a country seat. With the eyes of love and faith, he and Mary Elizabeth looked on the creaking panes and visualized plate glass, at the untidy old flower beds and saw fleur-de-lis and ribbons and stars of

---

* Removed in 1951.

clipped box. They founded a happy marriage on this harmony. Agreeing on everything, neither desired to mould the
other. *Her* spirits imparted buoyancy to him, *his* experience
guided her judgement. Having Charlecote as the object of
their mutual devotion, they found all paths led back to it.
They found, too, that where there is an assured income,
health, and a romantic background, the happy virtues—
spontaneous affection, modesty, goodwill—have room to
expand.

Mrs George Lucy noted the names of her first callers with
zest. The Warwicks from the Castle, 'ever after my best
neighbours and friends', Lord Willoughby de Broke from
Compton Verney, afterwards to be her brother-in-law, Sir
Grey and Lady Skipwith from Alveston—'I grew so fond of
Lady Skipwith and she did of me, I used to call her my
Warwickshire Mama'. The names in themselves conjure up
for us the secure Warwickshire they represented, which then
must have seemed safe for ever: the Shirleys of Ettington,
the Wests of Alscot, the Drinkwaters of Sherbourne, the
Bracebridges of Moreville, the Seymours of Ragley. . . .

Mary's own family came on a visit soon after Christmas;
if the Williams parents thought Charlecote draughty and
dimly-lit, affection repressed comment. Their son-in-law
was full of plans for restoring his old place—it was to be
made comfortable in the solidest sense. Already he had
banished almost all the old-fashioned furniture to the attics
and begun to replace it. There was to be a substantial addition
to the old house; there must be a library, to house the books
now lying jumbled on the Parson's study shelves and the
many more he meant to buy, and a dinner-room to seat
thirty guests, and kitchens large enough to provide the
dinners. His taste and Mary's would select wallpapers,
carpets, and curtains that would blend the old character of
the place with the new.

The Williams parents returned to Bodlewyddan well satisfied, leaving their daughter Margaret with her sister. The
Lucys and their guest visited the Clonmells at Weston, and
Mary, with George's permission, waltzed with Lord Clonmell till she was giddy. From there to Compton Verney—

'the old Lord did his best to entertain us, Miggy thought the place charming, and would rather like to be *its mistress*'. On 20 April George took a house in London, 10 Upper Grosvenor Street, for the season, and the Charlecote servants, the plate, the linen, four carriage horses, and riding horses were sent ahead. When George was obliged to return to Warwickshire as the Yeomanry had been called out on manoeuvres, Mary was as miserable on being parted from him for the first time as was compatible with her natural appetite for fun. He writes:

My darling wife, as you know I went yesterday to breakfast with Clonmell in Brook Street. We started at 7 o'clock and reached Stratford at 6; it was a very raw morning outside the Aurora Coach and I wished myself back again with you twenty times. Clonmell drove all the way, and a famous pace we went. He holds his Horses well together. How I wish you and dear Miggy could look at Charlecote from the room where I am writing, it is beautiful, and was to me last night on arrival quite enchanting, still it is not at its best. The Elms are not in full foliage, but the grass is like an Emerald in colour; one cannot be surprised at the backwardness of vegetation after the cold weather we have had, the night before last was so severe that 20 swallows fell benumbed and lifeless from the House top. . . .

And again:

I wish I could write as good a letter as you do. . . . How anxious I shall be to know how you get through the Drawing Room; be sure to arrive to a moment in Seymour Place, ¼ before 2 o'clock and take 2 Cards with these words written on them, 'presented by the Countess of Warwick, Mrs Lucy on her marriage'—one to be given when you enter the Palace, the other to be handed by Lady Warwick to the Lord in Waiting who will then announce the same to the King. . . . I regret indeed that I cannot have even a peep at you in your fine dress. I shall however in imagination. My Darling, the Trumpet is sounding for the field, afterwards I shall ride over to Charlecote and deliver your message about separating the Canaries. . . .

The dress she wore for the Drawing Room had been brought by her brother Hugh Williams from Lyons for the sister who married first:

. . . it was very beautiful, of White Tulle covered with small silver Stars, and round the skirt Flowers worked in shades of Lilac, the underneath Petticoat was of White Satin, and the Train too of the richest White Satin trimmed with broad Blond Lace and edged with a thick silver cord. On my head a plume of Ostrich Feathers, Blond Lappets and Diamonds, on my Neck the large Ruby (in form of a Heart) with Diamond centre and my splendid Diamond Earrings worn for the first time. . . .

I took Miggy to St James Sqr. To go with Lady Harriett Wms-Wynne, and then went to Seymour Place, my heart fluttering and beating like a Bird newly caged. I was ushered into the Drawing room where a party of Grandees, the Marquis of Hertford with the Garter, &c., were assembled to look at and admire and criticize each other. The Carriages were soon announced and the Warwicks took me with them, it did not take long to get to St James's Palace as Lady Warwick, who was a great friend of Geo. 4th,* had the private entrée. Then having passed through several rooms I stood before the King who sat upon his Royal Throne and was clothed with all his Robes of Majesty—And oh! how I trembled as I heard my name called out. The King stooped down and kissed my cheek, and I know not what I did but as I was about to move away, he stopped me, and said, 'What is your name? I did not catch it,' so the Lord Chamberlain in a loud voice cried out, Mrs Lucy. The King then gave me a most gracious smile, and allowed me to go, and I was too glad and thankful to hide my blushes and confusion and get away.

She missed her ruby locket in the crush and excitement, but found it safe hooked in the lace of her veil.

The breathless account runs on:

On the 23rd dear George returned and that same evening we all went to a Ball at Lord Willoughby de Broke's, 21 Hill St, Berkeley Square, given by his sister, the Honble. Mrs Barnard . . . it was a very good Ball and fine company and Miggy enjoyed herself greatly. Curious that her first London Ball should take place in a House that was to be her own. A few nights after, our next Ball was in Dover St Lady Maria Stanley's,† whose 2nd son, about

---

* Mary Elizabeth had been married very young. There is no indication in her journal that she had any idea that Lady Warwick and Lady Hertford were on terms of rather more than friendship with the King.

† Lady Maria Josephe Holroyd, mother of the first Lord Stanley of Alderley.

my age, was hereafter to be the husband of *my dear Sister Ellen*.
This week was a fearful one of dissipation, 4 Balls, Concerts, the
Play, Dinners, and Parties every night.

Life at Bodlewyddan had had its simple pleasures, but this
was iced champagne to home-brewed cider.

It was an age of rampant snobbery pushed to the limit of
vulgarity. Bad manners were thought highly diverting,
public drunkenness was the rule. The Palace set no example;
the unpopular, gross King was preyed on by disagreeable,
elderly, avaricious mistresses. Lady Louisa Stuart wrote of
George IV, describing a ball at Lady Hopetoun's:

. . . lo! At twelve o'clock in reeled his R.H., pale as ashes, with
glazed eyes set in his head, and in short almost stupefied. The
Dutchess of Cumberland made him sit down by her and kept him
tolerably peaceable till they went down to supper; but then he
talked himself into spirits, set all in motion again with the addition
of a bottle and a half of champagne, and when we went to supper
(for all could not sup at a time) he was most gloriously drunk and
riotous indeed. He posted himself in the doorway to the terror of
everybody that went by, flung his arms round the Dutchess of
Ancaster's neck and kissed her with a great smack, threatened to
pull Lord Galloway's wig off and knock out his false teeth, and
played all the pranks of a drunken man upon the stage. . . .

Though drawn into the rim of the fashionable orbit by
Lady Warwick and Lady Hertford, the Warwickshire
country neighbours naturally gravitated together and dined
and danced in each other's company. George and Mary
entertained with success.

We had a most accomplished artist as a Cook (equal to any Man)
Mrs Sharpe by name, who came from Boddlewyddan. She had an
Aunt who was Housekeeper to the King, and every 3rd or 7th year
(I forget which) she had as her perquisite all the Royal Table Linen,
and through Sharpe for £50 she offered me 30 of the finest Holland
Damask Table Cloths, very little the worse for wear, indeed some
seemed quite new and many large enough to dine 20 or 30 people;
of course we readily gave the fifty pound, there never was such a
bargain, 2 of the Cloths were worth all the money.

Mary's thoughts turned more and more toward Charlecote; she sent down instructions for Sarah, the still-room

maid, about bottling the early gooseberries; her canaries were not forgotten. The summer was slipping away. '[July 6th] Miggy has had dancing to her heart's content, and I am heartily weary of London and all its gaieties, and long for the quiet of the country.' And this is hardly surprising, for on 10 September, having driven in to Warwick Races three times in that week, Mary Elizabeth bore her first child, a son, William Fulke.

The pattern pleasantly repeated itself: dinner parties at neighbouring country houses, garden planning, babies, family visits, and for each Season a house was taken in London. A ball at Lord Heniker's is described agitatedly:

We had not been long in the room and I was standing alone, George having left me to speak to a friend in the adjoining room, when I caught sight of young Wilson Patten (later Lord Winmarleigh), whom I had not met since our parting on the 19th Sept. 1822. He had only just returned from abroad and had not heard of my marriage. He soon saw me, and his hand was clasped in mine, he must have felt it tremble. I strove to suppress my emotion, I almost gasped for breath: he looked at my costly Dress and Diamonds, and almost shrieked, 'I see I have *lost you*, you are no longer my *own sweet Mary*, and my happiness is gone for ever'; and he rushed out of the room, and I believe left London for I saw him no more. When George joined me I felt so faint and ill that I asked him to call for our Carriage and take me home which he did, and then I told him how dearly I had loved Mr W. P. and was beloved, before I had known him and become his Wife. . . .

George was not disposed at that moment to make a scene.

His hand was on my shoulder, I felt its touch was kind, his face looked fondly [down] and he smiled and said, 'I have no jealous fears. I fully trust you my dearest Mary.'

But later when—rather unwisely, one would think—Mr Wilson Patten was asked to stay at Charlecote, George showed signs of acute jealousy and, on being assured that there was now no cause for it, 'listened with visible emotion and pressed me to his heart'.

In February 1826 a daughter, Mary Emily, was born, the first daughter to be born into the Lucy family since Elizabeth,

who married Clement Throckmorton. In 1827 Mary Elizabeth met Mr Disraeli, 'who no one could have foretold
would have become Prime Minister and so great a Man. I
thought him in appearance an insignificant-looking person
and quite a fop, with his black *corkscrew* curls and his jewish
nose.' That was the year they took a house in Bryanston
Square, 'a very large House and beautifully furnished for
which he [George] paid 500 Gns. for the season, it was
charming for the dear children as the rooms were so spacious
and airy. . . .'

12th [of May] we went to a Party at the Ladies FitzPatrick, where
I was introduced to the old Countess of Cork★ who was dressed
in White Satin and a little white Satin Hat on her *old head*. She
never could go out without carrying off something, and when she
dined out she regularly put as many Silver Spoons and Forks as
she could in her pocket—the next morning a servant was sent to
get them back.

    In January 1828 another daughter, Caroline, was born. On
the 8th of April that year:

Sir Walter Scott and his daughter Anne paid old Charlecote a visit
so early that we were in bed, and were awoke by the ringing of the
Door Bell, and don't I remember our hurry to get dressed when
we heard who it was that had arrived and was waiting for
permission to see the House. When we went down he and Miss
Scott were intently surveying the Pictures in the Great Hall. I can
see him now in my mind's eye, advancing to meet us, with the
most genuine expression of benevolence and shrewd humour in
his face, his hair white as snow, and eyebrows very thick and
shaggy, and his crippled foot giving him a limping gait. He
remained with us about 2 hours, and ate a hearty breakfast; he
made me play some Welsh airs, he seemed delighted with the old
place and would fain have spent some days with us. . . .†

★ She was the last of the eighteenth-century eccentrics, and had been Miss
Monckton of 'the Blues'.
† 'Learning from Washington Irving's description of Stratford that the hall of
Sir Thomas Lucy, the Justice who rendered Warwickshire too hot for
Shakespeare, was still extant, we went in quest of it. Charlecote is in high
preservation, and inhabited by Mr Lucy, descendant of the worshipful Sir
Thomas. The Hall is about three hundred years old—a brick mansion with a

In July of the same year the artist, Benjamin Robert Haydon, that touchy, mistrustful genius, visited Charlecote and found very little to please him there. He set off from Stratford bursting with Shakespeare worship. In one long, breathless sentence he announces:

Every blade of grass, every daisy and cowslip, every hedge flower and tuft of tawny earth, every rustling, ancient and enormous tree which curtains the sunny park with its cool shadows, between which the sheep glittered on the emerald green in long lines of light, every ripple of the river with its placid tinkle

> Giving a gentle kiss to every sedge
> It overtaketh on its pilgrimage,

announced the place where Shakespeare imbibed his early, deep and native taste for landscape and forest scenery.

He was enraptured, as many have been before and since, by the park: 'Oh it was delightful indeed! Shakespeare seemed to hover and bless all I saw, thought of or trod on'— but was less pleased with his reception. He entered under the gateway:

Here was an iron gate, and inside a regular garden, the old front of the house showing at the end of it. A young lady and an old one

---

Gatehouse in advance. It is surrounded by venerable oaks, realizing the imagery which Shakespeare loved to dwell upon; rich verdant pastures extend on every side, and numerous herds of deer were reposing in the shade. All showed that the Lucy family had retained their "lands and beeves". While we were surveying the antlered hall with its painted glass and family pictures, Mr Lucy came to welcome us in person, and to show the house, with the collection of paintings, which seems valuable. He told me the park from which S. stole the buck was not that which surrounds Charlecote, but belonged to a mansion at some distance, where Sir T. L. resided at the time of the trespass. The tradition went, that they hid the buck in a barn part of which was standing a few years ago, but now totally decayed. This park no longer belongs to the Lucys. The house bears no mark of decay, but seems the abode of ease and opulence. There were some fine old books, and I was told of many more which were not in order. How odd if a folio Shakespeare should be found among them! Our early breakfast did not permit taking advantage of an excellent repast offered by the kindness of Mr and Mrs Lucy, the last a lively Welshwoman. This visit gave me great pleasure; it really brought Justice Shallow freshly before my eyes. . . .' J. A. Lockhart's *Life of Sir Walter Scott.* The discrepancy in the two versions is amusing.

were talking to a parrot, and a gardener was shaving the grass plot with a scythe. He referred me to the housekeeper; so fearing I had intruded I returned to the back entrance, and meeting a servant asked to see the house.

Chilled by this reception, he looked coldly at the collection of pictures—

with a good one or two amongst them—one a genuine Teniers of his marriage; a fine Hondekoeter and heads of Sebastian del Piombo and Hobbema [*sic*], all genuine. The Lucy family appeared to me shy. They may not be ambitious of showing themselves as descendants of the 'lousy' Lucy. That satire sticks to them and ever must as long as the earth is undestroyed. They sent for my card, but nothing came of it. Perhaps they had never heard of my name. . . . I left the ill-bred, inhospitable house, my respect for the Lucies by no means much higher than Shakespeare's; but the park amply compensated me, for a nobler, more ancient and more poetical forest I never saw. . . .

From Mary Elizabeth's journal, I find that her mother-in-law, Maria, Mrs Lucy, was staying at Charlecote at that time; the parrot, a white one with a lemon crest, lived to a vast age and was drowned when trying to drink from the flooded Avon.

Margaret Williams's marriage to Lord Willoughby de Broke took place in the following February, 1829. For the first time Mary permits herself a few small scratches:

. . . you cannot imagine the surprise, the talk of this marriage has made. Mr and Mrs Barnard (*she* is heir to the Title and Estate) are furious, Lord Willoughby it strikes me is *rather afraid* of entering the Holy State of Matrimony. He stayed at Charlecote till the 27th of Janry, his love making was *very mild*. . . . On the 9th Febry. we took Miggy to London to get her trousseau, and Lord Willoughby gave me *carte blanche* to buy her whatever jewels she wished and her Wedding Veil, and I did not spare his money. George and I gave her a very handsome broach and Earrings, but neither she or her rich old Peer gave us the smallest acknowledgement for all the expense we had been at on her account.

For this they had sat up yawning, till the dawn dimmed the candles in Hill Street; it was a fine marriage for Miggy, who only wanted an Establishment, but romantic warmth was missing.

All this time money was draining away—with so many preoccupations at home George found Parliamentary business more than ever irksome. Austen was obliged to write strongly from Fowey to remind him of his obligations.

Fowey Sept. 25th 1828
. . . I must beg that whilst you are in London you will represent to some members of His Majesty's Administration the enormous expenses which you were put to at the last general election to prevent Opposition men being seated for this borough . . . [your constituents] could never have contemplated that upwards two years would have elapsed without any Government patronage being given to them with the exception of a small place in the Customs here. . . . If yourself and Mr Eden were not Ministerial Men, Government patronage would not be expected by your constituents, but considering that you have represented Fowey nearly nine years as the known friend of Ministers without any patronage to bestow on them, they complain and certainly not without reason. When the Rashleighs had the patronage of Fowey Borough there was not an officer stationed in the port of Fowey without he was either recommended by them or his appointment known to them before he came. . . .

George had his hands full at this time settling up his father's estate and meeting debts from unexpected quarters. He had written to Austen from Bodlewyddan earlier in the same year: 'I am in much distress for Money. I owe some bills and interest money for which the Parties are urgent and dont allow me any rest . . . If you can Anyhow in the world assist me with the sum or a part I hope you will. I cannot leave this place till I can get it.' He dreaded returning to Charlecote to find creditors on the door-step. In spite of this, he was busy with architect's plans and builder's estimates.

The expenditure of a lifetime gives a fair picture of the character of the spender. George Lucy was both generous impulsive Lane and pound-foolish Hammond; beneath his amiable exterior there lay too a nervous unease, not often betrayed, never eradicated. He could be moody, and was easily unnerved by things which a robust person takes in his stride—weather, domestic mishaps, unpunctuality. He had, we know, a way of standing by in an agony of uncertainty when events took an unexpected turn. His wife soon learnt to take all irksome decisions on herself.

The architect of the improvements was a Mr Charles Smith, a clever young man who had studied at the Royal Academy school and become a pupil of Sir Jeffrey Wyatville, the author of the improvements to Windsor Castle. Smith had designed a modest Pump Room for Leamington Spa. George had seen a portfolio of suggested improvements for the Shirleys' house at Ettington drawn by him. After many and long discussions, it was agreed between them that the old domestic offices should be replaced. Entering old Charlecote from the court, all was darkness, for the oak screen of Jacobean design that supported the minstrels' gallery lay on the right hand and on the left a door opened into the servants' quarters. Once in the Hall it was not much lighter, for the windows were filled with old green glass and further obscured by coats of arms. The offices of noise and drudgery consisted of a common parlour for the entertainment of visiting servants, a larder, a butler's pantry and bedroom, a china closet and a staircase leading to bedrooms and a housekeeper's sitting-room. As far as it is possible to judge, there were twelve rooms on the south side. The kitchen, scullery, bread-room, and still-room occupied an outbuilding, probably seventeenth-century in origin, on the north side. It was all this that George proposed to sweep away. The lady of the house must have her drawing-room, and a morning-room for doing her accounts and writing to tradesmen. There must be linen cupboards, silver and china cupboards, a servants' hall large enough for tenants' dinners, and a spacious kitchen.

George Lucy had been alarmed by Wyatt's estimates; he paid Charles Smith £300 for his plan, and proceeded to be his own architect. While in London for her first Season Mary Elizabeth had chosen furnishing stuffs at Henry Miles and John Edwards of 134 Oxford Street, nearly opposite Hanover Square. The beautiful flourishes at the head of the account state that the firm are manufacturers of Persian Cloths, Embossed Moreens, Dimities, etc. From them she bought the 'Crimson China Damask' which more than a century's sunlight, and much handling, have hardly faded, complete with crimson Bullion Fringe, loops, tassels and cord 'for drapery'.

One hundred and sixty-five yards of 'drab ground and Bronze chintz' seems cheap at £19. 10s. The 'Ell-wide Geranium stripe Chintz', trimmed with geranium galoon and lined with glazed white calico, has not survived, but how perfectly of its period it is! As is the French Marigold rich Striped silk, the Yellow Bengal Print, the Gold damask (which still covers the drawing-room walls), the 'Emerald Green extra rich Broglio silk', lined with French Marigold taffeta, that in a sunless bedroom has kept its brilliance almost unimpaired.

George had a great respect for punctuality: like most undecided people he believed that if he could only fit life into a time-frame all its problems would be solved. So he caused the gatehouse clock, which strikes so musically and is as much part of Charlecote as the cawing of the rooks in the high elms, to face the court that the horses might not be kept waiting at the front door.

He had acquired at Fonthill, and was acquiring, all the time, furniture to replace 'the old bruis'd worn out'. Bronze hexagonal lanterns were hung in the Great Hall, and on the staircase. Oil lamps had not yet superseded the candles, with saucers of gilt glass to catch the grease; their wavering shadows lent mystery to the family portraits.

In the years before he took on the unrewarding obligations of a pocket borough, George had busied himself with collecting a vast mass of notes on Lucy genealogy. The Herald's College produced a splendid pedigree book, loaded with gold leaf, which gave much satisfaction to the old Reverend in the last year of his life.

Having economized on his architect, George decided to indulge his dearest hobby, and engaged Thomas Willement (Heraldic Artist by appointment to George IV) to piece together the scattered armorial glass for the new windows in the Great Hall. A good deal of it fell to pieces in the process.

Willement's account of his stained-glass work at Charlecote fills eight pages of his notebooks.* He was a most versatile artist and could advise and arrange about decoration as well. In 1832 he sent George in a bill for £611. 10s. for painting, gilding and paperhanging, with a letter:

I suppose your Paper Hanger is accustomed to the hanging of Flock and metal papers which require very great care; they should have very smooth and stout lining papers under them and the joints well rubbed down before the printed paper is applied; I trust that if well hung the effect of all three patterns will be very handsome and very well suited to the style of your house.

Patterns of these papers and many others have been preserved, and some are still on the walls. The 'Green flock on Buff and metal' survives, the gold faded but still discernible. 'Brown flock on Buff and metal' seems a curious choice for a sunless room that looked east. The Jacobean strap-work design in brown on gold, matched by chintzes of the same, is still in the library; the gold, blue and crimson flock and metal paper in the dinner-room, with its matching carpet, is scarcely less vivid today than when it was first hung.

After a short visit to the Continent while the old kitchen offices were being pulled down and the foundations of the new south block laid, the Lucys moved in to Coppington, a farm on the Stratford side, 'which we made most comfortable'. Mary Elizabeth writes in her journal: 'I had my Harp and Piano brought there with a Sofa, Arm Chairs, and lots of Flowers and pretty things to make our rooms look nice, and every day our riding Horses came for us to ride down to Charlecote to see how the workmen were getting on.'

George was privately uneasy. He wrote to Austen in February 1831 about it, saying that he was beset with demands from his Fowey tenants and 'to say nothing of the expenses in building new offices to this house, and the repairs of the old part of it . . . I have the Sherrifalty of this

* H. T. Kirby, *An Heraldic Artist's Notebook*, Apollo, 1946.

County put upon me, which is considered "an £800 poun-
der" and a Vast Boar . . . But there is no appeal.'

Again, in April 1833:

I am busy in adding two new Rooms, a Dinner Room and a Book
Ditto which have been long thought of, tho' I must say the work
is anything but convenient to me, for the period is now arrived (10
years since my Father's death) when I am called upon by my
Brother to pay him the Bequest, above £30,000 agreably to the
Will, a large sum in these times and as I am unable to do it I intend
assigning over an Estate. . . . I used to be able to raise money by
selling timber but since the introduction of foreign woods duty
free I can only sell at a very low price. . . .

He thought an alteration in the Free Trade system desirable. He had written to Austen as far back as January 1831:

There are faults in the present representative system, no doubt,
which might be amended with advantage to the State, and made
suitable to the altered state of the Times, and I hope there is
Wisdom and firmness in the Legislature to stop *there*. So far I am a
Reformer.

One must suppose that George, a High Tory in principle,
did not vote for the Reform Bill. His generation, 'educated
in a freer atmosphere, defended with reluctance the institutions which their fathers had supported with enthusiasm.'*
He saw that it was a victory for the new capitalist society;
and that all the expense he had been put to, to say nothing of
worry and alarm, by his electors, was to come to nothing.
He felt it necessary to write to Austen on the eve of Reform;
'. . . I fear there is nothing we can do to save Fowey from
disenfranchisement. . . . I am in fact resigned to this great
injustice which appears to be inevitable.'

He was, it seems, no longer an MP, but still the owner of
the Duchy Manor, and had seen his own nominee succeed
him. He was anxious about his property:

The houses now standing empty, are not I fear likely to find
tenants under the new, any more than they did under the old,

* Spencer Walpole.

order of things. . . . I suppose it will be impossible hereafter for idle men like myself to get seats in Parliament, and that none can enter Parliament who have not local interests in the places they sit for. . . . The future Governts, too, of the country, unless they pursue measures agreable to the passions of the people cannot stand. . . . They give the staff out of their own hands, and those of all future ministers, and rest for support on the favour and kindly feeling of the people which may be shewn while things go on smoothly, but never can when under pressure and distress, when I suppose the reign of anarchy will begin.

His tenements, the mines in which he had speculated, the ships he had shares in, continued to be a perpetual drain. The property was not sold off, nor the last accounts settled, till many years after his death.

As Mary Elizabeth wrote: '. . . a sad purchase it turned out; it cost a mint of money and an infinity of trouble and vexation of spirit (and gave me many a heartache in after years)'. George Lucy was repeatedly asked to represent the county of Warwick in Parliament, but he had finished with all that. Home affairs absorbed him more and more.

They moved into Charlecote on 2 October 1830, though the workmen were still in it. The work took seven years in all. By 1836, water-tight, air-tight, elegant, embellished, freshly painted, and trim, Charlecote presented a very different appearance to the ramshackle place it had been. You were confronted on approaching the front door by a fanlight designed by Willement, with the arms of Queen Elizabeth in the brightest colours. All the windows, several opened up after a long period of sightlessness since the repeal of the window tax, shone darkly with plate glass, and were neatly transomed in new stone. Gone were the worn mullions and small, curved panes that shook and rattled with every gust, banished with the screen and minstrels' gallery, the organ and the old wainscoting. Double doors of light oak opened on to the north staircase. The old windows in the Great Hall looking toward the river, paned with cloudy glass, had gone, and doors on either side of the fireplace now led to the fine new library and dinner-room with their flock and metal wallpapers. All the doors and shutters fitted with soundless precision, instead of a protesting screech of un-oiled lock and warped wood. The new oak used throughout was all light in colour: upstairs it was not oiled but painted and grained with bright brown varnish to imitate itself. The hall was painted light grey to imitate stone and pleasantly permeated with hot air, installed by Summers of Bond Street, which found its way through ornamental bronze grilles. Willement crowned his successes at Charlecote by altering the roof of the Great Hall from being arched and lofty to a flattened barrel vault supported by corbels, having along its centre ridge 'eleven large double roses crimson and White, the seeds (*sic*) gilt, large leaves green fully heightened with gold, the grounds pickt out with Cobalt Blue'.

The general effect of metallic gold and strong heraldic colours must have been dazzling. It is not difficult to understand how it affected George Lucy's contemporaries, who were unanimous in acclaiming his good taste and discrimination.

It followed that, having thus garnished Charlecote, the young Lucys would wish to show it off. In December 1836 they entertained for the first time in the new dining-room off the service of silver gilt bought from Rundell, Bridge, and Rundell* in 1824, and augmented in 1834 by silver-gilt knives, forks, and spoons and much elegant plate, all richly crested. Mary Elizabeth had to show off the jewellery her husband had bought her: the pink topaz bracelets, the pearl and emerald lily brooch, the wheat-ear combs of brilliants worn to form a hair ornament between her bunches of black curls, the coral cameos, the heavy gold bracelets set with rubies and diamonds. In the lofty room, the light of many candles caught a brilliant gloss from red and gold walls, gold epergnes, and brilliant white damask that had once covered the Prince Regent's dinner table at Carlton House.

* 'The sideboard was covered with glistering, gold, plate . . . like Rundell and Bridges' shop.' Thackeray, *Vanity Fair*.

CHAPTER 8

The Long Summer Afternoon

In the light of all we now know about the sufferings of the great mass of under-privileged at this time, it is a wonder for us that these good and well-meaning people appear to have been totally unaware of the political and economic state of the country. Our feelings have been played on by revelations of the slave conditions in the factories, the dreadful living conditions of the town poor, the slow degradation of the country people into pauperism, the ruthless, mangling turn of the huge industrial wheel. But in the still warm, if fading glow of their long day's afternoon, these children of the early nineteeth century, brought up as Christians, conscious of the responsibilities attaching to wealth and property, were apparently insulated from contact with these realities. George Lucy thought some sort of reform of the franchise desirable, but feared the power of the masses; even he saw that Toryism would have to change its character. Cobbett, blustering like a bee on a window pane about the wrongs of the yeoman class and, indeed, of all injured persons, declared that it would take less time to put out the privileged from their ancient estates than most people imagined; he reckoned it would take about six years at the rate they were being taxed. Cobbett's writings, naturally, did not find their way to Charlecote.

As in Jane Austen's novels, rumours of wars and economic unrest pass unremarked in Mary Elizabeth Lucy's journals. George might have his worries about money, but they lived handsomely. Being early Victorians, they had a strong moral sense and balanced their pleasures and their purchases for the house with church attendance and charity. Some part of every day was spent by the squire's wife and her daughters in visiting cottages; skim-milk puddings and bone broth were taken round; young girls going into service were provided by the ladies of the Hall with strong calico chemises. Charlecote was considered a model village. George Lucy replaced many of the ancient clay-and-timber cottages with neat brick dwellings, and his brother John, the squarson of Hampton Lucy, did the same for his village. William Howitt, writing in 1839, remarks:

It was a high and sincere pleasure to me to find the present descendants of Sir Thomas Lucy the very reverse of all that Shakespeare would persuade us that he was. On all sides, and from all classes of people, I heard the most excellent character of them. They were described as amiable, intelligent; as of the most domestic habits, and as spending the chief portion of their time on their estate here.

They were unware of the greatness of their epoch. Byron, because he was an aristocrat and his life was scandalous, was admired, but not as the spokesman of liberty. They contrived to be Romantics and highly moral at the same time. Writers of loose life who were not in the peerage did not lie, bound in crushed calf, on the *verd antique* tables.

Having built a handsome book-room, finished in light oak carved in a vaguely Tudor idiom, George set about furnishing its shelves. The books that in his father's day had rarely been opened were trimmed and given new marbled endpapers. From Pickering in Chancery Lane he bought books that he thought would 'go' with the house, but of contemporary writers only a very few—Kinglake, Gilbert White, Mrs Gaskell. (Not Keats or Shelley, Hazlitt or Coleridge.) His ambition was to dress his shelves, and this he did with a splendidly bound if not exactly selective collection of volumes, and some accidentally very rare ones.

Like his predecessor, George Lucy, he had natural taste. He allowed his wife to root up the untidy plots in the court and replace them with a fair imitation of an Elizabethan knot garden. Less happily, he removed the organ gallery and the Tudor screen from the Great Hall and put a light oak dado round it. More unhappily still, he allowed Willement, on whose judgement he had come to depend, to flatten the ceiling of the hall (the Elizabethan gallery that ran the length of the top storey had been divided up into servants' attics). Willement's heavy barrel vaulting with its outsize Tudor roses robs the hall of impressiveness. Never for a moment did the Lucys lose sight of Tudor England; even the door-handles were carved with Tudor roses. Twisted pseudo-Jacobean chimneys gave the roof the richly fretted and pinnacled outline which our great-grandparents so much admired.

The herald in George Lucy would not let him rest. Ignoring two immediately preceding generations of Hammonds, he delved with industry into the Lucy descent, and Willement, under his instructions, made stained-glass panels for the upper panes of the windows in the new addition, with Olde English inscriptions, not all correct. From a letter of Willement's, we gather that George had the idea of reviving the Barony of Lucy of Cockermouth, but was by someone unspecified dissuaded. Perhaps it was his own wife; she had a decided liking for 'people with handles to their names', as she often describes them, but too much common sense not to perceive the folly of litigation about a defunct title. Life was already sufficiently crowded with incident; she had a growing nursery and a big house on her hands; besides which, she worked every day at her music and was much in demand at country-house parties for her charming perform-ance on the harp. She was an early riser and was often out in the garden on summer mornings before six, revelling in her possessions—her canary house, the 'Wilderness' in the North Garden which she had planted with wild things, windflow-ers, and foxgloves and Solomon's Seal, her rose-garden which rides like the rounded prow of a ship above the green wash of the park, the ground dropping away to the Avon, with the tall tower of Hampton Lucy church beyond the trees. She hugged her possessions to her like a child cram-ming all its toys into its arms. Running back to the house with her hands full of flowers as the sun began to parch the dew that had soaked her slippers, she adored its rosy bricks, its now trim and tidy outlines; through the drawing-room window, where the maids were opening the shutters, she saw the sunlight throwing a reflection up the satin walls, where hung the Canaletto, the Clouet, the Schiavones, the Fra Bartolommeo of *The Descent from the Cross*, glinting on her harp and the *torchères* picked up for a song abroad, but regilt in London at the cost of one hundred guineas.

Reading her journal, I am conscious that life was much more exciting then. There being so little ready-made entertainment available, people were passionately interested in each other's marriages, childbeds, and violent deaths. Mary Elizabeth is horror-stricken, but relates with gusto, how her bridesmaid, Charlotte Hughes of Kinmel,* was laid out dead in her wedding dress at the very moment when a party below should have been celebrating her first wedding anniversary. After a visit to Lord Bradford—'I had the dreadful intelligence that the two eldest [daughters] were burnt to death going up stairs to Bed carrying a lighted candle. Lady Charlotte set fire to her sleeve and her Sister endeavouring to put it out was set on Fire herself. . . .'

The Lucys kept spirited horses, and every fine day the lacquered chariot, tilting high on its yellow-lined wheels, swung out of the drive to call on neighbouring great houses—the Gray Skipwiths at Alveston, the Throckmortons at Coughton, the Aylesfords at Packington, the Mordaunts at Walton, the Bradfords at Castle Bromwich, the Percys at Guy's Cliffe. Mary Elizabeth wrote for her grandchildren a gay description of her many accidents when riding or driving. Again and again she was thrown, rolled on, or nearly smothered, had a shoulder sprained, had both wrists dislocated, was all cut about the face, but was nothing daunted. A powerful bay horse called Mandor, driven in double harness for the first time, bolted, and galloped along the main Stratford road for a mile or more. The reins broke

---

* There is an entry in the journal for New Year, 1832: 'George and I went to Warwick Castle and met Lord and Lady Jersey, Sir Robert and Lady Peel and their eldest daughter, now Julia, Countess of Jersey. I remember so well the conversation turning on the Reform Bill, and the shame of creating so many men of straw Peers, to get it through the House of Lords, and Lady Jersey laughing and calling my old friends the Dinorbens, Lord and Lady *Dinnerbell*' (Colonel Hughes had been created Lord Dinorben).

and the horse tried to jump a ditch, flinging out Mr and Mrs
Lucy, two of their children and the coachman, with the trap
on top of them—

like an extinguisher. There we lay, and the Horse along with us,
but fortunately, so tightly wedged that he could not kick; the ditch
being narrow and very deep. My poor husband was under the
Coachman and the children were happily on top of me, so escaped
with a few bruises. There we were 'higgledy-piddledy' with
Oranges, Apples, bottles of wine, books, thimbles, scissors, pin
cushion, reels of cotton; the whole contents of my work-box
turned out, perfectly helpless, unable to stir. . . .

She begged for Mandor's life when George Lucy ordered
him to be shot, and he went in double harness for years.

That year, 1831, saw the marriage of Ellen Williams, Mary
Elizabeth's youngest and favourite sister. The family circle
at Bodlewyddan had sadly shrunk. Sir John Williams was
dead, and Brother lived there alone with Old Nurse, who
must have been a fabulous age, to darn his stockings for
him. Lady Williams had gone to live at Cheltenham, the two
eldest sisters were settling into self-sufficient spinsterhood,
Margaret was mistress of Compton Verney, Brother Hugh
was studying law, Brother William was trying to make
farming pay at Tyfry, and Ellen, with her auburn hair and
great eyes, had fallen helplessly in love with the Hon.
William Owen Stanley of Penrhôs, and he with her. They
met at the Gladstones at Hawarden, and the course of true
love ran smoothly from the first moment.

The years opened out before Mary with a happy vista of
visits to Penrhôs on the Menai Straits, and to stately Compton Verney, where Miggy was always waiting with a
Williams kiss of special warmth. Willement came to stay as
a guest (and at the same time overlooked the details of the
gilding and paper hanging), and was carried off by Mr Lucy
to stay with his farmer brother-in-law, William, at Tyfry,
for snipe-shooting. Fulke went to a private tutor to be
prepared for Eton.

There was one rowdy evening at Warwick Castle when
they all played blind man's buff in the large Cedar Room.

Lady Warwick said she would give a sovereign to any three gentlemen who would undertake to catch Mrs Lucy:

So my naughty husband said he would, and Lord Hillsborough and Lord Broke said they would . . . but I, who was then very slight and nimble, ran in and out amongst the chairs and tables till I tired them all. . . . Lady Warwick got so excited that she could not resist catching hold of my dress as I passed her, and it being muslin she tore it, but could not stop me. I laughed and said, 'Well you must give me a new one'; and they all cried out, 'Yes! Yes! you deserve one.' The three gentlemen sat down and said I had fairly beaten them, and I was so tired I had not a leg to stand on, so I was glad they gave up. Next morning before I was dressed, Lady Hillsborough came into my room with about 20 yards of a beautiful pale pink Satin for a dress, with Lady Warwick's love to me.

Victoria was soon to ascend the throne, but the romping manners of the Regency still prevailed.

There were now six children. Pale-tinted drawings show them large-eyed like tamed fawns, low frocks slipping off their shoulders.* Delicate, affectionate, precocious little creatures, spending their early years in a nursery looking on to a wall that got the early sun obliquely, and a schoolroom that was cold shade till late afternoon. They were bathed in hip-baths by candlelight on fluffy mats from the backs of the black-and-white Portugal sheep spread out in front of the nursery fire, where towels warmed on the brass fire-guard. The old-fashioned, long-handled pans that held hot coals for warming beds still survive at the back of a housemaid's cupboard, rightly looked on as objects of domestic utility and not as part of the antique-dealer's stock-in-trade.

So happy were George and Mary to be at Charlecote with their children that they generally confined their visiting to neighbouring country houses, hurrying home gladly to greet

---

* The grandmother of the writer, a child of the 1860s, when fashion had begun to overload children with clothes, buttoning and lacing them into long boots and redundant petticoats, remembered *her* mother telling her about the paper-thin kid slippers and off-shoulder muslins of *her* childhood, worn in and out of draughty passages and overheated rooms, resulting in bronchitis and pneumonia. A. F.-L.

the first buds of the Gloire de Dijon rose on the gatehouse, or a baby's first staggering steps, or a parcel of new books from Pickering.

Among the fragments in a portfolio of sentimental odds and ends, I find the visiting card of 'Prince Doria Pamphili'. In 1838 Mary Elizabeth wrote:

Lord and Lady Shrewsbury with Prince Doria on their way from London, slept at the King's Head, Wellesbourne, and drove over the next morning to spend the day with us, we were so sorry that they had not written to propose themselves to us, instead of going to a Village Inn. The Prince was in raptures with old Charlecote and so admired the large Florentine Table in the Great Hall, which had originally stood in the Borghese Villa at Rome; from whence it had been taken by the French in the time of Napoleon, ultimately being bought by Mr Beckford, and at the sale at Fonthill bought by my husband for one thousand eight hundred guineas. The Prince Borghese had recently married Lord Shrewsbury's youngest daughter and Prince Doria was engaged to Lady Mary Talbot, the eldest. At luncheon the Prince liked the *Charlecote Biscuits* so much, that I said, laughing, you must carry some away, and so I ordered a packet of them to be put in the Carriage; just after they had started I saw the packet of Biscuits had been left behind, so I took it and ran after the Carriage, and caught them up before they got to the Park Gate and gave them to the Prince. When we went to Rome, 3 years after, nothing could exceed the kindness of Prince Doria and his charming wife, and he said to me he would never forget my running after him with the Charlecote biscuits. . . .

A letter from her brother, Sir John Williams, written in 1844, seems to belong more properly to this happy period before tragedy had broken the charmed circle:

My dearest Mary, thanks many for your nice description of your return home, how refreshing to find yourself in easy slippers running from one flower bed to another in the fine old Court, little toes relaxed on the turf after the hard flags of London. How delicious to pick a Strawberry, and smell a Rose, and kiss the sweet cheeks of your chicks and turn about in ease and comfort, instead of walking up to a Glass to find out the blacks on your nose, or to shake off the Park dust from your beautiful ringlets. Still, London must be visited for Emy's sake, she must have a twirl in the swing and gaiety, although I expect it will turn upon some pleasant College friend of Fulke's to induce her to sigh under the shade of the old Lime Avenue. . . . I hope dear Emy will find her head in a circle of rose-buds, without any sharp points in the wires to prick her. I shall be so rejoiced to welcome you all here and so will Sarah.*

This kindest of uncles was always welcoming to his sister's children. Herbert Almeric, most tenderly loved because delicate from birth, was sent to Bodlewyddan after an attack of the whooping cough to breathe the health-giving air of Rhyl. He had the waxy, mature look and sad self-possession that seem so often to foreshadow early death. In his sedate little way he was pleased to have the big house full of worshipping servants to himself, without any romping, teasing brothers and sisters to make him run about and cough.

Just after Christmas, 1839, Herbert Almeric returned to Charlecote with presents from the Abergele toy-shop for all his brothers and sisters, but through the spring and summer months of 1840 he sickened, and 'faded away like a broken flower'. On 13 August he was buried in the family vault. 'The rooms he had seemed to fill with life, even while his own was waning fast, could know him no more.'

Five days later, prostrate with inconsolable grief, Mary Elizabeth gave birth to another baby, who was privately baptized by the name of Edmund Davenport.

They resumed the routine of their lives, but the spring had gone out of it. 'I had never recovered the death of my *beloved child*, nor indeed had his Papa, so we both thought a thorough change of scene would be the best thing, and we persuaded dear old Mrs Lucy to live and be mistress at Charlecote in our absence.' Maria, Mrs Lucy, had been living at a nearby farm called The Hill, furnished for her by her son, and drove behind her white pony almost daily down to Charlecote to embrace her grandchildren and her 'dear darling', as she called her daughter-in-law. She was by now very old, but still sprightly, though her memory was going.

* His wife, Lady Sarah Amherst.

The Charlecote household turned and hummed like a well-regulated machine while the old lady dozed in the sun, picked flowers and forgot to put them in water, or entertained the few elderly people living round in Wellesbourne and Barford who had been young when her husband, John Hammond, succeeded.

The foreign tour, at the prospect of which Mary Elizabeth felt very disconsolate, hating to leave the beloved place, lasted from October 1841 to May 1843. This chapter of her journal follows a well-worn pattern. There is much exclaiming over scenery and antiquities, for which enough adjectives cannot be found. When it descends from the sublime to the human it becomes interesting. The travelling party consisted of Mr and Mrs Lucy, Mr Drake the Tutor, Hughes the Nurse, Thomas Footman, Desirée the Swiss Courier, and the Lucy children—Fulke, Carry, Emily, Spencer, Aymer, and the baby Edmund. They took 'two Carriages, a Coach and Chariot, 2 Beds for the little ones, 2 Baths, Sheets, Towels, Pillows, and we had a sort of *well* fixed under the Coach which held lesson Books, Tea, Arrowroot, and every possible thing we fancied we might want'. On the Continent they were taken for travelling Royalty.

We arrived in Paris on the 8th [of November 1841] and staid there ten days, and got to Lyons on the 22nd, and there our darling beautiful Edmund Davenport was taken ill for the first time. . . . I was in agony, but Desirée tried to comfort me by saying that it was the milk and that it was the case generally, with English children, and that he would soon be all right. . . .

They crossed the Mont Cenis against advice, for there had been a heavy snowfall. The coach was held up for a considerable time while some 'Rude Waggoners' dug it out of a ditch. The cold was intense, and the baby obviously suffering from what we should recognize as the symptoms of gastro-enteritis. The chaise got through, being narrow, but the heavy coach swayed and toppled and George Lucy cried out, 'Oh my God, the Coach can never pass; it must go over!' ('I pressed my Baby to my breast and felt I was dying with him.') The coach righted itself and the immediate danger

was passed, but the long, cold, jolting journey had been fatal
to the ailing child. His frantic mother fed him on spoonfuls
of chicken tea and arrowroot and kept him under her shawl,
but he was past reviving.

I clasped him to my heart, I drowned him in my tears, I cried to
the Lord to have mercy on me, to send his little spirit back—in
my agony, my frenzy, I breathed into his little mouth as though
my breath could have reanimated him—but he was gone. . . .
Eleven long hours did I travel with its dear lifeless body in my lap,
ere we reached Turin at 3 o'clock in the morning. Never, never,
can I forget that night of anguish, seated in the Carriage with the
Moon shining bright through the Window on its pale but beau-
teous face, so calm, so still, so lovely in death.

The British Consul intervened to prevent the Italians
taking the remains of the child for immediate burial, as was
the custom. A sea-captain, one Turner, master of the brig
Matilda, agreed to take the body to Liverpool, and extorted
a stiff price for so doing ('. . . when he came and carried off
the Coffin, to part with it was like parting with a portion of
my heart'). George Lucy sent anguished orders about silver
coffin plates and a white velvet pall to his agent, and to his
brother, the Reverend John, at Hampton Lucy explicit
directions about the form of the burial service and the
commitment of the little body to the family vault. Already
the tour had thrown him into a state of agitation; it had
begun most inauspiciously. Unnerved, he visualized
draughty lodgings, damp beds, cheating foreigners, contagious illness. Thomas Footman has become ill with rheumatic fever. 'I fear it will be a long time before we can have
his services, and have in consequence been obliged to hire an
Italian footman to do his work, it is very unfortunate. . . .'

But they had come abroad to improve and distract their
minds, and gallantly they carried out their prearranged
programme. Portraits of chubby infants asleep reduced the
poor mother to tears in many a picture gallery. It is heart-
rending to picture them frozen in Florence in November,
scorched in Rome in June, but indomitable. 'Oh, the *sorrow*
of having *so much* to see', Mary Elizabeth exclaims in her

journal. She was deeply shocked by a great deal that she saw, and felt the colour mounting to her cheeks as she stole glances at lovely, naked goddesses: 'I fear much of my modesty will wear away before I return to England, as naked Statues & *shocking* Pictures meet my Eye in every Palace.' Emily and Carry were not allowed to look at Canova's Venus that they might not have their native innocence impaired. They stayed in Rome over Christmas, then most unwisely went on to Naples, where it rained steadily, and which they left without a qualm of regret. By March they were again settled in Rome in ten large rooms in the Palazzo Georgie, which they had to scrub and clean, as the previous occupant had been a Russian Countess with six dogs and every hole and corner was full of fleas. They soon acquired a circle of English acquaintances, some amusing, some bores— and a round of entertainments was added to those merciless sightseeing excursions.

After many delays the brig *Matilda* docked at Liverpool. Wallington, the agent, wrote from Charlecote in February 1842:

I hasten to give you the satisfactory intelligence of the safe arrival of the remains of the lamented child. . . . I trust shortly to hear now that Mrs Lucy is regaining her spirits and that you are all in good health and able to enter with zest into the new scenes around you. I was much disappointed to find you were not on the whole pleased with Italy, but trust that the grand object of your sacrifice will be obtain'd in the education of your family, and that we shall have you all return more fond than ever of Old England. . . .

The kindness of Prince and Princess Doria made their stay in Rome pleasant, and the Shrewsburys were met again. Lady Shrewsbury was sympathetic and encouraged Mrs Lucy to talk of the loss of her baby, and the burdened heart was for the first time a little relieved.

She picked violets in the Pamphili Gardens—'the colour of the violets is far richer than any I ever saw in England but they do not smell half so *sweet*'. The evening crushes at the Torlonias and the Borgheses were very grand, and the women's diamonds outshone the chandeliers. George often had a headache after sightseeing and recording in his sketch book minute details of mosaic and marble pavements (Charlecote was always in his mind: the worn stone paving of the Great Hall was to be replaced next), and she sometimes went alone with Princess Doria. It was not in Mary Elizabeth's nature not to respond to the stimulus of lights and music and florid compliments. She saw Byron's last love, Countess Guiccioli, at the Torlonias': 'I sat by her for some time and heard her talk in broken English. She has a profusion of reddish auburn Hair, and wears it in long ringlets down her face, looking very much like Titian's Magdalen in the Pitti Palace but not half so beautiful, indeed I cd. not see any beauty in her excepting in her fine Hair. She is shorter than I am and stout, but of course Time has laid his hand on her, as with all others. . . .'

The catalogue of picture galleries visited makes one ache for the children dragging tired little feet along endless marble corridors, or fidgeting and driving their elders mad in the confinement of the family coach. Mary Elizabeth is often ready to scream with fatigue, she is not 'antiquary enough to be enraptured with a place merely because it was centuries back a great City'; there is a hateful picnic expedition to Ostia when plans go awry, the children are out of humour, and she is 'cross and tired with walking over a flat and ugly marsh covered with Thistles which pricked my legs at every step'.

Florence, Bologna—in the stupor of June—'the heat is so overpowering that I can hardly hold my Pen—and at night one cannot sleep for hunting some cool corner for one's burning feet (though covered only with a single sheet). Oh, give me the climate of dear old England with its cloudy sky in preference to the bright blue one of Italy with its scorching sun.' Tempers are frayed: 'I wished very much to see the Cell [at Ferrara] where Tasso was confined, and Ariosto's tomb, his chair and Inkstand, but saw them not, as G. *cares not for Poets*, at least for foreign ones.' *Padua, Venice*: a visit to the Lido, to reflect sentimentally that here Lord Byron used to ride by the shores of the Adriatic. She wished to take back a Gondola 'and put it on the Avon with two nice

Gondoliers to row me at my pleasure'. *Verona, Milan, Lugano*, the ascent of *St Gothard, Lucerne.* . . . Scenery now takes precedence, though Lucerne is seen only through steamy mist. *Strasbourg*, and a glimpse of the Duc de Nemours bowing to the crowds that lined the streets 'but not smiling, his Countenance is of a peculiar grave cast, and no doubt the recent sad death of his eldest Brother shadows it with double Melancholy just now'.—*Nancy.* . . .

For the first time we are told that she was very poorly, which explains a good deal; she wished to reach Paris in good time for her confinement still six weeks away, to which end they had risen at five each morning and travelled all day in great heat. They were to stay one night in Nancy, but next morning, 'as Carriages were packed and the Horses, with the Postillions cracking their whips, impatient to start, I was taken so very ill that the Carriages were sent away and a Doctor sent for. . . .'

The commotion was terrific. The gruff old landlady ordered them off the premises, as the Duc de Nemours was hourly expected to occupy the very rooms they had just left. Already the officers of his entourage were crowding out all the lodgings in the town. Mr Lucy exclaimed: 'Well, Mary. This is indeed unfortunate,' and the children wept at the grown ups' long faces, and Hughes, the Welsh nursemaid, wrung her hands. A young French doctor was called in and said authoritatively that Madame must not be moved. The cross landlady was interviewed by Mrs Lucy, who tremblingly threatened to appeal to the Duke, and after some disagreeableness she consented to allow them to occupy a partially furnished upper room.

. . . I had to crawl up a steep flight of stairs to a large comfortless Bedroom. . . . I had no Baby Clothes, as both Clothes and an English monthly Nurse were to meet me in Paris—dear Emily and Carry set to work with their needle and Hughes cutting up some of my Linen and Flannel, they soon made a suit for the expectant Baby. I shall not easily forget the hour of his birth. The Doctor was in the next room talking French with my husband, whilst Hughes kept crying—'Sir, do let Dr Simonin come to my dear Mistress, who is so very ill!'

Dr Simonin had a dandified appearance, but was a clever doctor; '. . . he left Nature quite to herself, which was most agreeable to me as I had no *black doses* to torment me . . .' The child, when born, was a boy and appeared dead, but Desirée, the invaluable, plunged it straight into a warm bath and it breathed.

For five weeks they stayed at Nancy, while Mary Elizabeth slowly recovered; her strength was much tried by having to do everything for the baby herself, emotion having completely unnerved Hughes. 'We received the greatest kindness from Dr Simonin and everyone in the Hotel, even from the cross old landlady, who became so fond of us all that she was full of sorrow at parting with us.'

They arrived in Paris on 1 October and settled down in a hotel in the Rue de Rivoli for the winter. Fulke and the tutor returned to England; the girls had lessons in French and dancing, a harp was hired, and Spencer, a lively child, was sent to a day school. Routine re-established itself. The drawbacks of Italy would be forgotten: the dead trampled grass, the smells, the dust, the jolting on bad roads would mercifully recede, and the drifts of violets under the black cypresses in the Pamphili gardens be remembered. It was comfortable to be in Paris, almost as good as being in London. It was cold and rainy in a homely, English way, street lamps glistened on the wet roads, and the shops were full of new winter modes. The tempo of life slowed down; there was a baby in the family again, and with it the comforting familiar routine of the nursery.

George Lucy had done a good deal of business while abroad. From the Accademia delle Belle Arti at Florence he ordered white and coloured marble fireplaces to be made for Charlecote with the Lucy crest and the homely English pike on them. He bought, as well as pictures, Graeco-Roman vases, cabinets in Opera di Commesse inlaid with semi-precious stones, and an alabaster replica of the Vase with Doves Drinking found at Hadrian's villa.

On 20 May 1843, at seven o'clock in the evening, the coach turned in at the gates of Charlecote and the long, uncomfortable, exhausting, emotional tour was over.

Another little coffin lay in the family vault and a new baby would occupy the vacated cradle.

With what thankfulness they sank back into their daily life one can only imagine. Old Mrs Lucy remained with them at Charlecote, which she now could not remember ever having left, and died peacefully in November that year. 'Her death was most sudden and deeply affected us all, but it was a blessed end, really like the extinction of a light which had burnt bright in its socket to the end.'

In 1844 the flagstones of the Great Hall were taken up. The Venetian pavement of rose and white marble squares was laid down and the Fonthill table of coloured marble set in the centre. The family portraits, blackened by two hundred years of wood smoke, looked uneasily down on the transformation. The Florentine fireplaces were installed, and the rest of the bric-à-brac disposed about the rooms, which were still, by the standards of the day, sparsely furnished. With satisfaction, George felt that he was acting in the tradition of the Elizabethans who imported Italian stone-cutters and plasterers to beautify their English mansions.

The winter of 1844 was terribly cold. Edward Fitzgerald wrote to a friend: '. . . it has blown a most desperate East wind, all razors; a wind like one of those knives one sees at shops in London with 365 blades all drawn and pointed; the wheat is all sown; the fallows cannot be ploughed; what are all the poor families to do during the winter?'

For some time the master of Charlecote had been ailing. He still rode round the estate with Wallington his agent, and wrote letters but with increasing difficulty, his strength all the time draining away. The icy wind numbed him; he had to be lifted from the saddle. His passionate absorption in booksellers' and auctioneers' catalogues flagged; his last purchase for Charlecote was of two dark red porphyry pedestals, from a Roman palace. They stand, looking incomplete, in the Great Hall; we shall never know what his intention with regard to them was, for by the time they were installed he was in London, in the hands of a doctor named

Johnson. His wife had not 'been half happy about him for a long time'—in fact, since the closing stages of the tour.

In May 1845 Dr Johnson came down to Charlecote, and again in June. By this time George Lucy was too weak to dress himself or lift a book. His wife nursed him day and night. He was in pain now, and part of the time unconscious. From where he lay he could see the sun on the Renaissance carving of the porch and hear the children's voices from the court. He was fifty-six; they had thought Miggy's 'old peer' decrepit at the same age. The illness that deprived him partially of speech dragged out till the end of June, on the 30th of which month he composedly asked for his family to assemble round his bed for a last farewell. Aymer and little Berkeley were got out of their cribs in their nightgowns, for it was ten o'clock of the long, light June night. He repeatedly blessed them and kissed his favourite son, Spencer, and died as the clock on the gateway struck eleven.

The *Warwickshire Standard* for 5 July 1845 spoke eloquently of his public work and esteemed character: 'During the last few years Mr Lucy mixed but little in public life, preferring it would seem the far dearer pleasures of his own domestic circle, and principally devoted himself to the renovation and embellishment of his fine ancestral hall.'

Mary Elizabeth, writing some years later when the first bewildered passion of grief had been spent, says: 'He was beloved and lamented by all who knew him, for he was a well-wishing and kind friend . . . one who never passed a hard censure, his interpretation of what others did was always charitable, and in his tongue was the law of kindness . . . he was a most dear lover of Pictures and Sculpture and a most excellent judge of all things rare and beautiful.'

William Fulke Lucy was not quite of age when his father died. He was a gentle, delicate, affectionate boy, who had never known good health since an attack of rheumatic fever in childhood. Eton undermined both his constitution and his self-confidence: one can understand why his father, perhaps too openly, preferred the next son, the sturdier Spencer. William Fulke was his mother's favourite.

He was such a beautiful child that, when in London, his nurse was often stopped (and twice by Royalty) to enquire his name, etc., and I well remember one fine day in the Month of June 1829, he was running by my side in Kensington Gardens, when the Queen, then Princess Victoria, was tossing Hay with a little Rake, attended by her Ladies and he ran off towards her, when she, looking at him, exclaimed: 'What a lovely little boy', caught him up in her arms and gave him a good kiss—for which she received a reproof!

All that remains of him are his portrait by De Manana, the purple velvet dress he wore at a children's party at Stoneleigh, and a few rather pathetic letters. Eton is too rough for him; he does not like football or cross-country runs. Sitting through Chapel with wet feet, working without a fire in his room, getting soaked through on the river, bring on the cough and aches he dreads. Like all Eton boys, he is always short of money for tips and extras. He is laughed at for his girlish surname, which he supposes cannot be helped. He enjoys a ham brought from Charlecote, needs new trousers, is sick from eating damsons and syllabub, thinks all the time wistfully of his 'sweet home', wonders if Spencer has shot a woodcock.

He went from Eton to Cambridge, but was recalled to Charlecote by his father's last illness. There was some ambiguity about money affairs. Inconceivably George Lucy had not made a will before illness overtook him, which for so careful a man seems extraordinary. The doctors who attended him most officiously drew up a will on his behalf to which they set their signatures. The paralysis that attacked him at the end made it difficult for him to speak, nearly impossible for him to sign his name. We shall never know what was in that will, but we do know that Mary Elizabeth, on being shown it, rushed with it to her husband's bedside and begged to be allowed to tear it up. He had been too ill to indicate that it displeased him, but with a last effort he took it from her and tore it in pieces.

Hugh Williams, his brother-in-law, who had been Lord Willoughby de Broke's agent, undertook to look into the Lucy family affairs. What he found startled him so much that he exclaimed: 'Mary, you must let Charlecote, for you cannot possibly afford to live there, and the Pictures and valuable furniture must be sold to realize money for the younger children, for the Personalty will fetch so large a sum that it would burthen the Estate too much to borrow.' To which she replied with spirit that rather than leave Charlecote or part with any of her late husband's collection, she would live upon a crust. This was found not to be necessary. Fulke took over 'the Pictures, etc., at the price his Father had given for them, and as happily that cruel succession duty had not then passed, we were able to do as we pleased.' There was money still owing for the rebuilding and decoration of the house, rents were very low and the property in Fowey, still in George Lucy's name though the Borough had been disfranchised, had so deteriorated in value that he was negotiating not long before his death to sell it to Mr Treffry. The transaction was not put through in time, and the money went as Personalty to the younger brothers and sisters.

Mary Elizabeth did not come out of her heavy mourning till June 1847, but an invitation to the Duchess of Sutherland's Ball at Stafford House in honour of the Grand Duke Constantine of Russia could not be refused, for dear Fulke and darling Emily's sake.

Her description of Stafford House, of the garlands of roses slung from pillar to pillar, the marble basin of the fountain in the ballroom filled with real water-lilies, the hundreds of wax lights, the supper so appetizing, babbles on as did her account of her presentation to George IV twenty-six years earlier: 'My dearest Fulke looked so handsome in his dress Uniform, worn for the first time, dear Emily's dress was of White Tulle, double skirts looped up with apple-blossoms and in my eyes the prettiest dress there and herself quite a Pocket Venus.'

She had felt acutely the loss of husband and children, but her zest for life was still keen. In a short sentence rather self-consciously underlined, she mentions Mr Wilson Patten, now Lord Winmarleigh and a widower: 'We were *very devoted to each other*, but I would never marry again, though I had several offers. . . .'

Mary Emily, pink and white as apple blossom, married that year young Tom Fitzhugh of Plas Power, Co. Denbigh:

The day was lovely and for the time of year [October] very warm, for the Geraniums were still round the Court, and Dahlias and Hollyhocks in full bloom. We went in twelve Carriages to the quiet little Church in the Park, the Bride being with me, Carry and her Brothers in the *new Coach** with our own beautiful 4 Horses. The Village Bands of Charlecote, Hampton Lucy, and Stratford, united drumming and fiddling away along the road as we passed to the great danger of frightening the Horses . . . as the lovely bride and handsome Bridegroom returned to the Carriage their path was strewed with Flowers by the Village School Girls who were dressed in Pink Frocks, White Tippets, Straw Hats with Pink Ribands. About half past 12 o'clock after changing her Bridal Dress for a travelling one of Lilac shot silk and a Bonnet of White Terry Velvet, my most dear Emily left the home of her childhood . . . at 3 o'clock every Cottager on his [William Fulke's] Estate was regaled with Beef, Plum Pudding and *good Ale* in the New Loft over the Stables which held about 300. . . . At 9 o'clock the Tenantry, their wives and sons and daughters began to arrive for a Ball, they danced in the large Dinner Room and Supper was laid in the great Hall. There was an excellent Band and everything went off well and dancing was kept up with great spirit till 4 o'clock in the morning.

There had been an affecting scene before the ceremony in the Great Hall when the bride came in on her brother's arm and Wallington, the agent, had stepped forward and clasped a bracelet on her arm, the gift of the tenantry crowding into the Hall and court to cheer. The bright October day passed like a dream: 'and all was over, and my beloved Mary Emily was gone, and carried away with her my very right hand, yea, the very glow from our grate! the sunbeam from our panes!'

In less than a year the young squire, William Fulke, was dead of jaundice. 'On the 10th of July his loved remains were borne by six of his workmen along the Avenue of tall ancestral trees to the old Church of Charlecote to be laid

---

* Still in the coachhouse at Charlecote.

aside *his Father* who on the very *same day* of July three years before had been carried along the same Avenue to be laid aside *his Father*. . . .'

A silence fell on Charlecote, almost a chill. It had been so gay, bustling with workmen, humming with servants, musical with children's voices. Now there was only one little boy, Berkeley, alone in the deserted schoolroom, for Aymer was away at a tutor's and Spencer at Christ Church. Caroline slept in the dressing-room that had been her father's so that her mother might not be lonely—but so few could not reanimate the place. Mary Elizabeth, an apt pupil to her husband, turned to the solace of bricks and mortar and decided to rebuild the church in his memory.

Her choice of an architect fell on John Gibson, the talented pupil of Sir Charles Barry, who at this time was rebuilding the Houses of Parliament—according to the journal, 'quite a young man, little known to fame, but known by my Brother to be very clever and what was even better thoroughly honest and high principled'.

The *last Sunday* that Divine Service was performed in the old Church, and it was about to be pulled down, I could not help feeling very sorrowful . . . with Husband and Children I had prayed in that old family pew, with its large Oak Desk around which we had knelt together, then in the plain ancient Norman Font all our children had been christened . . . and the old Church Bell had rung its remorseless toll 4 different times and the burial service been read for my beloved husband and three beloved sons, and *once* had rung very merrily and the marriage service been read for my dearest daughter Mary Emily. The recollection of these things kindled at my heart and caused my tears to fall fast on the old building as it fell to the ground and there was not one stone left upon another.

She had written in her journal twenty-six years earlier of her first Christmas at Charlecote:

On Christmas Day we went to Charlecote Church. . . . I sadly missed the fine organ and Choir of St Asaph Cathedral. Our music was a Bassoon and a few voices mostly out of tune. The little old church itself seemed so poor, it was of Anglo-Norman origin, but not one architectural beauty remained; it consisted simply of a Nave and a Chancel and nearly the whole space of the latter was occupied by three Magnificent Monuments to the memory of the three last Sir Thomas Lucys. You entered the Church at the West end and descended two steps into it. The family pew seemed the only part cared for, it was quite a large room, wainscoted with oak and some carving and had comfortable seats and a fireplace.

Out came all the old wood which was thriftily converted into servants' furniture for the attics. A new set of communion plate was bought from Gerrards of Panton Street, Haymarket, who allowed £14 credit on the old silver flagon, chalice and paten, of undiscoverable antiquity.

The new church was dedicated on 2 February 1853: it had taken four years to build, and during that time the three great Lucy tombs were housed in a shed in the churchyard, wrapped in blankets from the house. When they were rehoused in a dark side chapel they seemed to have shrunk.

The new building was richly Gothic, and where the previous stone box had been plain there was now a profusion of ornament. Each of the children loyally presented a window. Gibson made a gift to the church of a window in the chancel, and the round window in the Lucy Chapel with the family arms was designed, executed and presented by Thomas Willement. Margaret Willoughby de Broke and her husband gave the white stone font, and the ancient Norman font was put out into the churchyard to be used as a birdbath. Where before small panes of dim glass had let in a grudged daylight, it now was tinged with yellow and blue and crimson, but the church was scarcely any less dark. The old man with the bassoon and the boy with a flute were replaced by an organ: hot air came up through gratings; there were crimson velvet pillows to the Squire's pew, filled with down from his own geese. The result of so much tender fervour was not, as its perpetrators imagined, a reconstruction of the Olden Tyme worthy of Charlecote's long history, but a mid-nineteenth-century period piece straight out of the pages of *The Daisy Chain*.

The rough grass of the churchyard had always been cropped by Wallington's sheep. The village hens scratched up the earth on the new graves, the tombstones were obliterated with lichen and ivy. Mary Elizabeth overcame the natural opposition of the villagers, and removed most of the old tombstones, laying them flat or substituting crosses. She fenced and planted the churchyard with roses, and longed to have the loved dead 'now resting in the Mausoleum to be instead under the soft green turf, that I might often water it with my tears, and pray by their graves, and plant Roses and Lilies on them and tend them with my own hand, and be buried by them, and know that my dear children would plant a Rose on me and sometimes water it with *their* tears. . . .'

Her dear Brother wrote to her on her birthday in November 1858: 'The birthdays, kept as they used to be with such happy kisses in our dear Mother's dressing-room, tap gently on one's heart for remembrance! Still the forms of our childhood flit before our eyes. That happy home rises up with all its enjoyments, such as few ever experienced, to pull tighter the cords of love on every succeeding birthday, before Time comes and sweeps us all into the Gulph!'

Afterword

In 1948 Charlecote, its Tudor Gatehouse, its deer Park, its Brewhouse and Stables, its collection of ancestral portraits, became the property of the National Trust. The contents of the Evidence Closet are now in the safe-keeping of the Warwickshire Archives.

Sometimes at the end of a day I stand aside watching the visitors depart as the hands of the Gatehouse clock move on to the hour of six. I get friendly looks and return them. The guides collect up their notes and follow the visitors out. I can almost imagine that I hear the creaking of released wooden floorboards which have been walked on all day by many hundreds of feet. The eyes of portraits going back 400 years from the original builder of the house and ending with the last Lucy heiress, look, perhaps, relieved not to be staring all day at strangers. One thing these portraits all have in common (other than family likeness) is confidence; a shared belief that they were representatives of a way of life that would last as long as time lasts. It could never have occurred to them that the house after two World Wars would open its doors to the nation.

Appendix

A Nineteeth-century Squarson, the Reverend John Lucy, Rector of Hampton Lucy and Vicar of Charlecote, 1790–1874

The earliest examples of photography impart to their subjects a sort of doom-full weightiness. John Lucy leaning against a stone pillar, a high folded stock hiding his chin, on his head a very tall, furry hat and round his tall thin person a frock-coat tightly wrapped, makes a far more seigneurial impression than does his milder brother George's bust in Charlecote's Great Hall sculpted by Behnes in the mock-Roman fashion. Cold and reserved by nature, he was more feared than loved by his parishioners. His sister-in-law, Mrs George Lucy, striving to be charitable, wrote of him in her journal: 'John Lucy was never an active parish priest in proper sense of the word, he belonged rather to a school of Clergymen now rapidly passing away, but he will be greatly missed, for if not beloved he was much respected and honoured by his parishers as their Rector for over fifty-nine years. He was bound to them and they to him by a link which length of time always rivets, with a strength of which we are unconscious till it is rent asunder. He was a most perfect Gentleman of the Old School. . . .'

He would sweep off his hat with punctilious politeness to an old woman picking up sticks; talked of a cowcumber and a balcōny, dined at two o'clock and rose at four, would not allow pork at his table or persons holding Radical views inside his house. He loved to entertain, for in common with his brother the Squire of Charlecote he was a passionate collector of *virtù* and liked to show it off. He possessed a notable cellar; his dinner parties were planned like campaigns.

But when in bad weather the Avon rose and covered the wooden footbridge that spanned the ford near the mill, invited guests often had to turn back in full view of the Rectory's glowing windows. Many a good dinner was lost this way, for in times of flooding a coach could not pass the ford. In 1829, at the Rector's sole expense, an iron bridge, cast at the famous Horsley ironworks in Shropshire, was erected, broad and high, with no pretensions to anything but usefulness.

By then Hampton Lucy village had undergone some drastic changes. The little low stone church and the cottages about it on the green had been pulled down and in their place a new church built, very unlike anything visualized by old Mrs Hammond in 1778 when she left all of her estate in trust for the ornamenting and beautifying of the church of which her late husband had been Rector. After the Civil War, when Fulke Brook's soldiers had burned the pews and torn up the brasses from the floor, the fabric had been patched, but there were still holes in the flooring where the brasses had been. Mrs Hammond had left explicit instructions to her executors that its floor was to be new paved with Wilmcote stone and it was to have new pews and a pulpit of mahogany. The original legacy of £900 had been accumulating in the Funds for nearly fifty years, and when the stock was sold amounted to over £9,000. In the lavish manner of the day, John Lucy decided to rebuild and pay the difference out of his own pocket.

The architects were to be Thomas Rickman* and his partner, Henry Hutchinson, of Birmingham, who were responsible for a dull but inoffensive block of new buildings at St John's College, Cambridge, and had already a number of churches to their credit. George Lucy had turned down Benjamin Wyatt's suggestions for the new wing at Charlecote. Architecturally his taste was unformed—over Charlecote, as we have seen, he hesitated and compromised. His brother saw no incongruity in replacing a fourteenth-century church with a nineteenth-century imitation, in what Rickman, in his new Dictionary of architectural styles, called the Decorated, with a tower 114 feet high that would be a landmark for miles round. He chose the yellowish-white stone of Gloucestershire, quarried at Postlip and Chipping Campden, and the combined talents of the two architects and of the stone-mason, Mr Oakes of Ombersley, with a good deal of advice from the Rector, produced a footnote to the Romantic Revival; its curiously impermanent air derives perhaps from the thinness of the walls and the

---

* Author of a series of lectures published under the cumbrous title: *Attempt to discriminate the styles of Architecture in England from the Conquest to the Reformation.*

shallow working of the stone. In 1856 Sir Gilbert Scott was unfortunately allowed to remodel the interior and refurnish it, which has spoilt the harmony of Rickman's original intention, while bringing it into line with mid-nineteenth century ecclesiology.

Undaunted by its dazzling newness and size (it had been built to seat four hundred people), the Rector continued his imperturbable practice of giving out fox-hunting notices from the pulpit. After wine and *virtù*, hunting was his passion. Later in the century he found it expedient to add to the Rectory a small bedroom and breakfast-room opening on to the stable yard, for his private use on cubbing mornings. (His groom, who was also his valet, called him.)

The house had an elegant white parlour lined with bookshelves which he found too small for his needs. He threw out a drawing-room at the back of the house, looking on to the cedar tree that his great-uncle, George Hammond, had planted. His dinners were lengthy, much wine was drunk, and guests were often obliged to stay the night; the housemaids taking down the library shutters in the great house across the park saw the lights in the Rector's drawing-room still burning. To house his curate he built a severe dark vicarage house in Charlecote. The curate had previously occupied a charming thatched and timbered cottage that stood in a corner of Dog Kennel Close, a fanciful Olden Tyme name for the field opposite the park gates, now used as a car park by the National Trust; it was as old as Shakespeare's England. (The fake tumbledown stile where the poacher was said to have been caught was in the same field.)

In the early years of John Lucy's incumbency the character of old Hampton Lucy village was altogether altered. Many sagging cottages disappeared; those that were allowed to stand were tidied up and given numbers. The old Grammar School built on a piece of land granted by Colonel George in 1710 was allowed to remain as the schoolmaster's house, and in the churchyard a low, timbered building was spared that had been the school-house in the third Sir Thomas's day.

Few nineteenth-century squarsons can have enjoyed such unquestioned authority as John Lucy had in his own sphere. The Church in the early part of the century was deeply unpopular— Radical reformers traced every abuse to the grasping 'tithe-eaters', entrenched in hereditary privilege and in a narrow orthodoxy that blocked reform. The alarmed Bishops in the House of Lords voted against the Reform Bill. After the Bill had been carried, it seemed as if disestablishment of the Church was inevitable. But the system rocked, righted itself, and through cautious compromise, spread over the next seventy years, inequality of endowment was more or less balanced. The incumbent of Hampton Lucy continued to hold the advowsons of Charlecote, Wasperton, and Alveston, received his tithes as before, rode to hounds, farmed, entertained the county to dinner, and put the fear of God, in the long black person of the Rector, into the schoolchildren whom he catechized, and into the backsliders of the village, to whom he was more terrible than the whole Bench of magistrates.

John Lucy was not regarded with affection by his nephews, to whom he was 'ever the close-fitted uncle', but they enjoyed his dinners. The younger boys, Aymer, who died of rheumatic fever at twenty-one, and Berkeley, holidaying from Eton, went out with the harriers, shot wood-pigeons, doves, blue-blacks, wood-cock, and snipe, netted sparrows, fieldfares, and thrushes, ratted and ferreted, bolted rabbits out of their holes, 'had capital fun', and dined with Uncle John, 'where Berkeley got screwed'. Getting screwed (drunk) was a sign of manliness, deplored by Mamma, but encouraged by bachelor uncles.

John Lucy's few letters, written in a galloping spider scrawl, are concerned mainly with the acquisition of *virtù*. He was seemingly unruffled by the fact that he was not a Lucy except by indirect descent, while his brother George, with too much of the twelfth century in him for his peace of mind, was hunting up parish registers all over England for details of Lucy births and marriages, to be set out later in the Pedigree Book.

Though lacking George's antiquarian fervour, John admired that independent spirit, William of St David's, from whose great-niece he was descended. A certain high-handedness characterized both clerics. William Lucy, after his elevation to the Bishopric, filled the stalls of St David's with non-residents who drew their salaries and did not attend, and concentrated his energies on rebuilding the Collegiate Church of Christ in Brecon with a handsome chapel in which he meant to lie with his family round him. Perhaps he was daunted by the hazardous journey to St David's, the absence of comfortable lodgings when he got there, and the vast problem of raising funds for its restoration. On that bleak coast stripped by the harsh Atlantic winds, there were only isolated farms and crofts scattered at long intervals; the salt-bleached ruins of St David's shrine had long ceased to be a place of pilgrimage. Silence and the crying of sea birds filled the shallow marsh where the Norman Bishop Peter de Leia had built the first Cathedral.

The William Lucys settled in thriving Brecon, where their daughters soon got husbands. Bishop Lucy's tablet by Stanton is in the ante-chapel of Christ's College, now a boy's school. He leans slightly forward, a book grasped in one hand, the other hand resting on a skull. The long, humorous nose, the drooping moustache, and the flowing hair give him a family likeness to the third Sir Thomas. He looks anything but an ecclesiastic, in spite of his Bishop's lawn.

By John Lucy's day St David's had undergone a remarkable transformation. John Nash, the architect of Regent Street, had been engaged at the beginning of the century to rebuild the west front. Church restoration was hardly Nash's *forte*, and the result was most unhappy. He increased the desolation of the place by plundering stones from what remained of the ancient Choir School or College. By the middle of the century enough money had been raised for the ubiquitous Sir Gilbert Scott to be approached for a new restoration. What more appropriate than that the Lucys, whose forebears' neglect had contributed to the decay of the fabric, should be asked to put their hands in their pockets to make restitution? John Lucy, on being approached by the Chapter, gave generously. Sketches were brought down to Hampton Lucy by Sir Gilbert, and it was decided that the three great lancet windows of the presbytery blocked in by the presence of St David's shrine on its north side (and by the lovely Trinity Chapel built at the beginning of the sixteenth century in Cotswold limestone) would be more worthily filled with glass. Modern Venetian mosaics were eventually chosen as being more striking (and much more expensive) than glass. Beneath them a now sadly neglected brass dedicated to the memory of Bishop William records the Cathedral's indebtedness to the Rector of Hampton Lucy.

This was in 1871, and John Lucy was by then in his eighty-first year. Old age had disabled him from fox-hunting, but he still attended the meets and waited to see the hounds throw off. His sister-in-law records in her journal: 'In the spring of 1873 he had several attacks of Jaundice and on the 15th of July [1874] I received a letter from Spencer saying he was not expected to live'. But his constitution was of iron. 'One day he overheard Dr Kingsley say there was no hope, when he turned himself round in Bed and said, "Doctor, there's life in the old Dog yet!" and verily he was a very "Mother Hubbard's Dog". The quantity of Nourishment, Turtle

Soup, Beef Tea, Consommé of Game and Meat, besides Champagne, Brandy and new Milk that he took every two hours in the day is almost incredible—he sometimes drank a Bottle and a half of Champagne during the 24 hours, as well as a Bottle of Brandy in 3 days; his Alderney Cow was milked at one o'clock in the early morning for a Cup of its Milk, with a spoonful of brandy in it, and his faithful and excellent Toogood gave it to him, whether asleep or awake. The Doctors ordered it, but I cannot help thinking they were wrong, for though it might keep him alive so much wine and spirit got into his head and made him say strange things. On the 11th October, ill as he then was, he would go to London to get a new set of Teeth, that he might be able to masticate solid food. Drs Kingsley and Pitt told him the railway journey alone would be his death, but go he did, got his Teeth and remained six weeks amusing himself, sometimes dining at his Club and having a few friends to dine with him at his Hotel. He had however during that time a very serious attack which nearly proved fatal and which left him very weak. He rallied considerably after that and on Xmas day dined here (Charlecote) and with his new Teeth thoroughly enjoyed the good things set before him. . . . As the Spring advanced he got better and was able to take Carriage exercise . . . about this time he was made one of the Canons of St David's Cathedral, he had given a splendid window to that Cathedral as well as large sums of money toward its restoration.*
August 26th he wrote to me to Penrhôs where I was staying [with the Owen Stanleys] saying that he was going to St David's to be present at the Installation of the new Bishop, and should stay there a few weeks—but before he went he overtaxed his strength and brought on his last and fatal illness. On Sunday 30th he did duty twice in his own Church—Monday, he got up at half past 4 o'clock in the morning, went to London with a return ticket, bought his new clerical costume and did various other things—Tuesday, he went to a Garden Party—Wed. to Hertford Bowling Green where he played, being supported by his man-servant whilst he bowled—Thursday, he gave a Dinner to his Curates, and was then in so weak a condition that his man Henry had to carry him down into his cellar for Wine—Friday, he drove to Warwick to get some money from the Bank to go to St David's, where he had forwarded

---

* He had the table tomb of Edmund Tudor that stands before the high altar of St David's restored and embellished with a brass inscription and coats of arms.

himself a case of Champagne and sundry good things—but alas! Saturday, so great was his weakness he was unable to leave his Bed.'

His sister-in-law nursed him in order to give the menservants a little sleep, but he would not allow her to read the Bible or any prayers to him, to her great distress. The thought uppermost in his mind was to recover sufficiently to get to St David's—he had perhaps some confused idea of laying his bones there. 'His narrow bed is alone, by the side of a Yew Tree, planted by himself in his own Churchyard of Hampton Lucy.'

The *virtù*, long coveted, did not come to Charlecote, but was dispersed and sold by auction. 'I never sat out five days of such excitement, cold and vexation of spirit', Mary Elizabeth writes, 'and I thought if the old Rector could have seen the dirty rabble crowded into his own beautiful Drawing room it would have driven him frantic, and more than all to have heard them bidding their shillings, yes! and sixpences, and the Auctioneer, seated on a table, knocking down his choice and highly-prized goods to people who he would not in his life time have deemed worthy even to have looked at them.'

Chronological Order of the Lucys of Charlecote, Warwickshire

The name Lucy derived from Luce-sur-Orne in the bailiwick of Passeis near Domfront in Normandy. By the end of the Middle Ages the Lucys of Charlecote were the sole direct descendants of this great Anglo-Norman family, which flourished all over England in the twelfth, thirteenth, and fourteenth centuries.

The de Montforts of Beldesert in Warwickshire descended from the de Montfort who came with the Conqueror to England. There was some degree of kinship between them and the Earls of Warwick of the Conqueror's creation.

1189.   Walter, son of Thurstan de Montfort of Beldesert, inherited Cherlecote. At the Conquest, Cherlecote had been granted to Robert de Meulan (Mellent), Earl of Leicester, whose daughter, it is believed, married a de Montfort of Beldesert, and who may have been Thurstan's mother. Thurstan received Cherlecote from his father or uncle and was holding it in fee to the Earl of Warwick till 1189, when his son Walter succeeded him, taking the name of de Cherlecote. A marriage between this Walter and an unidentifiable Lucy heiress founded the line of **de Lucy of Cherlecote**. The lands granted by Thurstan de Montfort to his son were confirmed to him by Richard I and again by John.

1204.   **Sir William de Lucy** took his mother's name. He farmed the Hundred of Kington (now Kineton) in which Cherlecote was situated for an annual rent of forty shillings. He married twice; by his second wife Maud Cotele, co-heiress of lands in Hampshire, he had a son, William. He founded the monastery of Trinitarian Friars at Thelesford.

1247.   **Sir William de Lucy** married a Herefordshire heiress, Amicia de la Fourches, who was some kin to the Fitzwarins, a line of Marcher lords of whom eleven sons in succession were named Fulc.

1263.   Her son, **Fulc**, held Cherlecote by the service of half a knight's fee to his kinsman and mesne-lord, Peter de Montfort of Beldesert. He assumed knighthood by virtue of his lands. He commuted his service to his mesne-lord by the payment of two hundred marks and died seised of the manor of Cherlecote. The first Cherlecote

Court Rolls date from his time and give a clear picture of the workings of the manorial economy.

1301. His son, **William**, held, probably through his wife, the manor of Cherrington on the Warwickshire Stour; it has been suggested that the unnamed tomb in Cherrington Church may be his, but as the effigy represents a franklin in the dress of his class, this seems unlikely. This Sir William represented the shire in four successive Parliaments.

1329. His son, **William**, was in the retinue of Warwick and received knighthood from the King. He carried a banner at Crécy and died of dysentery during the siege of Calais, when his eldest son, Thomas, was only nine. Thomas dying at eighteen was succeeded by his younger brother, another William.

1374. This **William** came of age in 1374 and entered the service of John of Gaunt. He sat in the first Parliament of Henry IV. He had married at sixteen, without licence of the King, Elizabeth de la Barre, and had a son, Thomas.

1404. This **Thomas** was in the retinue of Richard Beauchamp, Earl of Warwick, but, being in poor health, died in the summer of 1415 four months before the victory of Agincourt. His wife, Alice Hugford, was a Shropshire heiress, and had from her mother extensive lands in Bedfordshire as well.

1415. Her son, **William**, being a minor, was made a ward to John Boteler, to whom the mesne-lordship of Beldesert had passed. During the Wars of the Roses this William adhered to the House of York. He received a protection, or safe conduct, from his overlord, the Kingmaker, after the victory of Northampton in 1460. He married the sister of a Yorkist baron, Alianore, daughter of Lord Grey de Ruthin, and died seised of the Manor of Cherlecote, leaving a son, William, the first to call himself plain Lucy.

1466. This **William Lucy** was a Commissioner of the Peace for Warwickshire for four years in succession, and Sheriff of Warwickshire and Leicestershire. He married, firstly, Margaret daughter of John Brecknock, Treasurer to the household of Edmund Tudor, Earl of Richmond, and, secondly, Alice, daughter of William Hanbury. For his loyalty to the House of Tudor, he was created a Knight of the Bath at the Coronation of Henry VII's Queen. He quitted to the now impoverished house of Trinitarian friars at Thelesford all the claims his ancestors had had in it, and desired to be buried in the chancel of the Parish Church of the Holy Trinity at Stratford-on-Avon.

1492. His son by Margaret Brecknock, **Edmund**, died at the age of thirty-one, having been a Commander in the King's army. Edmund Lucy was summoned in 1494 to receive the Order of the

Bath with the King's son, Henry, but was prevented by ill-health, and died in the following April, desiring to be buried at Thelesford beside his mother. By his second wife, Joan, daughter of Sir Richard Ludlow, he had a son, Thomas.

1495. This **Thomas** had the wardship of William Catesby of Ashby St Ledgers, Northamptonshire, whose mother, Elizabeth, daughter to Sir Richard Empson, he married. He lived in London, in the parish of St Bride's, Fleet Street, and was a sewer, or server, to the King when the Court was in residence at Westminster. The King granted him the custody of the royal park of Fulbroke, across the river from Cherlecote. He reclaimed the rights from Thelesford which his grandfather had renounced, taking back the profits from the glebe lands of Cherlecote church and the advowson of the Vicarage. He also enclosed common land which the Brothers had had the use of for two centuries, and withheld the oblations left to Thelesford in his mother's will. He desired to be buried in the Church of the Grey Friars in Smithfield, London. He left three sons, dividing between them his manors of Cherlecote, Claybrook (Leicestershire) and Bickering and Sharpenhoe (Bedfordshire).

1525. His son, **William**, married Anne, daughter of Richard Fermor of Easton Neston, Northamptonshire, a merchant of the Staple of Calais. The second of their five daughters, Jane, married George Verney of Compton and is buried at Compton Verney. The third, Maria, married Christopher Hales of Meriden, friend of the reformers Bullinger and Sturmius, an exile at Zürich during the Marian persecutions with his elder brother, John Hales of Coventry. William Lucy, an ardent friend to the New Learning, connected by marriage with Bishop Latimer, engaged John Foxe the martyrologist to be his son's tutor.

1551. This son, **Thomas**, is first mentioned as attending a pageant in Banbury with his cousin, Richard Fiennes of Broughton Castle.* He was married at sixteen to Joyce Aston, sole heiress to her father, Thomas Aston of Sutton, in Worcestershire. With her fortune he was able to rebuild the old demesne house of the de Cherlecotes (now called Charlecote) in its present form, and there he entertained the Queen for two nights on her way from Kenilworth to Compton Wynyates.

He sat in two Parliaments, was a Justice of the Queen's Peace, a Commissioner of Musters at the time of the Armada, and for Recusancy, and a member of Burleigh's Council for the Marches of Wales. In the course of his routine duties as a JP he dealt out fines and a beating to some Stratford poachers caught red-handed on his land, in consequences of which action he has ever since been represented as the original of Shallow, of *The Merry Wives of Windsor*. His public life is on record, and that he was trusted by

* Stratford-on-Avon Minutes and Accounts.

Burleigh and the Privy Council is established. His effigy by Gerard Johnson in Charlecote Church is the first Lucy portrait.

1600. The Queen knighted his only son, **Thomas**, in his father's lifetime, in 1595. This Sir Thomas married as his second wife a great heiress—'first and last she was worth little less than forty thousand pounds to her husband' (her own words)—Constance Kingsmill, daughter of Sir Richard Kingsmill of Highclere, Hampshire. They had fourteen children, who are depicted kneeling on the painted tomb raised to Sir Thomas by his widow in Charlecote church. The fourth son, William, a divine, suffered much hardship during the Interregnum, and was rewarded by Charles II with the See of St David's. The sixth son, Francis, was MP for Warwick town.

1605. **Sir Thomas Lucy** (the third in succession) was educated at Magdalen, Oxford, and at Lincoln's Inn. He married Alice, daughter of Thomas Spencer of Claverdon, and had thirteen children. He was the friend of Donne and Drayton and perhaps of Shakespeare. He bought Fulbroke and emparked Charlecote. At the Herald's Visitation in 1619 his arms of three luces or pike *hauriant* were confirmed to him. He was Recorder of Stratford, a Justice of the Peace, and sat in six Parliaments; the last, a few months before his death in 1640.

1640. His son **Spencer** raised a troop of horse for the King and a regiment of foot. He took a degree as Doctor of Medicine while with the Court at Oxford. Dying without issue in 1649, he left his estate to his next brother **Robert**.

1649. Charlecote being entailed on the heirs male passed at Robert's death nine years later to his next brother, **Richard**.

1658. **Richard Lucy** had succeeded his uncle Francis Lucy as Member for Warwick town, and had sat in the Parliament of 1640 with his father. He was Sheriff in 1647 and a year later Member for the county. He was one of the forty-one members excluded from the House in Pride's Purge, but was summoned by Cromwell to sit in the Barebones Parliament of 1653.

1677. Richard's soldier son, **Thomas**, captained a troop of horse at the time of the Dutch invasion. He made elaborate improvements to the gardens at Charlecote, but died suddenly of the smallpox, leaving one daughter, a ward in Chancery.

1684. The youngest son of the third Sir Thomas, Fulke, brother to Spencer, Robert, and Richard, had married Isabella Davenport, a Cheshire heiress. His eldest son, **Davenport**, in default of a direct heir, now succeeded to Charlecote. He was a soldier, and followed William III to Ireland, where he was killed at the siege of Limerick.

1690. His only surviving brother, **George**, also a soldier, followed him at Charlecote, but died childless.

1721.   The estate passed to the next brother, **William**, a clergyman, who, being also childless, adopted the two sons of his youngest brother, Fulke, whom he disinherited in favour of the two boys. **Thomas**, the elder, was an epileptic and died unmarried at Charlecote in 1744.

1744.   The younger brother, **George**, did not marry. He lived at Charlecote for forty-two years, and during that time swept away the seventeenth-century layout of the gardens, employing Capability Brown to redesign the park. He diverted the Warwick road from passing under his windows. He was the last Lucy in direct descent from the first William. He made a will in favour of his secretary-companion, the Reverend John Hammond, whose grandmother, Alice Lucy, had been the daughter of Sir Fulke of Henbury.

The Hammond Lucys

1787.   In 1722 Dr William Lucy had entailed the estate upon the heirs male of his sister, Alice Hammond, if his nephew's line should fail, and directed that any Hammond so inheriting should take the name of Lucy. **John Hammond** received the King's Sign Manual in February, 1789. He married Maria, daughter of John Lane of King's Bentley, Staffordshire, and vested in himself the family livings of Charlecote and Hampton Lucy. He sent his eldest son **George** to Harrow and Christ Church, his second son, John, to Winchester and Trinity, Cambridge. George Hammond Lucy became MP for the pocket borough of Fowey in 1820 till the disfranchisement of 1832. He married in 1822 Mary Elizabeth, daughter of Sir John Williams, Bt, of Bodlewyddan, Flintshire. He entirely remodelled the interior of Charlecote and much of the exterior. In 1823 John Hammond Lucy died at the age of ninety, and his son John succeeded to the family livings. George Hammond Lucy died in 1845 in his fifty-sixth year.

1845.   **William Fulke Lucy**, his eldest son, left Cambridge in 1847, and died of jaundice at Charlecote the following year.

1848.   **Henry Spencer** succeeded his brother at the age of eighteen. He was Master of the Warwickshire Hounds from 1856 to 1858. He added oriels to the two wings of the house and restored the brickwork on the north side, refaced the stables, and continued the lime avenue to the Stratford road, where an arch in the Jacobean style was erected. After his marriage with Christina Campbell, daughter of Alexander Campbell of Monzie, Perthshire, in 1865, two rooms were built to the south block for his mother's use.

1890.   Henry Spencer Lucy died suddenly from a chill caught out shooting. The entail on the male line was broken in favour of the eldest of his four daughters, **Ada Christina**. She married in 1892 **Henry William Ramsay-Fairfax**, Lieutenant in the Second Life

Guards, eldest son of Col. Sir William Ramsay-Fairfax, Bt, of The Holmes, Roxburghshire, and great-grandson of Vice-Admiral Sir William Fairfax, who was with Wolfe at Quebec and who was created a Knight-Banneret for gallantry when Flag Captain to Admiral Lord Duncan at the Battle of Camperdown in 1797. (In consideration of his services to the Navy, a baronetcy was conferred on his son.)

On his marriage to Ada Christina Lucy, Henry Ramsay-Fairfax took by royal licence the surname of Lucy. Their eldest son dying at Eton, Charlecote passed to their second son, Sir **Henry Montgomerie**, who presented it in 1946 to the nation.

Thus in eight centuries Charlecote has three times gone through the female: through the obscure Lucy heiress who married Walter de Cherlecote at the end of the twelfth century, through Alice, daughter of Sir Fulke of Henbury, who married a Cheshire clergyman called Hammond, and lastly through the great-granddaughter of John Hammond Lucy, when it was joined to the no less historic name of Fairfax.

Index